MANAGING PROFESSIONALS

Managing Professionals deals with the tensions between managers and professionals within organizations such as hospitals, universities, banks and judicial organizations. Often managers rely heavily on the skills and expertise of the professionals in their organizations, yet these professionals consider management a source of bureaucracy and paperwork.

This tension is explored head on in order to answer the question of how to manage an organization effectively. With numerous real-world examples, the book analyses the problems and complexities of management in professional organizations and makes recommendations on how to manage professionals. The book focuses on a number of key issues, including:

- management as a problem
- management as a solution
- knowledge and innovation
- strategy
- cooperation
- performance

Managing Professionals presents an empirical analysis of the problems between management and professionals and offers solutions to this tension. It will be of interest to managers and to students of management, organizational behaviour and business administration.

Hans de Bruijn is a Professor of Public Administration at Delft University, the Netherlands. Much of his research and consultancy focuses on the role of managers in professional organizations. He is the author of *Managing Performance in the Public Sector* and co-author of *Management in Networks*, both published by Routledge.

MANAGING PROFESSIONALS

Hans de Bruijn

Routledge
Taylor & Francis Group

LONDON AND NEW YORK

First published 2011
by Routledge
2 Park Square, Milton Park, Abingdon, Oxon OX14 4RN

Simultaneously published in the USA and Canada
by Routledge
270 Madison Ave, New York, NY 10016

Routledge is an imprint of the Taylor & Francis Group, an Informa business

Typeset in Aldus by Pindar NZ, Auckland, New Zealand
Printed and bound in Great Britain by TJ International Ltd, Padstow,
Cornwall

British Library Cataloguing in Publication Data
A catalogue record for this book is available from the British Library

Library of Congress Cataloguing in Publication Data
Bruijn, J. A. de, 1962–
Managing professionals / Hans de Bruijn.
    p. cm.
  Includes bibliographical references and index.
  1. Conflict management. 2. Professional employees. 3. Executives. 4.
Organizational culture. I. Title.
  HD42.B78 2010
  658.3'044—dc22   2009053863

ISBN 13: 978-0-415-56508-0 (hbk)
ISBN 13: 978-0-415-56509-7 (pbk)
ISBN 13: 978-0-203-84827-2 (ebk)

CONTENTS

ILLUSTRATIONS

TABLES

FIGURES

BOXES

1

THEY CAN'T LIVE WITH EACH OTHER, CAN'T LIVE WITHOUT EACH OTHER

A BOOK ABOUT PROFESSIONALS AND MANAGERS

This book deals with a relationship full of tension: the one between managers and professionals. Professionals are the people who do what is called the 'real work' in our society. They are engineers, judges, medical doctors, teachers, police officers, actors, pilots, and so on. They maintain power plants, they pass verdicts, they operate, they teach, they catch criminals, and they move and inspire us. Their work often requires specialist knowledge, which they can only maintain by constantly gaining new experiences. For many professionals, their profession is their passion: they are strongly motivated because they love what they do.

In the past few decades, professionals have increasingly been confronted with managers: non-professionals who manage the professional organization. The often-heard complaint is that there are too many managers, and that they are too powerful while they know too little about the profession. The added value of all these managers is unclear to many professionals – especially when it concerns managers who do not come from within the profession. Management causes hassle, and as soon as managers are in charge, things no longer happen spontaneously.

PROFESSIONALS NEED AUTONOMY …

This is an often-heard wisdom that will appeal to many professionals. Professionals should be allowed to do their work and should be bothered with as little organizational and bureaucratic hassle as possible. Someone who performs complex tasks needs autonomy and has a right to be trusted with the responsibility to perform these tasks well. Managerial control mechanisms are superfluous in well-functioning professional organizations. Professionals are always embedded in a professional community, with its own codes that contribute to the quality of the service delivery. This mutual professional control has much more added value than managerial control mechanisms. In addition, there is the phenomenon of professional pride: professionals generally have a strong intrinsic motivation and take pride in their work. By definition they will make an effort to do their work to the best of their capabilities. Professional autonomy is the best guarantee for a high quality professional service delivery.

... AND THEREFORE MANAGERS ARE THE PROBLEM

Much of the hassle in professional organizations is caused by managers. Managers know less about the profession than their subordinates do, and therefore they resort to useless protocols, plans and procedures. Protocols, plans and procedures result in an enormous burden of proof imposed upon professionals. Before they can act, they have to prove that their actions meet the requirements of the protocols, plans and procedures. There is no room left for what is called 'professional audacity': acting professionally, also when there is limited information or time. Managers break the basic rule – that professionals need autonomy. Someone who seeks refuge in protocols, plans and procedures will deliver a sub-optimal professional performance in the end. The conclusion should be that fewer managers equals less hassle and more professionalism.

Of course no one will deny that there is a need for managers. After all, someone needs to take care of the buildings and the equipment – but the question in a professional organization should always be: what is the added value of the echelons above the professional? Professionally, a university professor is the one expert in his organization. His organization's *raison d'être* is to enable research, including his own. The logical question is: what is the added value of the echelons above the professor? What is the added value of the dean of his faculty? And of the board? Of the various staff departments? It is the managers who carry the burden of proof; in fact they should be the ones to go through the hassle of protocols, plans and procedures, instead of our poor professionals.

... AND THEREFORE MANAGERS ARE ALSO THE SOLUTION

So far this line of reasoning will be appealing, but it calls for a critical note. Society is becoming increasingly demanding and complicated. This gives rise to new questions, which do not always correspond with the interests and the values of professionals. Technological developments and the ageing of the population strongly increase the need for medical professionals, both quantitatively and qualitatively. At the same time, there is a strong cost increase. The logical consequence is that an effort is made to limit these costs. The strong demand for legal services – and other professions – is resulting in increasingly long waiting lists. It may therefore be necessary to introduce new standards that are different, sometimes even radically different, from the existing professional standards. We want our professional organizations to use new and often very costly technology, but some of them are too small for this and can only do this by merging with other organizations. We want teachers to listen to the parents; we are sometimes frustrated because they don't, and wonder why the school has not come up with a solution for this kind of situation. Cost control, new standards, mergers, complaint arrangements: they do not always spontaneously emerge from the professional community – professionals may even oppose them – and yet we want these issues to be addressed. Not addressing them may affect the quality of the service delivery. Moreover, some of these issues require a kind of expertise that differs from the professionals' substantive expertise. Or, put differently, they require another kind of expertise in addition. It is not unlikely that a professional, when asked for his initiatives in relation to these issues, will refer to the manager. The idea that professionals need autonomy can also be used as an argument in favour of more management. Questions that are directed at the organization and that have nothing to do with the content of the profession should be answered by managers. This will allow professionals to focus on the things that are important to them.

ABOUT THIS BOOK

If all of this is true, then there are two obvious conclusions. One: managers exist, they do useful things, and they will therefore always keep existing. Two: there will always be tension between professionals and managers – they are often each other's *countervailing power*. The doctor represents medical quality, the manager represents cost control, and both of them are right. The manager and the professional represent two different world views that are both correct. They often cannot live with each other, but they cannot live without each other either. And perhaps they are both unsatisfied in the end. The manager is unable to achieve the cost control that he envisioned, and the doctor has to compromise what he sees as quality.

In this book I will therefore assume that there are managers in professional organizations and that they can have a useful task. Managers and professionals cannot live without each other. This does not mean, however, that managers are always right. On the contrary: management can be a major problem in professional organizations – all too often, managers and professionals cannot live with each other. But we should keep a certain balance in mind: managers can also be a solution to problems that exist in professional organizations. Therefore

Chapter 2 will illustrate why managers are often a problem, while Chapter 3 will explain why they can also be a solution.

Reality, in other words, is often less simple than it appears to be. We will often have to look beyond simple *management bashing*, but also beyond the many all-too-simple tools and models that suggest that professional organizations are ordinary organizations.

Based on the observations in Chapters 2 and 3, I will deal with a number of themes: strategy (Chapter 4), quality (Chapter 5), coordination and cooperation (Chapter 6), knowledge and innovation (Chapter 7), performance (Chapter 8) and change (Chapter 9). Chapter 10 contains a few concluding remarks. The bottom line is that 'either/or thinking', whether from a professional or managerial perspective, yields a picture that is too simple. This means that some pictures that I describe may be counter-intuitive – for the professional, for the manager, or perhaps for both these groups.

2

MANAGEMENT AS A PROBLEM

MANAGERS CREATE BUREAUCRACY, introduce unnecessary procedures and place too much confidence in management gurus and their model talk. Too often they resort to the paper reality of their planning and accountability systems. They create so much hassle that they prevent professionals from getting to the core of their work. Managers, in short, are a problem rather than a solution – in contrast to what they often believe.

All of this can be true: management can become a power that leads to nothing but deprofessionalization and bureaucracy, and doesn't add any value to the profession. In this chapter I will look into the causes of this. These can easily be found by examining three central characteristics of professional organizations: professionals' expertise, variety within the professional organization, and the way professionals innovate.

FIRST CHARACTERISTIC: TACIT KNOWLEDGE – A PROFESSIONAL DOES NOT RECOGNIZE HIS OWN INTELLIGENCE

The central characteristic of professionals, of course, is that their activities are knowledge- and skill-intensive.[1] The classic example is the medical doctor. Having completed his graduate degree in medicine, he has to spend several years gaining practical experience as a resident. The process continues after that: a doctor can only maintain and renew his knowledge and skills if he is professionally active. Each year he has to perform a certain minimum amount of medical interventions. Apparently a doctor who does not succeed in this can lose his skills despite many years of study and practice. This leads us to an important characteristic of professionals: the skills they need are knowledge-intensive and *they maintain and develop these skills through the daily practising of their profession*.

There is more: many professionals are hardly aware of this process of maintenance and development. It just happens. The surgeon just operates and is often unaware of the fact that he is learning continuously. In addition, the knowledge that he gains is so natural to him, so intimately connected to his person, that he often doesn't even know all the things he knows. This is what we call *tacit knowledge*.[2] Professional knowledge is often tacit or implicit: it has grown slowly by continuous professional action, and a professional often finds it hard to make this knowledge explicit and explain to others what he knows and why he acts the way he does.[3] In other words, he doesn't recognize his own intelligence.

WHY A NON-NATIVE SPEAKER KNOWS MORE ABOUT A NATIVE SPEAKER'S LANGUAGE THAN A NATIVE SPEAKER

The simplest example to illustrate this point is a person's knowledge of his native tongue – a metaphor that helps us to understand the tension between managers and professionals. Almost everyone speaks his or her own native tongue fluently and almost flawlessly. We do this naturally. We have learned the language from birth, first at home and then at school. We use this knowledge on a daily basis. Without further consideration we produce the most complicated grammatical constructions.

My native language is Dutch. In class I often meet German students. I have often asked them if they can name the prepositions that are followed by the dative case in German. I have never met a German student that could. I am much more likely to hear the right answer from Dutch students. Effortlessly they produce the dative-case prepositions: 'mit, nach, bei, seit, von, zu, aus, ausser, gemäss, zuwieder, entgegen en gegenüber'. This difference also relates to tacit knowledge. Of course the German student speaks the language much better than the Dutch student. The German student's mastery of the language is so good that he is unaware of his intelligence. These prepositions are naturally followed by the dative case. Dutch students are much less confident with the German language and have to rely on learning the underlying grammar rules if they are to speak the language correctly. They have to learn the sequence by heart, and the fact that they can recite it doesn't indicate that their German is good. On the contrary. The Dutch student knows these prepositions because he *lacks* a certain skill. The German student lacks that knowledge because he *has* a certain skill.

We can apply this example to the relationship between a professional and a manager. In this case, the native speaker is the professional and the non-native speaker is the manager. When the non-native speaker (the manager) asks for the prepositions that are followed by the dative case, the native speaker (the professional) will not only be unable to provide the answer; he will also be completely uninterested by it. Making these prepositions explicit is difficult for the professional/native speaker. It is a hassle and it is pointless: it will not improve his language skills. To the manager/non-native speaker, on the other hand, this will appear to be a very useful activity. Many managers will conclude that everyone speaks German, but that there are no protocols that explain the underlying grammar, and that the use of the dative versus the accusative case is completely unclear to them. They will also conclude that no one can explain to them why, and that everyone seems to choose randomly between the two. Finally, they will determine that this results in an urgent need to spell out the underlying grammar, so the next generation of professionals will know what to do.

This example illustrates part of the tragedy of managers and professionals. Both lines of reasoning are powerful, and both can be convincing. Both the professional and the manager have their own intrinsically logical line of reasoning, each from their own perspective, while these lines of reasoning are like water and fire. Later in this book I will come back to this issue.

So there is something we call 'tacit knowledge'. There are, of course, many types of tacit knowledge. The following four phenomena – which are not intended as an all-inclusive list – may be helpful to understand tacit knowledge.

PATTERNS: THE CHECKERS MASTER

There have been interesting studies on the question, what enables a checkers master to play a blindfold simultaneous game? A checkers master is crazy about playing checkers; he spends the majority of his time playing checkers, and his memory appears to contain an enormous variety of associations with other games. This is his tacit knowledge. During a blindfold simultaneous game, he continuously uses these associations. The checkers master Ton Sijbrands, for instance, played a blindfold simultaneous game referring to the '15th match Deslauriers vs. Kouperman at the 1958 World Championships'.[4] It is one of the many matches that he stored in his memory. Rather than reconstructing the situation based on a photographic image of the board, in each game he refers to patterns that have been stored in his memory. This enables him to retain the positions on a particular board and present intelligent reactions to the moves of his opponent.

This type of tacit knowledge is easy to visualize. It can be compared to a library catalogue: a seemingly endless row of titles, catalogued by, for instance, year of publication, author or genre. The checkers master has a mental library just like that, which he can activate when he is playing a blindfold simultaneous game. The library is dynamic: as long as the checkers master remains crazy about checkers, it will expand. But what will the checkers master reply when asked which games are stored in his library? He won't know. A physical library can make its collection explicit. The checkers master can activate his games when he needs them, but will not be able to present others with a perfect overview of the thousands of games that are stored in his head. They represent tacit knowledge.

SEARCH SYSTEMS: THE NURSE IN THE INTENSIVE CARE UNIT

Patterns can be visualized as a long list of titles or as a file system, in which each file lists a title and has a logical order. We'll go one step further when we use another analogy: the Google search engine. By entering certain keywords in Google, we can perform a very focused search in an almost endless amount of information. The keywords will lead us to the information we need. Google allows us to select the right information from the enormous amount of information on the Internet. Professionals are like that: they have the ability to use a limited amount of data (the keywords) to produce exactly the right information.

Doctors have a special clinical way of looking at things. If a patient is admitted with chest pains, these can be the symptoms of a heart attack. The doctor will use certain 'keywords' to see if this is indeed the case: pain that radiates to the arms, neck or back; a family history of heart failure; blood pressure; is there extra pain between the ribs if the doctor exerts pressure on the chest? This limited set of 'keywords' leads the doctor to a first diagnosis.

Another example is the tacit knowledge of nurses. Premature infants are very vulnerable. If they develop an infection, it can quickly be fatal if antibiotics are prescribed too late. There is some interesting research that shows that nurses are very good at predicting an infection. Sometimes they predict an infection, even when the first test turns out negative, while a second is positive after all. Apparently the nurses possess a special expertise – 'expertise that the person clearly has but cannot describe'.[5] What is this expertise? What clues do nurses use? It took a large number of interviews to reveal these clues. One of them was that a child that consistently cries when it is picked up, but not at other times, may have an infection. These and other clues were then presented to experts. Some of the clues appeared to be in the textbooks – in other words, they were not tacit knowledge, but explicit knowledge – but other signals were new. In some cases they were even counter-intuitive. This, too, is an example of tacit knowledge: it is richer than textbook knowledge, and the nurses could not make this knowledge explicit themselves.[6]

REFLEXES: THE SPORTS HERO AND THE MARINE OFFICER

A soccer player past the age of 30 will have an increasingly difficult time in challenging international competitions. Interestingly enough this is not true for goalkeepers. David – 'Safe Hands' – Seaman, for instance, was the goalkeeper of the English national team until he was 39, while 39-year-old Edwin – 'Jolly Green Giant' – van der Sar still plays for Manchester United. Of course the first explanation is that they depend less on their physical abilities than players in other positions. But there is more. They have accumulated tactics and reflexes that a younger goalkeeper generally lacks. Something similar is the case for boxers. Older boxers are physically less strong, but they have better reflexes, which they have developed through years of experience. In the case of soccer we generally speak about 'ball sense': through years of experience, a soccer player has developed a wide range of reflexes that make him better than an inexperienced player.

A completely different and fascinating example comes from the Gulf War in the early 90s. Michael Riley, officer on board the HMS *Gloucester*, was on duty and suddenly saw an object approaching on the radar screen. He had only tens of seconds to decide how to react, and he decided to fire at the object. A few moments later the captain examined the radar data and broke into a sweat. He was convinced that the British ship had taken down an American airplane. All available clues did seem to indicate that it was indeed an American plane. In reality, however, the object was an Iraqi Silkworm missile. Michael Riley had made the right decision and saved the HMS *Gloucester* from destruction.

On the basis of what information did Michael Riley make the right decision? Experts who scrutinized the data afterwards all reached the same conclusion as the captain. On a radar screen, airplanes and missiles appear to have the same size and in this case they were approaching from the same direction. There was no communication between the HMS *Gloucester* and the American airplanes. The only important difference was the altitude: missiles fly at 1,000 feet, and airplanes at 3,000 feet. Michael Riley, however, did not have any information about altitude when he made his decision. Then what information did he have, in addition to – or apart from – the radar data? Or: how did he interpret the radar data, other than in the usual way? Apparently he acted differently from the experts, who had plenty of time afterwards to analyse the data.

Michael Riley was of course subjected to extensive interviews, just like the nurses who could predict infections. There was, however, an important difference between Michael Riley and the nurses. Riley's own analysis of his decision was that he saw within five seconds that the object was accelerating, and that it therefore *had* to be a missile. An airplane flies at a more constant speed. But here's the point: this self-analysis was wrong. In fact the missile was not accelerating. Michael Riley was not able to make his tacit knowledge explicit. In the end it was a defence specialist who solved the puzzle. Both airplanes and missiles came from the same direction, and became visible on the radar screen as soon as they passed the coastline. The missile, however, had become visible slightly later, when it was already above sea. The weather was cloudy at that time. The object, therefore, must have flown at a much lower altitude than an airplane, being hidden from the radar a few seconds longer. It was tacit knowledge that helped Michael Riley spot this one small difference, upon which he based his decision. It was a professional reflex, and it was true tacit knowledge as well: after the event, Michael Riley was unable to reconstruct how he came to the right conclusion. What's more, he made an incorrect reconstruction. He did not recognize his own intelligence.[7]

Tacit knowledge can often only be used by the *acting* professionals. Tacit knowledge is not only difficult to describe, but it also has the risk of being reconstructed in the wrong way, as illustrated by the Michael Riley example. The examples of the goalkeeper and the boxer make clear that some types of tacit knowledge cannot be reconstructed at all. It is of course impossible to condense their reflexes or a player's ball sense into a flow chart or a list with underlying competencies – to name a few management buzzwords.

INSPIRATION: 'IT COMES FROM HEAVEN' – 'I JUST MESS AROUND' – 'I HAVE NO IDEA WHAT I'M DOING'

A fourth type of tacit knowledge is inspiration, another phenomenon that is difficult to comprehend. In his book *Musicophilia: Tales of Music and the Brain*, the famous neurologist and publicist Oliver Sacks recounts conversations with people who 'suffer' from musicophilia: they are completely possessed by music. One of them, Tony Cicoria, is a composer. He explains to Sacks what happens to him almost daily when he plays the piano. Sacks writes:

> His own music "would come and take me over. It had a very powerful presence." Was he having hallucinations? No, Cicoria said, they were not hallucinations – "inspiration" was a more apt word. The music was there, deep inside him – or somewhere – and all he had to do was let it come to him. "It's like a frequency, a radio band. If I open myself up, it comes. 'It comes from Heaven,' as Mozart said." His music is ceaseless. "It never runs dry," he said.[8]

A similar case in this respect is the sculptor who sets to work and finds that his statue is taking control over him. Apparently the sculptor has the sensation that he is not making the statue, but it is creating itself. His creativity stems from somewhere, but apparently not even he knows where it comes from – it seems to come from the statue itself. Perhaps Karel Appel's famous confession – 'I just mess around' – is rooted in this experience. He cannot describe in words what he does, and what the secret of his art is.

Another example. The actress Carice van Houten has acted alongside famous actors like Tom Cruise, Jude Law and Forest Whitaker. Her fellow professionals say about her: 'She is a natural. She doesn't know exactly what she's doing.' 'She acted entirely instinctively, and yet it was immediately right on.' 'When she came to me the first time, she kept saying "I don't know anything, I can't do anything, I don't understand anything".' 'She often says: "I have no idea what I'm doing".'[9]

The tacit nature of these concepts – inspiration, passion, creativity – is clear. Apparently Tony Cicoria and Karel Appel did not know where their talent came from. Therefore they relied on something lofty – 'It comes from Heaven' – or on something vulgar – 'I just mess around'. An average manager will not be particularly pleased when he is told that the professionals in his organization are just messing around. When those professionals, however, are creative minds such as Tony Cicoria or Karel Appel, the main recommendation for the manager is to give them all the space they need to just mess around.

WHAT IMPLICATIONS DOES TACIT KNOWLEDGE HAVE FOR MANAGEMENT?

How does all of this affect management? Imagine a professional organization that is faced with a manager from the outside world, who is not very familiar with the profession. Imagine that tacit knowledge is a major factor in the professionals' work. Why does management in this context soon become problematic?

MANAGEMENT IS A TACIT ACTIVITY TOO: MANY THINGS IN PROFESSIONAL ORGANIZATIONS ARE NATURAL

Tacit knowledge implies that there are many things in professional organizations that happen spontaneously. Coordination and knowledge sharing, for instance, are spontaneous activities. Professionals closely cooperate with one another and need very few words to coordinate their activities. The arrangements they use are tacit, like their knowledge. Knowledge management and learning often happen tacitly, in the interaction among professionals. When doctors cooperate, they continuously learn from one another and share their knowledge. Judges in a full bench (when a case is addressed by three or more judges) share their knowledge and learning. This is no different for researchers working on a project in a team. Learning and sharing knowledge are implicit processes. They take place during the action, even without professionals noticing. This is how the new generation of professionals learns the trade: the medical resident who assists the doctor, the young judge who resides in multiple courts together with older judges, and the junior researcher who works together with the senior.

Now imagine that a manager is hired to be in charge of human resources management (HRM). The manager doesn't always realize what happens in terms of the development of young professionals – which, after all, often takes place implicitly and is therefore hardly noticeable. A natural reflex would be to demand the development of learning and training plans for each employee, which specify the planning on a yearly basis and justify what has happened. Of course, one needs to be able to compare these plans, and therefore they are moulded into a format. To a professional this will soon seem like bureaucracy and paperwork: just as useless as asking a German student to explain the grammatical structure of German. Learning takes place during action, and therefore a good manager will make sure that a young professional has sufficient opportunity to work alongside seniors, in varying contexts.

The same thing will happen when it comes to cooperation. Professionals working together will make many implicit decisions that contribute to the quality of their cooperation. They just do that, because they share the same professional values and competencies. Cooperation comes spontaneously, without any structure supporting it. The manager who is unaware of these tacit processes, however, might conclude that the cooperation practice lacks structure. It seems to be too dependent on coincidences, too much shaped by history, and insufficiently thought through. In early days organizations could get away with such informal arrangements, but today protocols are needed to secure a sufficient degree of cooperation. Again, this is like telling a German that his German is perfect, but that his use of language is not, and that he needs to take a grammar course to ensure the quality of his German language skills.

Plans and protocols hardly have any added value in this case. A manager who nevertheless introduces plans and procedures often creates two realities: the paper reality of plans, procedures and protocols, and the 'real', informal and tacit professional reality. The practical meaning of this paper reality is very limited. From a professional perspective, making plans, procedures and protocols is a ritual that has to be passed. They remind us of a rain dance: the ritual is performed, but of course there is no relationship with reality. If it starts to rain, it is definitely not because of the rain dance.

MANAGERS DAMAGE THE HIDDEN INTELLIGENCE OF THE PROFESSIONAL ORGANIZATION

A manager who does not realize that many professional activities are organized in a tacit way not only causes a lot of hassle, but can also damage this tacit organization. Table 2.1 explains this.

When activities are organized in a tacit way, an organization will, by definition, have a lot of invisible, hidden efficiency. Many activities – learning, knowledge management, coordination – come spontaneously during the work. They do not demand any extra effort by a manager, and in this case management does not have any added value.

Sometimes this hidden efficiency is also visible for the manager. He notices, for instance, that young judges who are members of a full bench have ample opportunities to interact with older, more experienced judges and gradually improve their performance. Put differently, the young judge learns tacitly. He will decide that there is no need for knowledge management or knowledge managers. But a typical characteristic of hidden efficiency is the fact that it often remains invisible for the manager. From a managerial perspective, there may even be a situation of inefficiency.

An example of this is a study on the time spent on various activities in nursing homes. This analysis showed that washing a client took a lot more time in one of the homes compared to the others. At first sight, this seems to be a sign of inefficiency. In the home where the staff took more time for washing the clients, they used this extra time for some informal chatting. This made the clients feel more comfortable; consequently, they were more likely to participate in social activities, which improved their physical and mental condition. Moreover, the informal chat was a valuable source of information on the physical and mental condition of the patient.[10] In other words, there is usually a lot of hidden, albeit

Table 2.1
Efficiency and inefficiency, visible and tacit

	Hidden, tacit inefficiency	Hidden, tacit efficiency
Visible inefficiency	I Stimulus: Change the existing, undesired situation	II Stimulus: Change the existing, desired situation
Visible efficiency	III Stimulus: Maintain the existing, undesired situation	IV Stimulus: Maintain the existing, desired situation

ambiguous, efficiency, which isn't always visible from a managerial perspective. If the management imposes norms and reduces the time available for washing, this will result in visible efficiency (less time for washing) but hidden inefficiency (less information, more difficulties in stimulating people to participate in social activities). In Table 2.1, the situation changes from quadrant number II – hidden efficiency – to number III – hidden inefficiency. At a first glance this may result in a better service, but in reality the situation will get worse.

Table 2.1 shows something else also. Quadrants number I and IV are unproblematic. In quadrant number II, however, there will be a process like the one described above: there is a stimulus to change an existing and desired situation. In quadrant number III there is hidden inefficiency: because there is no time for a chat, there is no information and the clients will feel lonelier. This is a situation that does require managerial action, but in this quadrant there is no stimulus for action and change, because this inefficiency is not visible. So when we combine hidden and visible (in)efficiencies, change is always to the profession's disadvantage. This is in fact logical: visible efficiency and inefficiency are clear and therefore easy to communicate – in charts, in spreadsheets, in model talk, in pep talk, during an elevator pitch. Hidden, tacit efficiency and inefficiency, on the other hand, are often more ambiguous and more difficult to communicate.

MANAGERS WANT TO MAKE THINGS EXPLICIT – BUT THIS IS UNNECESSARY AND EVEN RISKY

Many managers think it is important to make their professionals' tacit knowledge and expertise explicit. Sometimes it is. This book will mention many examples of managerial reasoning that are centred on making tacit knowledge explicit. Knowledge management is an example of this. Knowledge is in the minds of professionals, and it needs to be made explicit if an organization is to be less vulnerable if, for example, one of the professionals is hit by a bus. Benchmarking is another example: professional organizations should make their best practices explicit, allowing other professionals to learn from them. Quality management requires making explicit what knowledge is, and what is needed to improve that quality. However, as mentioned before, from a professional perspective, making things explicit may bring a lot of bureaucracy and hassle to a professional, just like a native speaker will find it a hassle to have to spell out the grammar of his own language.

Moreover, if professionals do not see their own intelligence, they most probably will not be able to explain why they perform so well. They will even make mistakes when they try, as illustrated by the example of Michael Riley above.

The Finnish education system is currently enjoying worldwide attention because it performs so well. Would Finnish teachers be able to explain why this is? Probably not. Many things are so natural to them that they do not see them as a contributing factor to their success. If they are forced to describe their own intelligence anyway, there is a chance that they will give an incorrect or oversimplified explanation for their success. Anyone who tries to learn from the Finnish system by benchmarking it against other systems will run the risk of deriving the wrong lessons. Ridderstrale and Nordström therefore state in their study that benchmarking is a risky activity. It is like karaoke: it is always a bad copy of reality (see Chapter 7).

THE MORE TACIT KNOWLEDGE, THE MORE MANAGERS RESORT TO PROCESSES AND STRUCTURES

When it comes to substantive expertise, of course almost every manager is less knowledgeable than the professionals in his organization. This notion may be rather uncomfortable for a manager. The natural reflex of someone who is supposed to take the lead while he lacks substantive knowledge is to resort to processes and structures.

Processes: Imagine, for instance, EFQM-like procedures and protocols.[11] Take a manager in a consultancy firm, who lacks the expertise the consultants have. To safeguard the quality of the consultancy, it might be attractive for the manager to introduce protocols that should be conducive to this quality. Such protocols, for instance, can require that a consultant keeps a particular kind of record for each project: three copies of the project description, and reports of each conversation with the client or with the people he interviews. These requirements have nothing to do with the contents of his work, and do not necessarily improve the quality of his consultancy. To the managers these procedures can be useful: they feed the notion of influence and control, if only because of the availability of uniform records for each project. To the professional, however, they feed the notion that the profession is regressing towards bureaucracy and paperwork. Or even worse: an increased level of procedures can lead to a decreased level of professionalism. New professionals can get the impression that people who conform to these procedures are automatically good professionals.

Structures: Someone who cannot rely on substantive knowledge often retreats towards discussions on organizational structures. Is there insufficient cooperation among professionals? Then the organization needs to be restructured. Do executives and managers have insufficient influence on the profession? Then the governance model needs to be adjusted. Did something go wrong between a professional and a client? Then the competencies and responsibilities need to be more clearly defined and a structure is needed to monitor this. This too feeds the notion of influence and control, but to professionals it is often a hassle (it costs time and energy), tedious (new structures solve old problems and create new ones) and it only distracts from the real professional work.

SECOND CHARACTERISTIC: VARIETY AND AMBIGUITY

A second important characteristic is the variety of professional organizations and the ambiguity of professional action.

The variety of professional organizations is almost proverbial. Imagine a university with all of its professional disciplines, or a hospital with all of its specializations. To limit myself to a university: the professional disciplines do not only differ in terms of the content of their work, but they also have entirely different 'cultures of publication'. In one discipline there is a wide range of journals, and a researcher can publish an average of four articles a year. In another discipline, there are just a few journals and two publications per year would be an exceptional accomplishment. Also, there are differences in possibilities for acquiring external funding: in one discipline these may be plentiful, while in others they may be limited. In addition, the potential for innovation may differ among professional disciplines. One may have room for continuous innovation, others are more inert. It is no coincidence that I mention publication, acquisition and innovation, since these are currently the main themes at universities around the world.

How does this affect management? Generally speaking there are two potential managerial reactions to variety, and both feed the impression that management is a problem.

THE MIRACULOUS MULTIPLICATION OF MANAGERS

Every manager has a certain span of control. Defined simply, this is the number of people that report to one person (in this case: the number of professionals that report to one manager). As the variety of professionals and professional units increases, the span of control decreases. Every managerial intervention, after all, requires that exceptions need to be made for some units, that adjustments are made, or that unwanted side effects are corrected. Imagine that a university judges its employees by the number of their publications. An allocation model is designed that pays the employee a certain amount of money per publication. In an environment with a large degree of variety, a simple measure like this soon requires tailor-made solutions.

Is it fair that a professional discipline with twice as many publishing opportunities will be allocated twice the amount of money? That a discipline with many journals is treated in the same way as one with very few journals? Should there be a distinction between fundamental and applied disciplines? And what about new, multidisciplinary disciplines? And disciplines that have no publication tradition, rather a design tradition? The answer to each of these questions can result in tailor-made solutions for the intervention. The more fine-tuning, the more complicated the intervention will be, the more limited the span of control of a manager, and thus the more managers are needed to implement the intervention.

When this happens, one can easily predict the complaints made by professionals. First, managers intervene in an organization full of variety. Second, given this variety, the intervention becomes an overcomplicated set of rules, specifications, exceptions, temporary exceptions, compensations, etc., that make the intervention incomprehensible for the ordinary professional. Third, the complexity created by the managers themselves requires more and more managers to understand, maintain and implement the intervention. Call it the miraculous multiplication of management: someone who aims to control an organization with a large degree of variety creates the need for additional control mechanisms and additional managers.

'ONE SIZE FITS ALL' – ON FRIDAYS WE ALL EAT FISH

Another well-known phenomenon is the fact that managers are insufficiently tolerant towards variety, and indiscriminate in their interventions. From a managerial perspective this is actually understandable. In an organization with a large degree of variety there are always arguments why something is impossible for a particular unit, why it should be done differently, why it requires an exception, etc. We should be aware that in terms of substantive knowledge, professionals are always superior to managers, and therefore always capable of constructing a storyline that justifies why they should be exempt from the intervention. A manager that has often experienced this may become insensitive to the argument of variety: the managerial costs are high, as illustrated by the earlier example of tailor-made solutions.

If there is limited tolerance towards variety, and a similar intervention is applied in very different situations, the professional criticism is also predictable. It is too much of a 'one size fits all' paradigm. It is like a university dining hall: on Fridays there is fish on the menu, so every guest has to eat fish. Units are being forced into a mould that limits their functioning, rather than increasing their professional performance. And they are right: people who are forced into the mould of another profession can be quite bothered by this. Imagine that an applied discipline is forced to invest much effort into publishing in international journals – in other words, that it is forced into the mould of the more fundamental disciplines. The result may be that an applied discipline, which should be open to society and sensitive to societal issues, becomes too focused on the scientific community and develops a one-sided and internally oriented position.

MANAGERS CANNOT DEAL WITH PROFESSIONAL AMBIGUITY

And then there is the ambiguity of the profession. The difference between a bureaucrat and a professional is that a bureaucrat's actions can be caught in a number of 'if, then' formulas. To a bureaucrat, reality is unambiguous and therefore it is clear which actions are needed in which situations. To a professional, however, reality can be multifaceted. For a professional, reality is often ambiguous and subject to different, sometimes conflicting demands. This will be addressed in more detail in the chapter on quality; here I will limit myself to a simple example of a judge. A judge is acting professionally when his verdict (1) is in line with legal quality demands and jurisprudence, (2) is well and understandably motivated, (3) is reached within a reasonable time limit and (4) results from a fair trial, in which all parties had been able to provide their views. It will be immediately clear that there may be conflicts among these demands: between fast and good or between understandable and legally correct or between fast and fair. Professionalism, in other words, is an ambiguous concept for a judge. It cannot be reduced to simple 'if, then' formulas. What to do if a case is (1) legally very complicated and adequate jurisprudence is lacking, (2) if there is a lot of media interest, (3) if financial interests call for a quick decision, and (4) if the stakeholders are at serious conflict with one another? Again, 'if, then' formulas are useless here. The only answer is to trust in the professionalism and autonomy of the judge.

There are many other examples of conflicting demands. Professionalism in the case of a hospital implies reducing the waiting lists. Waiting lists compromise the well-being of the patients and may entail health risks. It is therefore a professional value for a hospital to prevent waiting lists. On the other hand, waiting lists have positive functions as well. In some cases they give patients time to reflect on their situation. They contribute to efficiency and cost reduction – if every patient is always helped immediately, the hospital runs the risk of creating over-capacity that may be useless elsewhere.

Now why can management, taking into account this ambiguity, be a problem in professional organizations? Because managers by definition cannot deal with all aspects of the profession, and with the trade-off among these aspects. Only the professional can do that. Managerial interventions always run the risk that they focus on just a few aspects of professionalism, usually those aspects that can be defined relatively easily. As a result, the balance of the profession can be disturbed: a one-sided emphasis on productivity and throughput times, for instance, may compromise values such as quality time (as illustrated by the waiting list example). A one-sided emphasis on speed can compromise legal quality (as illustrated by the example of the judge).

THIRD CHARACTERISTIC: SPONTANEOUS CHANGE

A third characteristic of professional organizations is the fact that many changes happen spontaneously or emergently. Again, they rather result from professionals' actions than from top-down planning. The explanation for this is simple. When an organization consists of well-functioning, competent and enthusiastic professionals, they will jump at every opportunity for improvement. If these professionals are granted autonomy, and the number of interventions remains low, the organization will automatically change in the right direction. Again, it becomes apparent that such a change will occur implicitly (the first characteristic of professionals), without too much planning, just because professionals do what they have to do. Processes of change are therefore mainly tacit processes.

Moreover, the variety of a professional organization (the second characteristic of professionals) can be a source of renewal. In his famous book *The Wisdom of Crowds*, James Surowiecki describes a number of conditions under which 'crowds' – groups of individuals – can be innovative.[12] He describes three of them:

- variety – allowing the contribution of different opinions and types of knowledge;
- decentralization and the absence of hierarchy – preventing people from dictating what the 'crowd' should do; and
- autonomy – preventing the members of the 'crowd' from influencing one another too much.

These are exactly the characteristics of a professional organization; respect for these characteristics allows for spontaneous change.

Perhaps this sounds a bit lofty. Therefore I will illustrate this point using a simple example of a history teacher at a secondary school. In his first year, the teacher develops his curriculum, offers it to his students, and will undoubtedly discover that it has some start-up problems. Some of the subject matter will not get through to the students, while for other aspects they will need less time than he had anticipated. He finds out which examples make his students enthusiastic and which evoke no reaction.

These are the usual experiences for a teacher. In the second year of the course he uses these to his advantage: he adjusts the curriculum in order to make it relate to his students' world.

Over the years, the teacher also has other experiences. At a certain moment he notices that the students' prior knowledge is different from what it used to be. He is forced to adjust his curriculum. When he speaks with teachers at institutions for higher education, however, he finds out that they complain about deficiencies that surface in their classes. Again, the teacher has to critically examine his curriculum.

As the years go by, the teacher sees his students change. They are more visually oriented than before, they are better at multitasking, and they know their way around the Internet. The simple fact that they can copy entire papers from the Internet forces him to think about different kinds of assignments. He confers with colleagues who teach other subjects, but who are facing the same challenges. He discusses the matter with fellow history teachers, and together they design a new type of assignment, which is less focused on factual knowledge and more on interpreting facts and making meaning. It works, but it also appears to have some downsides. There are some facts that are indispensable in order to deal with the endless stream of information on the Internet. So again, the teaching method is adjusted.

Over the years, the composition of the school's neighbourhood changes. There is an increase in the number of students with behavioural and concentration problems. The teachers of mathematics – which many students find dry and boring – have been familiar with this problem for a while, and they have adjusted their teaching method. The history teacher has heard them discuss this over lunch, and uses their ideas as inspiration for his own curriculum. He starts experimenting with simulation and gaming, and searches for IT applications that will make it easier for the students to stay focused.

The point of this example is that this professional is actually doing nothing more than his job. He innovates by doing, and after ten years he will conclude that his curriculum has changed drastically. The change occurs tacitly as well as incrementally: step by step. There have been no plans, nor strategic visions nor innovation policies. Apparently Surowiecki's three conditions are met. The teacher is functioning in an environment with a large degree of variety: his fellow history teachers, his colleagues for other subjects, different types of students, etc. He can make decisions decentrally, which allows him to quickly react to the changes that he notices, for instance, in the student population and in relation to the risks of certain changes. And he has autonomy: he can either accept the strategies of his fellow teachers, or ignore them. We assume that he accepts them if they work, and ignores them if they don't.

In this example there is a single teacher. When the school consists of several dozen of such teachers, the accumulation of their actions can lead to major changes. Such changes are not publicly announced beforehand, so they are not always visible, but they just happen. It makes a school exceptionally adaptive: because professionals are active on the ground, they are the first ones to be confronted with new societal developments and because they have autonomy, they can react to them.

MANAGERS ARE BLIND TO SPONTANEOUS CHANGES

If changes in professional organizations often occur spontaneously, then why is management often a problem?

Since spontaneous change occurs implicitly, continuously, and incrementally, it is also hardly visible to the manager. That is a first reproach to managers: they don't notice spontaneous changes. They have insufficient insight into the intelligence that is stored in the capillaries of the organization and that requires very little guidance.

A second reproach is similar to this. Managers like change – it is partly their *raison d'être*. The notion that change occurs naturally does not correspond with this *raison d'être*, and therefore managers will want to interfere with change. There is a strong temptation for them to formalize this spontaneous process. People who want to change are forced into a procedure. Our history teacher has to state each year what he wants to do, and what he is planning to do differently. He has to spell out his arguments and his proposal is assessed by the newly established 'Quality Control' commission. It is an often-heard complaint by professionals: even the most logical change requires all kinds of hassle before it can be introduced. From a managerial perspective, such a procedure may not seem unusual, but to the professional the added value isn't always clear. Among themselves, professionals proceed completely differently. How do they assess a proposal by the history teacher? If he has proven to be able to make the right decisions in the past – in jargon: if he has a 'proven past performance' – they will probably rely upon this proven performance and support him. If the teacher has been proven to make the wrong decisions, he will probably have gained insufficient confidence among his fellow professionals to be able to make the change.

A third reproach is that changes initiated by managers, unlike spontaneous changes, are not inspired by professional experiences but sprout from the world of the manager. Examples include management considerations such as re-organization, process redesign, the introduction of formal procedures, of performance management systems, and so on. There is nothing inherently wrong with measures like these, except if they make the manager blind to what really happens within a professional organization, and if they leave no room for professional experiences and considerations.

THE TRAGEDY OF MANAGEMENT AS A PROBLEM

In summary, there are in fact two worlds, or systems. There is a managerial world, featuring executives and managers, and there is a professional world. The problem-solving power of the managerial world is highly limited – management is a problem rather than a solution.

How can all of this happen? Are managers really so ignorant that they do not recognize the mechanisms described in this chapter? Sometimes they are. But there is a deeper, underlying reason. When we make a distinction between a managerial world and a professional world, the following 'law' presents itself: interventions that have a high 'feel-good content' in the managerial world, and are then implemented in the professional world, often appear to have a high 'feel-bad content' there.

Imagine that executives and managers advocate for more transparency, more accountability or more quality. All of these are pleas that no sensible person will oppose – the concepts have a high 'feel-good factor'. However, these concepts have to be made operational, have to be translated into daily practices. Professionals will be faced with procedures that prescribe the need for detailed accountability reports, preferably supported by quantitative data. Examples include the vast volumes of numbers that some professional organizations have to produce in light of the need of transparency and accountability. Or imagine that executives and managers advocate for more competition for research funding in order to reward good research. This also has a high 'feel-good factor' in the managerial world. How to translate this into an instrument to assess the quality of research? By establishing a procedure which forces professionals to make detailed plans, to submit these plans and then wait for a committee's decision. Professionals will perceive this as time-consuming bureaucracy and paperwork. It does not feel good – it feels bad.

This 'law' explains why professionals' complaints about the increasing bureaucracy are so strong, why the managerial world always promises to address this, and why the bureaucracy and hassle increase anyway. Bureaucracy and hassle result from good intentions, and not from someone's conscious decision to create more bureaucracy and hassle.

NOTES

1 For literature about managing professionals, I refer to Henri Mintzberg's (1979) classical work, *The Structuring of Organizations*, Englewood Cliffs, NJ: Prentice Hall; as well as Russell D. Lansbury (1978), *Professionals and Management: A Study of Behaviour in Organizations*, Englewood Cliffs, NJ: Prentice Hall.

2 Michael Polanyi (1966), *The Tacit Dimension*, Garden City, NY: Doubleday.

3 Another famous work is I. Nonaka and H. Takeuchi (1995), *The Knowledge-creating Company*, Oxford: Oxford University Press.

4 Douwe Draaisma (2004), The checkers master's memory: Conversation with Ton Sijbrands. In: Douwe Draaisma, *Why Life Speeds Up as You Get Older*, Cambridge: Cambridge University Press.

5 Gary Klein (1998), *Sources of Power: How People Make Decisions*, Cambridge, MA: MIT Press, p. 40.

6 Ibid., pp. 39–41.

7 Ibid., pp. 35–39.

8 Cited from Oliver Sacks (2007), A bolt from the blue: Where do sudden intense passions come from?' *The New Yorker*, 23 July, pp. 38–42.

9 Dutch newspaper article 'Gekoesterd als een breekbare vaas. Actrice Carice van Houten is ontdekt door Hollywood, ze speelt met Tom Cruise en Leonard di Caprio', in *NRC Handelsblad*, 22 October 2007.

10 As shown in the following publication (in Dutch): M.C. van Poortvliet *et al.*, (2007), *Kwaliteit van leven in de V&V sector: De samenhang tussen kwaliteit van leven van cliënten en kenmerken van de instelling*, Utrecht: NIVEL.

11 EFQM stands for the *European Foundation for Quality Management*, which promotes several frameworks for organisational management systems.

12 James Surowiecki (2004), *The Wisdom of Crowds: Why the Many Are Smarter Than the Few and How Collective Wisdom Shapes Business, Economies, Societies, and Nations*, New York: Doubleday.

Chapter

3

MANAGEMENT AS A SOLUTION

S O FAR, SO GOOD. Management is a problem, and many people will find that the situations described in Chapter 2 are a daily reality. There is another reality, however: management can in fact be the solution to problems caused by professionals.

FROM BAD ORGANIZATIONAL HYGIENE TO PROFESSIONAL SLOPPINESS

Even the most fanatic 'management basher' will admit that there is a role for managers in professional organizations. After all, there are regular management functions – human resources (HR), finance, facilities – that are delegated to non-professionals in every organization. Many professionals will still identify these functions as 'support': their aim is only to support the professional in carrying out his profession. If there aren't enough managers in these functions, the price is high: eventually it will result in the expensive doctor or scientist doing the job of the support staff. Moreover, this will compromise what is called the 'organizational hygiene': the adequate implementation of basic functions like HR, finance, facility management and so on. Examples include simple matters such as the organization of annual performance evaluations, an adequate overview of the costs of professional services, or clean and safe buildings.

Inadequate organizational hygiene can affect the professionalism of the service delivery. Underperforming professionals can continue to do their work (as there are no performance evaluations), secondary processes are too costly at the expense of the core of the professional service (as there is no financial overview), or the service is inadequate because of bad facilities.

The extent to which bad organizational hygiene can affect the profession is illustrated by a study on the consequences of cardiac arrest in patients in American hospitals. Many hospitals turned out to be inadequately equipped to deal with cardiac arrest. Especially patients in smaller hospitals and patients who suffered cardiac arrest during weekends were the ones who bore the negative consequences. The explanation lies in the way these hospitals were organized, rather than in the competencies of the medical staff.[1] In some hospitals there is simply not enough staff – for instance, due to their small size. This is a management issue rather than a professional issue. Other hospitals only have classical defibrillators available, rather than the modern ones that can be used by laymen – a matter of bad facility management. Hospitals that perform well, however, have a rapid response team, or they invest a lot in safety procedures and drills to keep the staff alert. That too is not very complicated, but it has to be done and requires managers.

A similar example: Dutch researchers analysed all complaints about surgeons that were found valid by the medical disciplinary board between 1996 and 2007. The board concluded that the number of mistakes resulting from organizational failure was increasing, while the number of mistakes related to medical practice was decreasing.[2]

OLD AND NEW ORGANIZATIONAL HYGIENE

There are classic management functions – the well-known POSDCORB – that aim to support professionals and create an attractive working environment. These functions can be regarded as the old organizational hygiene: *internal* functions aimed at supporting professionals. There is also a new organizational hygiene, which is characterized by an *external* orientation and comprises issues like client focus, corporate responsibility and public relations.

In contrast with the old organizational hygiene, this second category involves more than just supporting professionals. It also relates to the position of the client, the sponsor or society as a whole. Let us take a look at one of these themes: client focus. An important part of new organizational hygiene is the correct treatment of customers, for instance in healthcare or justice. A correct treatment is not something that happens spontaneously. Take, for instance, the problems associated with waiting time in several professional sectors. Take a student that has to wait too long for his paper to be graded.[3] Apparently it is not self-evident that teachers conform to the maximum term for grading papers. In this case managerial intervention can be quite wholesome. Take someone who seeks justice, and who has to wait for the judge's verdict: serious attention to lead times of judicial decisions is, at least partly, dependent on managerial interventions.[4] Google 'patient' and 'wait for hours' and read the stories of many frustrated patients that have to wait for medical treatment in the ambulance, in hallways, in the A&E, etc.

A common line of reasoning among professionals is that students, people who seek justice, and patients are not really clients. They are dependent on the teacher, the judge and the doctor, who possess certain knowledge and skills that these 'clients' do not have. Moreover, the teacher's knowledge, the judge's verdict and the doctor's intervention can conflict with the client's wishes and beliefs. All of this is true, but the same applies when I buy a few bottles of wine at the wine store, and there I expect a correct treatment as well.

TACIT KNOWLEDGE CAN BE DECEPTIVE: THREE CLASSIC MISTAKES BY PROFESSIONALS

In Chapter 2, I introduced the concept of 'tacit knowledge'. A professional's tacit knowledge is the source of his professionalism. Without tacit knowledge a professional is someone who speaks a language, but who has to be constantly aware of the underlying grammar. The likelihood of mistakes increases, the speed of action decreases, and learning new words and rules costs a disproportionate amount of time. Tacit knowledge is the lubricant of a professional organization. However, it also entails certain risks. Professional intuition can be deceptive. Some mistakes are typical for professionals who rely on their tacit knowledge.[5]

THE REPRESENTATIVE ERROR

This error is made when a professional uses his tacit knowledge to interpret information and make a decision that is correct in the vast majority of situations. However, he ignores the fact that there are always exceptions to the rule, in which case the information needs to be interpreted in a different way.

Take a doctor who is seeing a patient who complains about chest pains.[6] The patient is in excellent health, in his forties, and an outdoor enthusiast. He feels pain in the centre of his chest, but this pain does not radiate towards his arms, back or neck. He tells the doctor that there is no family history of heart failure or diabetes. His private life is good, and he enjoys his job. His blood pressure appears to be normal. The doctor exerts pressure to the area between the ribs and the sternum, which doesn't give the patient any extra pain. An X-ray of the chest shows a normal situation, as does a blood test: there is no sign of chemicals that can indicate heart failure. The doctor concludes that there is nothing wrong with the patient. In reality, however, the man has suffered from acute cardiac arrest. The doctor has made a representative error. The group of patients with these symptoms usually don't have any radiating pains, no family history of heart failure, normal blood pressure, and so on. As the patient shows these same symptoms, the doctor considers him to be a representative of this group of healthy people. This type of error involves a professional who is too much influenced by what is correct in the vast majority of situations, but not in all cases. The same thing can happen to a teacher, who doesn't understand a certain thesis and concludes on the basis of the representative error that the student is not very bright, while he is in fact a genius.

THE AVAILABILITY ERROR

This type of error happens when a professional derives too much guidance from information he recently used or situations he recently experienced. Take the example of a doctor who sees a 60-year-old lady with a high fever and breathing problems. Her lungs seem to be alright, and so does the amount of white blood cells. Her blood does turn out to have a high acidity, and the doctor concludes that she has a sub-clinical pneumonia – sub-clinical meaning that it is not sensorily perceptible and requires further investigation – and that she is in the early stages of an infection. Her actual condition, however, is a medicine poisoning. The doctor in this story was notified of this and immediately understood his error. He realized that this would have been the best diagnosis on the basis of the available information. Then why did he fail to make this diagnosis? Because by coincidence he had recently encountered many cases of sub-clinical pneumonia. As there was a lot of information available in his head about sub-clinical pneumonia he had an implicit inclination to make that same diagnosis in this case.

THE AFFECTIVE ERROR

The affective error is the result of a doctor identifying too much with a patient in one way or another. In the first example – the patient with heart failure – the doctor indicated afterwards that the athletic appearance of the patient reminded him of his own past as an Olympic rower. His incorrect diagnosis was partly caused by this – athletes do not have heart problems, and this was a fellow athlete. Another example is that of a doctor who identified strongly with a cancer patient who suffered seriously. When a new symptom manifested itself and the patient complained about the continuous discomfort and pain, the doctor limited his examination and skipped the most painful part of it. As a result, he overlooked a new, serious complication.

THE PROFESSIONAL HABITAT DOES NOT WORK ...

In a professional organization, the most important mechanism to prevent errors like these is horizontal or mutual professional control. The doctors in the examples above were eventually corrected by their fellow professionals. Who else would be able to do that? This illustrates the importance of a professional habitat: an environment with a sufficient amount of good professionals. The presence of such a habitat allows for implicit learning processes as well as mutual professional control – when professionals make mistakes, they will be corrected by their fellow professionals. A well-functioning professional habitat will always have a richly developed *feedback culture*: professionals comment on one another's work, which contributes to the continuous improvement of their service delivery.

However, there are a few possible reasons why the professional habitat does not work and why, as a consequence, the mechanism of mutual professional control is failing.

... BECAUSE THE PROFESSIONAL HABITAT IS TOO FRAGMENTED

First, a professional habitat can be too fragmented. The professionals are preoccupied with their own activities and there is insufficient communication among them. This is a well-known phenomenon in professional organizations: mutual control is unlikely to happen, simply because there are insufficient connections among the professionals.

In the year 2004 the mortality statistics of the cardiac surgery department of Radboud Medical Centre in Nijmegen, the Netherlands, turned out to be very high. Why? The professional habitat was too fragmented. Patient care is a chain in which the different disciplines need to cooperate. Research showed that the professionals did not work together, did not coordinate their actions and hardly communicated with one another. They were focused on their part of the chain, not on the impact of their work on other professionals in the same chain. There was no structured consultation between the referring doctor and the thoracic surgeons. This negatively affected the quality of the information provided to patients before and after their operations. The feedback of postoperative data was also lacking. The handover moments proceeded sloppily at the hospital and there was no adequate interdisciplinary communication about the complications. Therefore the mutual professional control had no chance to develop. Concerning the anaesthetics policy, there were no arrangements among anaesthesiologists, surgeons and intensive care specialists. Cardiac surgeons performed their medical-technical operations and left the preparations and follow-up to cardiologists.[7] The result of this fragmented environment was that patients died. There was absolutely no tacit cooperation and a managerial intervention was needed to restore cooperation.

... BECAUSE THE PROFESSIONAL HABITAT IS TOO HIERARCHICAL

Second, the relationships in the professional habitat can be so hierarchical that the mechanism of mutual professional control no longer works. In his study *Intensive Care: A Doctor's Journal*, John Murray describes the relationships in an intensive care unit.[8] There is a strong hierarchy, with surgeons at the top who are not sensitive to signals of their subordinates, such as the nursing staff, who are often better informed about the patients than the surgeons are. The attitude of the surgeons is one of 'often wrong, but never in doubt'.

Another example is the largest airplane crash in history: a collision between two Boeing 747s at Tenerife Airport in 1977. A KLM aircraft started its take-off on an airstrip where a Pan Am aircraft was still taxiing. The two aircrafts collided and 583 people died. This disaster was caused largely by the hierarchical relationships between the pilots of the KLM aircraft. The captain of this aircraft was a highly experienced pilot – some sources identified him as one of the best KLM pilots, who was nicknamed 'Mr. KLM' – while the co-pilot only had a limited number of flying hours under his belt. In addition, the co-pilot had been trained by 'Mr. KLM', which made the authority relationship between them even stronger. This hierarchy proved to be destructive in the cockpit: the co-pilot did not take action when the captain took off without 'take-off clearance', although his communication with the air traffic control tower showed that he was surprised by this. The pilot also ignored signals about the position of the Pan Am aircraft given by his aircraft mechanic. The strong hierarchy disabled the mutual professional control. Karl Weick phrases the position of the subordinate as follows: 'I am puzzled by what is going on, but I assume no one else is. After all, they have more experience, more seniority, higher rank.'[9] One of the most important lessons that were drawn from this accident is the need to diminish the hierarchical relationships in the cockpit and to establish the rule that important decisions require mutual consent.

... BECAUSE THE NON-INTERVENTION PRINCIPLE APPLIES

Third, there is the well-known non-intervention principle. Professionals strongly depend on one another, they constantly meet one another, and therefore they tend not to follow one another's actions too critically. Today professional A is assessing his colleague B, but tomorrow professional B will assess his colleague A, and vice versa the day after that, and so on. Such repetitive interdependencies are a breeding ground for the non-intervention principle: when A doesn't interfere too much with what B is doing, then B won't interfere too much with A, and both of them will have what seems to be an easy life. This is called the non-intervention principle, which will harm the mutual professional control. The implicit rule of the game is to leave each other alone. There is no room for opposing views.

In a park in the Dutch city of Schiedam, on 22 June 2000, a ten-year-old girl named Nienke was murdered.[10] The perpetrator also tried to kill her friend Maikel, who stood face to face with him. Maikel managed to escape, and warned a passer-by, Kees B., a man with paedophile inclinations. The police investigation team suspected Kees B., who was then accused by the Public Prosecutor and sentenced to prison – wrongly, as it turns out.

There were quite a few indications that Kees B. could not have been the perpetrator. No DNA of Kees B. was found on Nienke or Maikel. Maikel did not identify Kees B., who happened to walk through the park when he was calling for help, as the perpetrator. Kees B. was an unstable personality, a type who easily confesses when being interrogated. He had withdrawn his original confession. Then what can explain the fact that a team of 30 police professionals and the Public Prosecutor still reached the conclusion that Kees B. was the perpetrator? Why did no one draw their attention to these contra-indications? Why did the mutual professional control not function?

An evaluation of this failure shows that the non-intervention principle applied. No internal or external contradiction had been organized. There were no critical questions from the police management or from the Public Prosecutor's team. The Public Prosecutor, who should always be critical towards the police, was involved with the police investigation on a daily basis and could therefore not perform this role.

All of this is understandable: police and Public Prosecutor were operating under a lot of public pressure to solve the murder, and the mistakes mentioned above are lurking around the corner. Kees B. had paedophile inclinations and had made a confession. That caused a representative error. Paedophiles who confess in this type of situation turn out to be the perpetrator in 99.9 per cent of all cases. The investigation team was therefore strongly reduced after the confession. This also seems to be an example of an affective error. The Public Prosecutor had been in personal contact with Nienke's parents on several occasions. The evaluation commission concluded: 'Perhaps it may have been an extra burden for the Public Prosecutor, and possibly also for the officer in charge, to have such intensive conversations with Nienke's parents and maintain distance from the case at the same time.'

THEREFORE, PROCEDURAL AND STRUCTURAL INTERVENTIONS ARE USEFUL …

Managers do not have the expertise professionals have and therefore they resort to structural and procedural interventions – as has been shown in Chapter 2. However, when the professional habitat is not functioning, there is often no other option than to intervene procedurally or with structural measures. The remarkable thing is that many of the explanations for the malfunctioning of the mutual professional control have a managerial nature: insufficient contradiction in the investigation team (in the case of the park murder), insufficient opportunity for subordinates to make their voices heard (in the case of the intensive care unit and the cockpit), and insufficient cooperation (in the case of Radboud Medical Centre. Apparently management can also be a solution, namely when professionals don't seem to be able to maintain their habitat. Structural interventions and procedures can help in restoring the professional habitat.

… IN ORDER TO PREVENT FRAGMENTATION

In the Radboud Medical Centre example, the recommendations are obvious. For instance, ensure that there are good handover moments, and ensure that doctors are actually present during these moments. That is a very simple managerial measure aimed at improving the healthcare process. Structural interventions can also be useful in the case of over-fragmentation. A professional unit can simply be too small to be a functional professional habitat, and mergers can therefore be conducive to professionalism. Professionals are usually very heedful of the disadvantages of scale enlargement, but a small scale can be problematic too.

… IN ORDER TO PREVENT HIERARCHY

Procedural interventions can also be useful to break through the hierarchy. In the case of complicated criminal cases, there is a bench of three or more judges. The judges make their decisions in the privacy of their chambers. In order to prevent the senior judge from having too much influence on the final verdict, the younger judge is the first one to speak. It is a simple procedure that prevents the hierarchical relationships disturbing the professional habitat.

... IN ORDER TO PREVENT NON-INTERVENTION

NASA is an organization of technical professionals who operate in various, often different, disciplines. Of course there is a low tolerance towards errors: every error can have fatal consequences. How can it be guaranteed that the mutual professional control – the most important mechanism for minimizing mistakes – is functional?[11] NASA works according to 'challenging' procedures: engineers working on a project have to continuously subject their designs and constructions to critical evaluation by a competing team of engineers, following prescribed procedures. These procedures aim to trace weaknesses in design and construction. They are used to prevent the non-intervention principle from playing a role, and to guarantee that the mutual professional control can take place. Which solution is presented to prevent errors like the ones in the case of Kees B.? A procedural one: organize contradiction in the team by allowing a third party to take a critical look at the file. This is how the professional inter-relationships can be strengthened.

VARIETY AND THE PROBLEM OF POOR COOPERATION

The variety of professional organizations is the logical consequence of the ever-increasing complexity of society, which continually gives rise to new specializations. An organization's variety may be a source of innovation: the most exciting innovations often originate at the interfaces of different specializations. The more variety, the likelier these innovations are, as Chapter 2 has shown. At the same time, variety can be a source of problems, like in youth care: a variety of organizations can be involved in the treatment of one child, and adequate cooperation is not self-evident.

Caroline Wilkinson is a 'facial anthropologist' at the University of Dundee who reconstructs faces with *clay*. In 2006 she was asked to reconstruct the face of a young girl who was found in a river in Rotterdam, murdered and cut into pieces. This 'Rotterdam girl' was subsequently identified and it turned out that she was a client of youth care and a pupil at a school in Rotterdam, but no one had reported her missing. The Dutch Healthcare Inspection writes about this case: 'The various professionals work at their own initiative, and fail to ask one another focused questions, despite the presence of relevant signals.'[12] The same phenomenon is common in secret services. 'One fight, one team' is one of the mottos of the American 9/11 Commission, which investigated the functioning of the American secret services.[13] The underlying reason for this motto: too much fragmentation, too little cooperation. And then there is the chain concept. Many professional organizations form part of a chain-like process that crosses the borders of the individual organizations. The Public Prosecutor determines how much work a court should have, the judge determines the amount of work for the rehabilitation authority. If there is sufficient coordination – for instance between Public Prosecutor and judge – then the consequences are clear: the court either suffers from lack of capacity, which leads to waiting times, or it has over-capacity, which leads to extra costs.

This organizational variety can hardly be avoided. Every organization has its own specialization and often all of these specializations are needed to provide adequate and professional service. Given this variety, a professional working in a network of organizations should be able to make *connections* with other professionals.[14] What, in this case, does 'connections' mean?

A PROFESSIONAL CHERISHES HIS AUTONOMY, WHICH OFTEN MAKES COOPERATION PROBLEMATIC – EVEN WITH 'PROXY PROFESSIONALS'

First, making connections is the ability to maintain relationships with the 'proxy professionals': the professionals who operate in the same professional field. For a doctor these can be the public healthcare service or a private health-care foundation; for the FBI these can be the CIA or the police; for the Public Prosecutor these can be the police, the court, or the rehabilitation authority.

Second, making connections is the ability to make a trade-off between the interests of proxy professionals and one's own interests. It is possible that a psychiatrist has made an intervention plan that does not correspond with the professional beliefs of a medical doctor. The FBI may be interested in arresting a suspect, while the CIA prefers to postpone the arrest because the suspect can lead the way to an international terrorist network.

Making connections means balancing interests, so someone who makes connections will sacrifice part of his autonomy. What's more, for some professionals this will affect their professionalism. The psychiatrist has made an intervention plan on the basis of his professional beliefs, but the medical doctor's professional beliefs may be different. The CIA agent who has to share knowledge with the FBI agent knows that the FBI may use this information in a way that does not correspond with the CIA's professionalism.

Tacit knowledge is a source of professionalism, but also a source of non-professional action, as illustrated by the three types of errors. The same goes for autonomy; it is a source of professionalism, but at the same time it is a source of non-professional action – it may result in insufficient cooperation, which may affect the quality of professional action.

When cooperation and making connections are perceived as a limitation of autonomy, even as a decrease in professionalism, it is logical that connections will not always be initiated by the professional himself. Bad professional service can be the result. When a necessary change does not originate in the profession, this is a breeding ground for management as the countervailing power for the professional. How to make managerial interventions will be the subject of Chapters 6 and 9, which also deal with the risk of over-management. For the moment we will stick with the notion that management can be a solution.

'MASSIFICATION' AND THE NEW VALUE OF PRODUCTIVITY

In the past few decades, many professional sectors have been facing 'massification': a massive demand for service. Unavoidably, this enormous increase has resulted in an increased focus on productivity, which in turn has developed into a new professional value. The 'eternal student' may have been amusing in the 50s, but large numbers of students are simply too expensive. The same thing is true for healthcare and justice – and many other sectors. Focus on productivity will mean that a judge may not only have to reach good verdicts, but a large number of verdicts, while lead time is also a value. A hospital may put effort into reducing the length of hospital stays.

Productivity is sometimes seen as an opposite of quality, but it is also an element of quality. Someone who seeks justice wants a good verdict, but he also wants to hear the verdict soon. A patient waiting for a hip operation wants it to be done correctly, but he doesn't want to spend a lot of time waiting, and actually benefits from a fast treatment and recovery.

The new value of productivity can have a major impact on an organization. A court that has to be productive has to make a distinction between types of cases, and develop a norm for the amount of time needed to conclude each type of case. The next step is determining the production capacity of the judge. Production norms can be developed, they can be monitored, and so on. This jargon alone is an indication of the impact of the rise of productivity as a value. A professional will have to make new trade-offs. Is it the 'professional beauty', or the fast conclusion of the verdict – simply put, should every verdict have a 90 per cent score in terms of substantive quality, or is 70 per cent sufficient if it means that more verdicts can be reached? Should every case have its own individual written verdict, or can there be standard texts for simple verdicts? Should every judge reach his own conclusion about the punishment for every case, even the simplest one, or can he use a list of standard punishments? Should a bench of three or even more judges be the standard, or, in light of productivity, the exception? Questions that are a bit more down-to-earth may also surface – nothing human is alien to a professional – for instance whether or not a judge can make the unilateral decision to go on vacation, even if this increases the lead time of certain cases.

What happens when a professional organization does not want to adopt the new value of productivity? In the case of the court, there is an increase in the amount of cases and in waiting times; cases aren't dealt with for an irresponsibly long time, and eventually this can result in the loss of legitimacy, despite the 'professional beauty' of the verdicts that *are* reached. What happens when an organization adopts the value of productivity, but an individual professional does not conform? All that is left for him to do is to complain incessantly about the new professional jargon and the downfall of the profession. This is the slightly sour type of professional that can be found in almost every organiza-tion. More serious is the fact that the denial of the new value can block the discussion that is central to professional organizations: how can the service quality be guaranteed while productivity is maintained as a value?

The introduction of productivity as a value evokes questions that are mostly managerial by nature – as illustrated by the court example above. Management can in fact be a solution. Management is also a solution if professionals do not accept productivity as a value, but regard it as a restriction of their autonomy and even as a threat to professionalism. This can lead to bad professional service, and eventually to loss of legitimacy. This situation, too, calls for a countervailing power for the professional.

CHANGE HAPPENS SPONTANEOUSLY, BUT NOT ALWAYS, AND AUTONOMY CAN FEED DEFENSIVE BEHAVIOUR

In professional organizations, change occurs spontaneously – as shown in Chapter 2 – because a professional continuously receives stimuli from his environment, to which he reacts professionally. Autonomy allows him to adequately react to new developments – like in the case of the history teacher in the previous chapter.

There is, however, also another reality. First and in short, a main aspect of this other reality is that professionals are ordinary people, and therefore there are not just hardworking, passionate and innovative professionals, but there are also passive and routine-driven professionals. Spontaneous, tacit change is not self-evident in the latter case. And there is more.

Autonomy – one of the sources of innovation – can degenerate into isola-tion. For example, a group of professionals' total insensitivity to signals from the outside world, *because* they come from the outside world. Isolated groups often show 'defensive behaviour': there is no room for new perspectives and beliefs. New professionals are only admitted to the group if they share, or are prepared to share, the group's professional beliefs.

A further example: the use of a nuclear weapon results in blast damage as well as fire damage. The fire damage is much greater than the blast damage. A 3,000-kiloton bomb hitting the Pentagon would create devastation within a 50-mile radius. The lack of this knowledge has had far-reaching implications for the United States' military planning, namely the underestimation of the devastating effect of nuclear weapons and a resulting development of a nuclear weaponry that was much too large. Why did the expert and research communities underestimate the consequences of fire damage?[15]

The explanation is that blast damage belonged to the domain of physicists, while fire damage belonged to that of fire protection engineers (FPEs). The FPEs were less embedded in the academic world, had less computer infrastructure and calculating capacity at their disposal, and therefore had fewer opportunities to model and predict fire damage. The physicists focused on their own fields of expertise (such as predicting blast damage), and ignored the consequences of fire damage because in view of their expertise it is much more difficult to predict. Eventually this determined their view on reality: blast damage is important, and fire damage is not. There is cognitive fixation because the community of physicists is too isolated, and does not allow any room for the viewpoints of FPEs. These viewpoints are met defensively: things that do not match their professional belief are not accepted.

Another example is the high mortality statistics of Radboud Medical Centre. Many people died, due to a sloppy organization. The interesting thing was the primary reaction of the hospital when these mortality statistics were made public: these statistics were irrelevant, it was argued, as Radboud Medical Centre, an academic hospital, was facing an over-representation of high-risk cardiac patients and therefore a high mortality rate. It is a typical example of defensive behaviour: we, the professionals, have the expertise and outsiders, especially the spreadsheet managers with their statistics, should stay out of our professional domain. It was much too simple an attitude.[16]

Management can play a role in breaking through this defensive behaviour, for instance by:

- Involving professionals with other perspectives and beliefs. These can perhaps break through the defensive routines. This is illustrated by the fact that the situation in Radboud Medical Centre was first flagged by a newly appointed surgeon coming from another hospital. Involving new professionals is often much more effective than trying to change the minds of the existing professionals.
- Implementing managerial interventions. For instance, interventions in the

organizational structure can break through the isolation of a professional community. Changing the financing structure can be a simple managerial solution to break through isolation: fewer funds for existing initiatives, more for new ones.

• Bringing in a third, non-professional party. A businessman may have a different way of approaching disabled care, and may achieve results that are out of reach for professionals.

This is not an exhaustive list of interventions, but serves to illustrate that managerial interventions can contribute to better professional service. Management, in other words, can be a solution, especially when it appears that the quality guaranteed by professionals is insufficient.

THE TENSION BETWEEN INDIVIDUAL AND COLLECTIVE PROFESSIONALISM

Individual professionalism, of course, refers to the performance of the individual professional; collective professionalism refers to the performance of the collective. In many cases there is no conflict between these two. If a surgeon operates well, a television maker makes good television, and a teacher provides good education, this will promote the quality of the hospital, the broadcasting company, and the education programme. This is how the problems of managers and professionals are sometimes represented: if professionals just do their jobs, everything will be alright.

The total of good individual performances, however, can result in collective underperformance. The quality of a broadcasting company also depends on the programming: which programmes are broadcast at what times? Is there a logical flow in the evening? Does the company have a certain typical profile? How does the programming relate to that of other companies? These are matters that transcend the level of the individual professional. Moreover, decisions that are made in view of collective quality can compromise the autonomy of the individual professional.

The quality of an education programme does not only depend on whether or not there are good teachers available. It is also important that knowledge is accumulated, that there is a common theme in the programme, and that there is a balance between theory and practice. The need for knowledge accumulation, for instance, can compromise the autonomy of the individual teacher.

The need for collective professional quality can result in a need for managerial interventions if professionals are unable to improve the collective quality themselves. Relationships among professionals are often horizontal, and often the non-intervention principle applies, with the associated risk that collective professionalism is ignored.

An example: a simple innovation being implemented in many universities and colleges is the opportunity for students from faculty A to spend half a year taking a minor at faculty B. Any university or college wanting to introduce this option will have to standardize its education programmes. Every curriculum has to include a six-month exchange period in the same year of study and at the same time of year. This is a kind of innovation that is often not initiated by individual teachers or individual faculties, but by the higher echelons in the organization. It is also a kind of innovation that can affect the well-being of an individual teacher. He may have to sacrifice teaching time, for instance. It is an intervention that cannot simply be regarded as an empty managerial intervention. The introduction of minors, after all, can contribute to the classic ideal of the broadly educated scholar.

PROFESSIONALS DO NOT ALWAYS SEE THE CONSEQUENCES OF THEIR ACTIONS ON THE COLLECTIVE LEVEL

One of the notions in Chapter 2 was that change often happens emergently, under the radar of the manager or the politician in question. The example there concerned a history teacher who gradually improves his programme. The series of gradual improvements eventually results in a dramatic change.

However, this mechanism has a mirror image. There is a distinction between the macro- and the micro level. The micro level refers to the professional work floor. The macro level transcends that of the individual professional. This can be the level of the professional organization as a whole (the school, the university, the hospital) or that of the system as a whole (the education system, the healthcare system).

Sometimes, the impact of small decisions made at the micro level is not very visible at the micro level, but rather at the macro level. At the macro level, the

Table 3.1
Visibility at the macro- and micro levels

	High visibility at the macro level	Low visibility at the macro level
High visibility at the micro level		The rise of a new type of student
Low visibility at the micro level	Increasing costs of the healthcare system	

impact of hundreds of thousands of individual actions by professionals does become visible and this impact may be very negative:

- In the Netherlands around 1,700 cases of mortality in hospitals are considered to be 'potentially avoidable'.[17] From a macro point of view this statistic may be alarming, but when this number is translated into the number of 'potentially avoidable' mortality cases per doctor, this risk is almost negligible at the individual level. From a macro perspective, in other words, the alarming statistic should result in a sense of urgency regarding the improvement of patient safety. From the perspective of the individual doctor this is not the case, and hence the sense of urgency will be a lot less significant.
- Imagine a healthcare system: every individual action can be good according to professional standards, and still lead to undesired outcomes at the collective level, such as unacceptable costs. Or imagine a police intervention: every action by an individual police officer can meet all professional standards while the collective result can be unsatisfactory from a societal point of view – such as an inadequate level of crime investigation due to a certain prioritization of tasks.
- When someone with an ankle injury reports to an emergency room, the person may have a fracture. To exclude that possibility, the staff usually takes an X-ray. This is understandable at the individual level, but since ankle injuries are a relatively common condition in emergency rooms, the total costs are high. In the end only a limited number of ankle injuries turn out to be actual fractures. At this individual level there is hardly any stimulus to find alternatives to the X-ray, although these do exist.[18]

The total of individual, good performances can result in collective underperformance. Professionalism is therefore more than just individual professionalism. Attention should therefore also be paid to the larger system in which the professional performance is delivered, as well as to the impact of this larger system on professionals' individual actions. The question always remains, to what extent do professionals feel responsible for this collective level? Professionals can be in 'smaller mind': they focus on their own tasks and have no overview of the collective professional performance. Attention to collective professionalism calls for professionals in 'larger mind'. Attention to this collective quality can be very painful for the professional in 'smaller mind'. It can mean that a judge has to produce more verdicts, and that it is alright if the quality of these verdicts is not perfect – mediocre quality is sufficient as well. It can mean that a high-quality television programme is not broadcast because it does not fit with the programming and the profile of the broadcasting company. An assumption behind the idea that underlying professional control happens naturally is that there are sufficient professionals in 'larger mind'. As mentioned before, this is not always the case.

When the need for change is not visible at the micro level, macro-level action is required. This is usually the domain of executives and managers. Of course this can happen in different ways: top-down, against the wishes and beliefs of professionals, or in a process in which professionals are involved and have a say in the outcomes. This will be addressed further on in this book. The point here is that necessary changes do not always originate spontaneously or emergently from within the profession, and may therefore require an intervention by executives or managers as the professionals' countervailing power.

SUPPORT STAFF ARE PROFESSIONALS TOO

As mentioned before, non-professionals in professional organizations often used to be considered as 'support staff'. Support in the traditional sense of the word – such as the classic typing room in many organizations – had at least three characteristics. The non-professional served the professional; the professional was practising a profession, the non-professional a more bureaucratic activity; and the relationship between them was hierarchical: to perform his trade, the non-professional depended on the professional. This bureaucratic activity, however, has evolved dramatically. Support is becoming more and more a professional activity.

First, it has become more complex. In the old days there used to be a staffing department that mainly dealt with formal regulations, for instance in relation to commencement and termination of employment. The tasks of what today is called human resources management (HRM) have become more comprehensive and complicated. The variety of positions has increased, the labour market can be tight, professionals ask for development trajectories, labour disputes are sometimes less easy to soothe or buy off, compensations vary more than they used to, and organizations require professionals that have more competencies than just the traditional ones (but also managerial, communicative, acquiring competencies). These and similar developments automatically lead to expansion and diversification of the HRM department's duties. These departments are confronted with more complex development trajectories and trajectories of commencement and termination of employment, and with requests to mediate in case of labour conflicts, to develop acquisition strategies, to design remuneration trajectories, etc. The growth of these departments is there at least partly as the result of developments within the profession.

Second, the relationship between professional and non-professional has changed. This relationship is no longer strictly hierarchical, but one that is characterized by interdependence. Sometimes non-professionals are directed by professionals, but the opposite is also possible. This sometimes feeds the professional's notion that he is no longer the one that carries the organization, and that the organization is no longer serving him, but rather limiting his functioning.

Third, the non-professional has also professionalized. In the case of HRM, it is obvious that this area has gained the characteristics of a profession: it has professional associations, magazines, congresses, a shared jargon, etc. This too has an impact on professionals – in the interests of clarity I will keep distinguishing between professionals and non-professionals. If this trade develops into a profession, then new standards of good professional HRM will originate from this new profession. In that case, the relationship between the professional and the non-professional is not only determined by the wishes and instructions of the professional, but also by these standards, which may conflict with the professional's wishes.

An HRM department that is comprised of various consultants may conclude that much time of these – costly – consultants is taken up by answering simple questions by professionals, who call them non-stop, and who tend to put their HR problems on the HRM department's plate. As part of its professionalism, the HRM department can introduce a 'click, call, face' system: whenever possible, questions are answered via Intranet or email (click), and by telephone if they are too complicated for that (call). If the matter is even more complicated, the person can make an appointment with an HR consultant (face). The introduction of such a system is understandable from the point of view of the HR managers' profession. It may, for instance, increase the efficiency and prevent money that is intended for the profession being spent on the non-profession. It allows the HRM department to spend more time on the complex questions that it is presented with. Professionals, however, can get the impression that the service is decreasing: the HRM department is less accessible, professionals have to take a more active stance, and the service is perhaps more standardized.

Increasing the professionalism of the supporting departments also results in the supporter becoming a countervailing power of the professional, rather than 'just' giving support, like the old typing room used to do. A countervailing power can diminish a professional's autonomy, while leading to better overall professional service.

NOTES

1 Paul S. Chan *et al.* (2008), Delayed time to defibrillation after in-hospital cardiac arrest. *New England Journal of Medicine*, 358, 3, pp. 9–17.

2 R. Crommentuyn (2008, in Dutch), Fouten zijn geen natuurverschijnsel. *Medisch Contact*, 63, 21, pp. 908–11.

3 Yearly questionnaire among university students (in Dutch): *Elsevier Thema Studeren*, October 2007.

4 Study by Roland Eshuis (2007), *Justice in Better Times: On the Effectiveness of Measures to Accelerate Civil Proceedings*, Rotterdam: Erasmus University.

5 Nassim Nicholas Taleb (2007), *Fooled by Randomness: The Hidden Role of Chance in Life and in the Markets*, London: Penguin Books, pp. 195–96.

6 Example from Jerome Groopman (2007), Medical dispatches: What's the trouble? *New Yorker*, 29 January, pp. 36–41.

7 Report by an external healthcare review commission (Externe onderzoekscommissie) (2006, in Dutch), *Een tekortschietend zorgproces. Een onderzoek naar de kwaliteit en veiligheid van de cardiochirurgische zorgketen voor in het UMC St Radboud te Nijmegen*, Zwolle: Inspectie voor de Gezondheidszorg, pp. 41–42.

8 John F. Murray (2000), *Intensive Care: A Doctor's Journal*, Berkeley: University of California Press.

9 Karl E. Weick (2001), The vulnerable system: An analysis of the Tenerife Disaster. In: Karl E. Weick, *Making Sense of the Organization*, Oxford: Blackwell Publishing, pp. 124–47, quote on pp. 141–42.

10 Information on this case based upon the evaluation report by F. Posthumus (2005, in Dutch), *Evaluatieonderzoek in de Schiedammer parkmoord, Rapportage uitgebracht in opdracht van het College van Procureurs Generaal*, The Hague: Openbaar Ministerie.

11 Dianne Vaughan (1996), *The Challenger Launch Decision. Risky Technology, Culture and Deviance at NASA*, Chicago: University of Chicago Press.

12 Report by the Dutch National Healthcare Inspection (Inspectie voor de Gezondheidszorg) (2007, in Dutch), *Zorgverlening door Jeugdgezondheidszorg, GGZ en huisartsen aan Gessica vanuit het perspectief van een veilige ontwikkeling van het kind*, The Hague: Inspectie voor de Gezondheidszorg.

13 National commission on terrorist attacks upon the United States (2004), *9/11 Commission Report*, New York: W.W. Norton.

14 Report by the Dutch Scientific Council for Government Policy (Wetenschappelijke Raad voor het Regeringsbeleid) (2004, in Dutch), *Bewijzen van goede dienstverlening*, Amsterdam: Amsterdam University Press.

15 Lynn Eden (2004), *Whole World on Fire: Organizations, Knowledge, and Nuclear Weapons Devastation*, Ithaca, NY: Cornell University Press.

16 Report by an external healthcare review commission (Externe onderzoekscommissie), op. cit., p. 39.

17 Through the Utrecht University Hospital's website: http://www.umcutrecht.nl/subsite/ Patientveiligheid/Onderwijs/Cursus+aios/deel-2---Achtergrond.htm (last consulted 20 June 2008).

18 Lucas M. Bachmann *et al.* (2003), Accuracy of Ottawa ankle rules to exclude fractures of the ankle and mid-foot: Systematic review. *Bristish Medical Journal*, 326 (7386), pp. 417–19.

4

STRATEGIC MANAGEMENT

WHY PROFESSIONAL ORGANIZATIONS NEED STRATEGIES

Strategy development beats any other subject when it comes to management lingo and model talk. It is often assumed that without a strategy an organization will not survive in the long run. After all, professional organizations are confronted with long-term trends that can have a major impact on their functioning. The ageing of the population will change the nature of healthcare, and massification has changed the nature of education – and will change it even further. Sectors that are confronted with such developments have to analyse them and develop a strategic response.

Strategy development is also closely linked to leadership: the real leader knows how to 'present a vision' and make 'strategic choices', of course for the long term. Leadership without a strategic vision is unthinkable, particularly in dynamic and uncertain times. Our use of language also shows that we value strategy. We speak about a consultant and a strategic consultant, a choice and a strategic choice, human resource management (HRM) and strategic HRM. Someone who adds the word 'strategic' to a managerial function or activity suggests that the function or activity is of a higher order.

Remarkably, many models that are used in the world of other management functions – human resource management, knowledge management, quality management, and so on – imply that there is a strategy. Many HR models, for example, are based on an organization's strategy. A description of this strategy is a prerequisite for a meaningful discussion about things like the desired composition of the workforce of employees. 'Alignment' is the key concept. The HR policy needs to be aligned with the strategy. The same is true in knowledge management. A simple Google search will yield several models for knowledge management that include as a first question: what is the organization's strategy? Apparently someone who knows an organization's strategy is able to identify the knowledge need and to address knowledge management. Strategy thus becomes the starting point or the origin of the other management functions.

Without a strategy it is apparently useless to talk about these management functions. Having a strategy implies assigning a goal to the organization; strategy is the origin of the other management functions, and it gives meaning to the organization's actions. Origin and goal and meaning: it almost seems religious.

LIPS AND HIPS: NO STRATEGY, EXCELLENT PERFORMANCE

It is possible to construct an entirely different picture of the concept of strategy. In their bestseller *Built to Last*, Collins and Porras (1997) make a remarkable observation. Many of the dozens of companies that they studied appeared to have neither a charismatic leader, nor a strategy.[1] What's more: not having a strategy is not just a possibility – a strategy can even hamper an organization. The explanation for this is that strategies can affect an organization's agility: they force an organization into a direction that may be sensible today, but senseless tomorrow. They also affect professionals' autonomy, as it prevents them from using promising strategic opportunities that they run into, because these do not fit into the originally chosen strategy.

So there are two realities here. Strategies are needed, given long-term developments, and strategies can harm an organization's adaptiveness or agility. The reconciliation between these two realities comes from the concept of 'emergent strategies'.

If professionals *are* given autonomy, this creates room for emergent strategies: strategic changes are not planned, but happen spontaneously.[2] Professionals react to external developments by making a series of small decisions, and the sum of these small decisions is a major change. Today's microtrend, which is only visible at the operational level, may be tomorrow's macrotrend.[3] Some of these developments will be successful, others will be aborted. Many of these developments will take place under the radar of managers.[4] Often the consequences of these developments only become visible at a later stage.[5] Certain units suddenly turn out to be much larger than others, or an idea turns out to have become generally accepted. A well-known metaphor to explain this development is the lifecycle of a virus. Viruses spread among the population at a slow rate, and are therefore not visible, but at a certain moment there is a tipping point and suddenly there is an epidemic.

Put differently, strategy development is a tacit process. Professionals who act intelligently and anticipate and react to dynamics surrounding the organization spontaneously create major strategic change, perhaps even without realizing. From a managerial point of view, this process – many small initiatives and many initiatives aborted – can be seen as a kind of muddling through. This muddling through, however, protects organizations from a major change on the basis of a strategic analysis that may prove to be incorrect in retrospect and may have disastrous consequences.[6]

In view of this line of thought, 'strategy' has a much less weighty connotation – strategies emerge, they happen. When Lee Iacocca once asked an employee if she knew what the company's strategy was, she answered that she wasn't interested in Iacocca's lips, but in his hips: not in his opinions, but in his actual movements. When this is applied to professional organizations, strategic changes are not the result of the manager's lips, but of the professional's hips.

This strips strategy development of much of its grandeur. Readers of this book who work at a professional organization should ask themselves the question, whether the strategy department is actually the influential, authoritative department where brilliant minds reside? Or is it the department that has never really known how to assert its position, and where staff members reside who were never really trusted with the key functions of the organization, and who were therefore assigned to doing 'some strategy stuff'?

These observations imply that we need to be cautious of the simple and often far-too-simple model talk on strategy development. Take for example the difference between strategic and operational decisions. In simple language: strategy is about *what* should happen, while operation is about *how* it should happen. Strategy is about doing the right things, while operation is about doing things right. Many management books still present the view that the difference between strategic and operational decisions is of major importance, and that it is the higher management that deals with strategy: 'Strategic decisions touch upon the entire organisation. Therefore they should be taken at the highest level of the organisation.'[7] It will be clear that reality is often different. There is usually no difference between the two types of decisions. Operational actions – the hips of the professional – can be of major strategic importance, while strategy papers, strategic decisions and strategic choices – the lips of the manager – are, and might remain, a paper reality.

STRATEGY PARADOXES

In addition, the idea that strategy development is a linear process – perform a SWOT analysis, formulate strategic goals, make implementation plans – is of course much too simple. When strategic changes happen through the hips of the professional, strategy development is not a linear process. What never ceases to amaze me – the reader will have to decide whether or not this is recognizable – is that many executives will immediately admit that top-down, linear models are much too simple, but use them eagerly all the same. Why is that?

The first reason is that linear models are clear and easy to communicate, which often makes them attractive in a complex and dynamic environment. This can be called the first strategy paradox: the more complex and dynamic the world is, the more attractive simple and linear models are. Of course, the question remains whether an organization can base its strategy on these models.

The second reason for the popularity of top-down, linear strategies is again a paradox. In professional organizations facing many dynamics and many uncertainties, there may be a call for visions or even for top-down strategic visions. At the same, these dynamics and uncertainties can limit the possibilities for such strategies. What may seem like a sensible strategy today may be quite senseless tomorrow. The more uncertainties, the larger the need for clear, strategic top-down visions, but the smaller the chance that these will succeed. In view of this paradox, our way of thinking about top-down strategies should be refined. Strategies turn out to have two functions: providing a direction for necessary change, but also meaning making in a world full of uncertainties. They are necessary in terms of providing meaning, although their capacity to change the direction of the organization might be limited. Later in this chapter I will explain the implications of this observation.

The third reason is that emergent strategies might yield unwanted results. The hips of the professionals can lead to new strategic directions under the radar of the managers, but these directions can be very undesirable. An example is waiting lists in the healthcare sector. Waiting lists are the result of thousands of small decisions of individual professionals. They develop emergently, no one wants them and they may evoke a top-down reaction. When emergent, bottom-up developments lead to an undesired result, the natural reaction is to develop top-down counter-strategies. Put differently, when emergent strategies, professionally initiated, do not work, they may be replaced by managerial interventions with their inherent top-down character.

WHY STRATEGY DEVELOPMENT BY MANAGERS IS SO DIFFICULT IN PROFESSIONAL ORGANIZATIONS, AND WHY IT OFTEN BECOMES A DULL PROCESS

Strategy development by managers, as we have seen, is sometimes inevitable, but certainly not always successful. What happens when managers in a professional organization intend to develop a strategy, perhaps even with assistance from the key professionals? A simple exercise will clarify this. Suppose that a professional organization's management gathers the key professionals for a strategic meeting. The participants of the meeting make a SWOT analysis: what are the external opportunities and threats faced by the organization, and what are its own strengths and weaknesses? Why is there often a misfit between the

SWOT method and the characteristics of professional organizations? What are the risks of making a SWOT analysis in a professional environment?

- An important characteristic of many professional organizations is *variety*: there are major differences among professionals. Probably one professional's ideas about opportunities and threats do not correspond with another's.[8] Suppose this is the case at a university, and the government has decided that the societal relevance of research is a new criterion for future funding. This may be a major opportunity for a faculty of an applied discipline, while it may be a threat for a faculty of a fundamental discipline. One organization, two faculties, two different opinions on opportunities and threats.
- The same is true for internal strengths and weaknesses. Suppose a small and specialized professional organization makes a SWOT analysis. One person may consider the size and degree of specialization a weakness of the organization: it is vulnerable and its service is too limited. Another may consider these characteristics as strengths: the organization is a 'niche player' that can provide high quality and personal service because of its small size.
- Even if there is consensus about a SWOT, it may be unclear which strategy is the one to choose. The question is always whether to follow or to oppose external developments. Should a university, for instance, follow the development towards more applied research? Or should it conclude that, given the increasing call for more applied research, it is strategically sensible to invest in more fundamental research? There is no unambiguous answer to that question, and therefore it is likely to evoke disagreement.
- Professional organizations are characterized by the large number of mutual dependencies – between management and professionals as well as among professionals themselves. In addition, professionals have a large degree of autonomy. As a result, disagreement about the SWOT analysis or the chosen strategy is almost always problematic. Suppose the university mentioned above chooses a strategy of developing more applied research. Such a choice always activates a mechanism that is often underestimated: it activates the opponents of the strategy, and will therefore limit the impact of the strategy. In the example above, to professionals in fundamental research, the choice for a focus on applied research can be a stimulus to increase the profile of their own research. They are stimulated to raise more external funding, to develop more external relations and seek external support. This may cause the strategy to gradually disappear.
- This is another situation in which the strategy paradox becomes apparent. The more dynamic the environment, the more need for a strategy, but also the more limited the durability of a strategy. Today's adequate reaction to these developments may be obsolete tomorrow.

Consequently, strategy development soon becomes a dull activity. Meetings about these issues often reach the conclusion that any opportunity may be seen as a threat, and any threat also offers a potential opportunity. If people have different opinions on the desired strategic direction, organizations frequently resort to abstract language when designing their strategy. As a result, the strategy will be empty and often hardly distinctive. David Maister analysed the strategic plans in a commercial professional sector. He found that everything seemed to be the same. 'Their strategic plans could have been reshuffled and redistributed, with the firm names replaced.'[9] Another interesting question for readers working in a professional organization: who actually knows the contents of their own organization's strategy?

STRATEGY AS THE ORIGIN OF OTHER MANAGEMENT FUNCTIONS

As noted above, many management models see strategy as the origin of the other management functions. A Google search for 'strategic human resource management' will yield statements such as 'The strategic human resource manager bases the HR strategy upon the organisational strategy' or 'A smart and professional HRM policy calls for perfect alignment with the organisation's strategy' or 'How can the HRM policy best be aligned with the (strategic) company policy as a whole?'. These are quotes from brochures for workshops on strategic HRM; they all presume that an organization's strategy guides the HRM. A Google search for models on knowledge management will result in the same type of quotes: an organization's knowledge need can be deduced from this strategy, and knowledge management can then be shaped in several steps.

These lines of thought are very common, and they are also common in literature on other management functions, but they can easily be criticized:

1 When strategies emerge, and therefore do not (yet) exist on paper, they will be of less guiding value to other management functions. This is especially the case when there may be several strategies that emerge in different places, or when a top-down strategy is merely a paper strategy that some parts of the organization hardly support, and so on.

2 The models are also based on the assumption that HRM, for instance, is a derivative of strategy. Is this really the case? Is the hiring of new staff, for instance by a university professor, based on his organization's strategy? Or does he have more factors to weigh: the more or less random supply on the labour market; the unexpected chance to attract a prominent scientist; an external project that was brought in and that doesn't really fit into the

strategy, but does call for new staff? Sometimes it will become apparent that HRM is not the result of a top-down strategy, but top-down strategy is the result of a number of HR decisions. The random labour supply, the prominent scientist, and the new project staff can change the nature of the research group and result in a new direction, which may eventually be promoted to be the organization's strategy.

3   The power of models like these is that they are easy to communicate. They can be immediately understood. They confirm the notion that strategy is important: without a strategy there is neither good HRM nor good knowledge management nor any type of good management. They imply control: if the steps in the model are followed, the management function in question will be adequately shaped. But they are also annoying: they are simplified models that occupy the minds of many people – consultants, managers, staff departments – and they often lack a link with professional reality. Perhaps the conclusion could be that a good professional does not need such models, while a bad manager is excessively dependent on them and may therefore become oblivious to the reality of professional organizations.

WHAT CAN MANAGERS DO?

If it is true that strategies emerge and happen, even under the radar of managers, then we can wonder about the implications for the roles of managers. What can they do to promote meaningful strategy development within an organization?

The logical answer appears to be: 'nothing'. Rely on the professionals. Strategies emerge from the bottom up. They happen. That, however, is also too simple. There is the second strategy paradox: on the one hand, uncertainties and external dynamics limit the possibilities of managers developing strategies, while on the other hand they can result in a call for leadership and strategies. How to deal with this tension? What to do when emergent developments take an undesired course – for instance in the case of waiting lists? Five answers to these questions are provided below.

1. THE BREEDING GROUND FOR EMERGENCE: PEOPLE AND PROCESSES

The first answer: strategy development under the radar means that successful strategy development strongly depends on the degree to which an individual professional is able to think and act strategically. This is not self-evident: after all, professionals may also develop a defensive attitude, and lack interest in innovation. This means that strategy development is an important HR question: are there enough professionals who think and act strategically? Are there professionals who are able to detect long-term trends in their discipline, or who have the intuition to trace promising developments? Professionals who can make connections with other disciplines, who have external networks, and who can use those? Professionals who are able to translate top-down strategies into actions that are meaningful to professionals?[10] Sometimes strategy development can be very simple: a manager should create a context that is attractive to this kind of professional. The possibilities are plenty: employment conditions, secondary employment conditions, exemption from managerial tasks, adequate support, comfortable housing, and so on. An attractive context like that often attracts new, high-quality professionals, who think strategically and, more importantly, act strategically, and who can therefore contribute to an organization's strategic capacity. Good operational conditions for such professionals have thus become of strategic importance.

A second answer: strategy development under the radar implies that managers' attention shifts from the *content* of strategy development to *processes* to detect what strategies happen under the radar.[11] The attention shifts from substantive analyses of the opportunities and threats surrounding the organization to the process of activating the strategic potential of the organization's own professionals. What is the essence of such a process?

- A manager invites professionals to participate in a process of strategy development.
- A manager accepts the fact that a professional organization is characterized by variety, and that the external developments can vary among different units. Every unit of professionals should therefore be allowed to develop its own strategy.
- The manager is not the one to offer strategic answers and solutions, but rather the one who presents questions to the professional units: what are the major developments that these units are facing, and what are the potential reactions that they identify? What are the microdevelopments of today that can become the macrodevelopments of tomorrow? What are the professional niches in which the promising developments are taking place? The questions can be 'sceptic friendly',[12] and serve the purpose of challenging professionals and getting strategic information out of the capillaries of the organization: what possible strategic directions do the professionals see? What strategic choices have they already made?
- Based on the answers, the manager can assess the strategic directions that units choose, and evaluate whether he sees possibilities for making

connections among these directions. In a next round of the process, these can be presented to the professionals. The manager can consider promoting certain developments through financial support. He can consider which strategic developments are sufficiently mature to be publicly presented by his organization, and which ones need a little 'incubation time' in order to flourish and require some extra time 'under the radar'.

- Of course this process is continuous, rather than a one-time activity. Discussing these matters on a regular basis will keep everyone's strategic awareness alert. Moreover, strategies need to be adaptive, and constantly adjustable to changing circumstances.
- A manager who goes through this process several times will develop his ability to learn. The answers provided by one unit can serve to formulate questions to the other. He learns about the commonalities and differences between the units. He will notice different reactions to external developments: some units move along with current developments, others oppose them. He will even be able to deduce a strategy for the entire organization from the strategic choices of the professional units.
- During these processes he can also exert influence: by asking intelligent questions; by asking professional units to provide a common reaction to his questions when he identifies possibilities for cooperation; and by giving hints as to which kind of activities he aims to support through extra funding. A manager in a professional organization can sometimes achieve better results through intelligent questions than through intelligent answers.
- Strategic plans are of minor importance, and in many cases they 'only' represent the codification of the outcome of this process. It is much more important that key professionals are continually stimulated to think strategically. How? By challenging them in this kind of processes – and, of course, by hiring good professionals.

2. STRATEGY DEVELOPMENT IS OFTEN A RITUAL OF REFRAMING WHAT ALREADY EXISTS – AND THAT IS FUNCTIONAL

One of the strategy paradoxes says that there are strong incentives for managerial strategy development, not only *in spite of* complexity and dynamics, but also *because of* complexity and dynamics.

Suppose a strategy is formulated by the board of an organization. Suppose the organization has a high degree of variety, which implies that there will probably be dissensus on opportunities and threats. Suppose the organization's environment is continually changing. How does the board's strategy affect this professional organization, knowing that professionals are not only focused on their board's opinions and beliefs, but also on those in the professional field?

A well-known reaction of professionals is called reframing. A process of reframing develops as follows. Suppose a board of a university, for instance, decides to turn a number of research themes into strategic 'spearheads', including the theme 'Sustainability'. Faculties are invited to make proposals for research in the field of sustainability, and the board will evaluate which proposals will be chosen.

What will the faculties do? Some will initiate new research on sustainability. Others will reframe their existing research: it will be presented as research into sustainability. A group that does research on public transport might reframe this as research in sustainability: an increase in public transport will contribute to a more sustainable world. The same thing can be claimed about a variety of other disciplines: research into lightweight materials, consumer preferences, energy sector reform, food production, geopolitical developments: all of it can be reframed and related to sustainability. The strategies of most of the applicants will likely lie between new research and reframing: they will submit proposals that are mostly reframing and only partly new.

Reframing means that much of the existing research is merely reframed to fit into the strategic spearheads. Insiders will recognize this game. Their analysis will be that the introduction of the spearhead has not brought the major strategic change, but instead it has caused a hassle: everyone had to reframe their existing activities and frame them in new plans. It is all true, but the picture is more nuanced.

First, the outsider's perspective might be different. From this perspective the university will seem to have an entirely new research portfolio, in which sustainability plays a prominent role. This can have positive consequences: external parties seeking to commission sustainability research may be more likely to turn to this university.

Second, after some time, even from an inside perspective, reframing can become functional. Existing research is reframed in sustainability terms. This might attract sponsors who are interested in sustainability, which can force professionals to adjust their research a little bit. Although the researchers on public transport merely reframed their research, they now have to pay more attention to sustainability than before. In their publications about sustainability they will have to refer to the state of the art in the field of sustainability – and therefore researchers will have to familiarize themselves to some extent with this state of the art. The scientific discourse will increasingly be conducted in the language of sustainability, which will affect the researchers, particularly new ones. All of these are small changes, comparable to an unwieldy oil tanker that shifts its course by just a few degrees but that will reach a substantially different destination in the end.

Third, there is always the possibility that the board was entirely mistaken in its judgement. Sustainability may not be a lasting theme in society, for instance, or all universities may develop programmes centred on sustainability, taking away the theme's competitive advantage. Or new, successful research that has nothing to do with the spearheads is given too little chance to develop. Or there is no room for other research which is much better suited to be linked to external developments than sustainability. If the strategy really implies a change of direction, then the board's mistaken judgement would be a disaster. The strategic change of direction, however, largely consists of reframing existing research, and therefore the mistaken strategic judgement is a lot less disastrous. If the direction is suddenly supposed to be entirely different, the reframing process will start all over again.

What does this example teach us about strategy development? First, that it is something of a ritual. On paper there may be a decisive strategic choice and strategic focusing, but in reality there is much reframing. By reframing their research, professionals feed the manager's impression that the strategy is working. In reality, they will insert the existing research portfolio into the new strategy.

Second, this ritual can be meaningful. In many indirect ways it will lead to an adjustment of the research – the change of course of the oil tanker. The strategy only has some impact on the implementation, and this is exactly the strength of the strategy. The potential disadvantages of the strategic choice are being mitigated. There will be sufficient room under the management's radar for developments that may not fall within the chosen strategy, but that are promising nonetheless.

Third, a sensible manager is conscious of all of these processes. Strategy development (1) induces the development of rituals, which (2) in turn limit the effect of the strategy, and which (3) are even functional. People who believe in the model talk of strategy development may find this counter-intuitive, but I hope to have provided sufficient evidence in this book that such model talk ignores the characteristics of professional organizations.

3. STRATEGIES OFTEN HAVE A LIMITED IMPACT ON THE DAILY OPERATION – WHICH IS HOW IT SHOULD BE

A third answer is that a manager would be wise to make a 'loose coupling' between his strategy and its implementation. A loose coupling means that professionals always have an opportunity to make their own choices; they don't have to implement the strategy without any critical reflection. The reason for this is that the operational truth is always much more complicated than can be planned from the top down. A loose coupling means space. It gives professionals an opportunity to learn and to take into account their own, local circumstances. This, too, may be counter-intuitive: strategies work because they are not fully implemented. I will use the problems surrounding healthcare waiting lists as an example to illustrate the importance of loose couplings.

Healthcare waiting lists seem like an operational problem, but they are regularly placed high on the strategic agenda. Let us take a classic approach towards strategy development and position the Minister of Public Healthcare as the strategic leader of healthcare. The healthcare institutions are the operational units that implement the Minister's strategic decisions. There is a lot of societal pressure on the Minister to put an end to the waiting lists.

Suppose the essence of the Minister's strategy is that all healthcare waiting lists need to be reduced. Such a strategy is clear, but the operational truth is always ambiguous. This is a sector with an enormous variety: hospitals with a wide range of specializations; homes for the elderly; organizations that have and have not made an effort to reduce waiting lists, and so on. Therefore there are large differences between waiting lists and the seriousness of the problems. A few observations:

- There is an obvious tension between waiting list reduction and healthcare cost. When waiting lists are eliminated entirely, this may compromise the efficiency of the service (there will be a large amount of expensive 'slack' in the service). Waiting lists allow for an efficient use of personnel: there is always a 'stockpile of work'.
- Waiting time also turns out to be reconsideration time. People on a waiting list sometimes decide that they abandon their resolution. Waiting lists also give rise to 'temporary healthcare': people on the waiting lists are offered lighter kinds of healthcare, which may cause them to withdraw from the waiting list.
- There are interdependencies among the various types of waiting lists. A hospital with waiting lists can cause an increase in the waiting lists for homes. Cuts in the field of domestic assistance may lead to longer waiting lists for nursing homes. Elderly people that would be able to live independently with simple forms of domestic help may be forced to turn to a home. In other words, reducing the problem in one step of the chain may aggravate it in another.
- This may result in tension between individual and collective responsibility. Do healthcare providers accept a collective responsibility? Are they prepared to adjust part of their capacity planning to the capacity in the chain, the region or the sector? To perform sub-optimally as an institution to allow the collective to perform optimally? Or do they only optimize their

internal processes, such as the capacity and healthcare quality in their own organization?

- There are institutions that will do anything to reduce waiting lists, and institutions that are indifferent to the problem. Simply put, there are hard workers and lazy workers. There is a fair chance that the strategic importance of this issue will cause the hard workers to work even harder, thus allowing the lazy workers to develop into free riders.
- Institutions are faced with the need to reduce waiting lists, but also with developments that may cause waiting lists to grow. Medical innovations lead to new preferences on the side of consumers, who will then apply for treatment. New laser technologies for eyesight correction will increase the waiting lists. Labour union arrangements about a reduction in working hours have a direct impact on hospital productivity. More working-hour reduction means fewer personnel and may result in longer waiting lists.
- The simple fact that the Minister places waiting lists high on the agenda makes them likely to grow. Clients in healthcare will start to show strategic behaviour. They will make sure to be put on one or more waiting lists in advance, causing them to grow autonomously.

What happens when the strategy is implemented without giving room to these observations? When a strategy is not loosely coupled to implementation, but tightly coupled? When the message is that waiting lists have to be reduced, irrespective of these observations? This will have many undesired side effects: healthcare that is much too costly, waiting lists that increase because of the strategy, temporary care that is used too little, more incentives for free-rider behaviour, and so on. These effects can be different for each discipline. There is therefore a need for space between strategic choices and operational implementation, allowing professional organizations to learn, to be adaptive and to act at their own discretion. Formulating a strategy is not very difficult, but reality imposes a large number of limiting conditions.

Loose coupling and offering room in the implementation phase are not self-evident. After all, a manager may interpret this as creating opportunities to ignore the manager's wishes. But room and loose coupling of strategy and implementation is often functional. It contributes to the strategy's effectiveness because the strategy can be adjusted to the complexity of the operation. An alternative might be that a manager takes into account all possible operational complications when formulating his strategy. But this manager will probably end up with an over-complex strategy that will not be very appealing and impossible to communicate.

4. TOP-DOWN STRATEGIES MIGHT WORK – WHEN AIMED AT SECONDARY PROCESSES

Many changes in professional organizations, including strategic changes, are effectuated through secondary processes.

Let's start with a simple example. The board of an educational institution makes a SWOT analysis and reaches the conclusion that the organization needs to reposition itself strategically. It needs to offer students an opportunity to develop themselves broadly and thus shape the classic ideal of universal education. In a rapidly changing society, educating super-specialists will not do: today's super-specialization will be obsolete tomorrow. Moreover, a society of super-specialists will require generalists who are able to make connections among the specializations.

Suppose the educational institution has a portfolio with a large number of specialist education programmes. This may result in a lack of support for the strategy among professionals. They will have to give up their programmes and the new strategy has nothing in it for them. As a consequence of their resistance, the strategic change process might fail. However, there are also secondary processes in an educational institution, such as scheduling, and the semester structure. The board can decide that every education programme must follow the same semester structure (education in the same weeks, exams in the same weeks and study time in the same weeks), and it can decide that every education programme must include a course-free period of 14 weeks to allow students to take a minor in another programme. This change may not be possible without resistance, but it is easier than trying to change the contents of education programmes. This measure can result in large numbers of students choosing to take minors in other programmes, in which case the management is taking an important step towards its strategic goals after all. If a minor is successful, the step from a minor programme to a Master programme may be easier to make – resulting in a broad Master through the simple route of a new structure of the academic year.

The point of this example is that an intervention in secondary processes is often easier than in primary processes, and such interventions can have a much more important strategic impact than may be obvious. In essence, the manager uses this method to effectuate the desired change in an emergent way.

5. ALL BLESSINGS COME FROM ABOVE: WHY TOP-DOWN STRATEGIES CAN BE NECESSARY AND EVEN FUNCTIONAL

Suppose a manager believes that strategic change is needed and that it will not come from the professionals. Suppose this manager is right: the professionals are too defensive and management is the solution, as illustrated in Chapter 3. Emergent strategy development is no option since the professionals do not want to change their routines.

This results in a challenging situation. Emergent strategy development does not result in the necessary change, but planned top-down strategy change has little chance of success in professional organizations. Suppose a manager has to rely on his planned, top-down strategies. What options does he have to employ these without the risk of these strategies failing due to the characteristics of professional organizations?

A top-down strategy has little chance of success, as mentioned before, because of the variety among and within professional organizations. Variety, however, also offers opportunities. The more variety, the more chance that some professionals *will* be responsive to a top-down strategy. These professionals may be able to activate the others.

In his research into lead times in courts, Roland Eshuis makes a remarkable observation.[13] Reducing lead times is high on the strategic agenda of the Council for the Judiciary: the legitimacy of justice can be compromised by lead times that are too long. There are top-down efforts to reduce the lead time of lawsuits. Certain courts have already made an effort to reduce their lead time, and they appeared to be sensitive to the top-down strategy. Others, however, have regarded lead times reduction as a non-issue, and they were not sensitive to the top-down strategy. So there are fast courts and there are slow courts. What was the impact of the Council's measures to reduce lead times? The fast courts were sensitive to these measures, the slow courts were not, so the fast ones became faster and the slow ones, in relative terms, slower. The conclusion might be that this strategy failed. It failed to do what it was supposed to do: influence the slow ones. This effect, however, can also be interpreted in another way. As the Council's strategy is embraced by some professionals, the gap between fast and slow will grow and this will result in peer pressure: if a critical mass of professionals does regard lead time reduction as important and does actually succeed in this, there is an increasing pressure from fellow professionals on the 'slow ones' to join in the effort. The bigger the gap, the more pressure.

The intelligence of this strategy is the fact that it may not be embraced by all professionals. This, however, is not really necessary. When a critical mass joins in the effort, eventually there will be a process in which professionals that are lagging behind will experience peer pressure. A variation to this theme is the fact that some professional sectors are characterized by a large amount of copying behaviour. If a professional unit implements an innovation, others will usually follow automatically. If this is true, top-down strategy will require nothing more than influencing one or more professional units. The rest will follow automatically.

THE FAMOUS FIGURE OF HENRI MINTZBERG, AND WHY IT CAN BE MISLEADING

Many publications on strategy refer to a figure of Henri Mintzberg,[14] which indicates that there are two types of strategy development: planned strategy development, which is often top-down, and emergent strategy development, which usually originates from the capillaries of the organization. The eventual, realized strategy is an amalgam of both planned and emergent strategies.

The idea of planned and emergent strategies being mingled into the ultimate realized strategy is attractive, but it will be clear by now that reality can be less than harmonious:

- It is possible for an organization to operate strategically without any planned strategies (Figure 4.1).
- It is possible for an organization to operate strategically without any planned strategies (Figure 4.2).
- Emergent strategies don't always conform to the stream of planned strategies; their direction can be entirely opposite (Figure 4.3).
- There may be multiple and mutually conflicting strategies in an organization (Figure 4.4).
- Planned strategies may only be codifications of what is already happening in an organization (Figure 4.5).
- Planned strategies can push away promising emergent strategies (Figure 4.6).
- A professional organization can be comprised of two worlds: the planned strategy and the emergent, actual strategy (Figure 4.7).
- A large number of emergent strategies take place under the radar of the manager (Figure 4.8).
- Strategy development can be 'just' reframing what is already happening in an organization; it is a ritual that may result in a small change of direction (Figure 4.9).

A formal strategy, a strategy on paper, in other words, may hide a whole range of processes, which means that the question always is: what is behind the formal strategy?

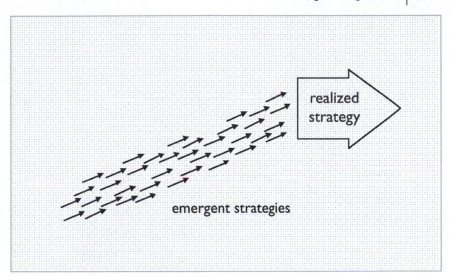

Figure 4.1
Planned strategy follows emergent strategy

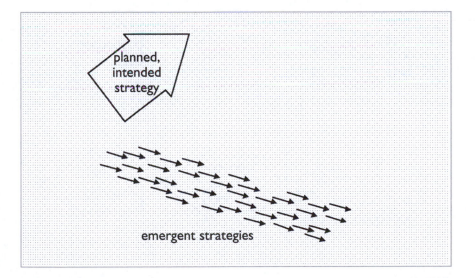

Figure 4.2
Planned strategy and emergent strategy diverge

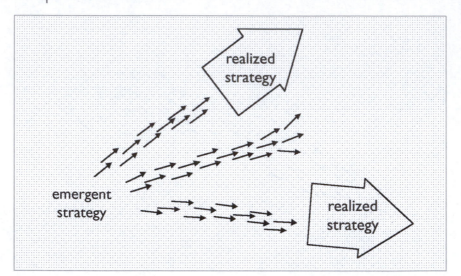

Figure 4.3
Multiple, mutually conflicting strategies

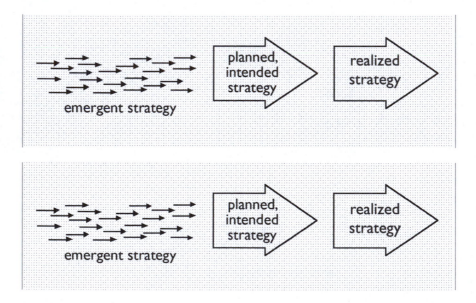

Figure 4.4
Planned strategies may sometimes be nothing but codifications of what is already happening in an organization

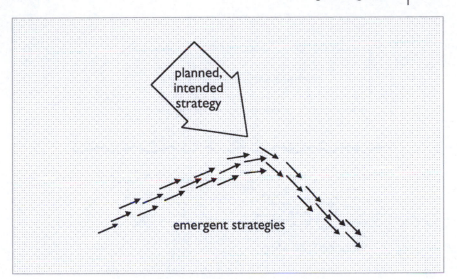

Figure 4.5
Planned strategies push the emergent strategies away

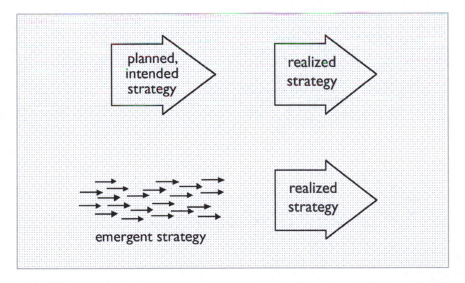

Figure 4.6
A professional organization can be comprised of two worlds: the planned strategy and the emergent, actual strategy

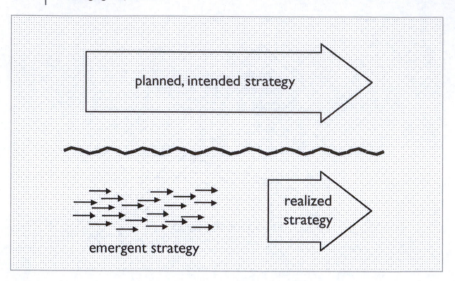

Figure 4.7
Strategy development under the radar of executive board and management

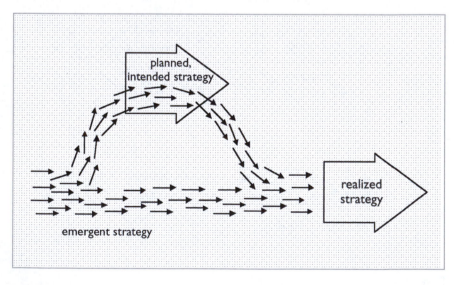

Figure 4.8
Strategy development as reframing existing activities

NOTES

1 J.C. Collins and J.I. Porras (1997), *Built to Last: Successful Habits of Visionary Companies*, New York: Harper Business.

2 Henri Mintzberg and J.B. Quinn (2003), *The Strategy Process: Concepts, Contexts, Cases*, Upper Saddle River, NJ: Prentice Hall; Henri Mintzberg (1994), *The Rise and Fall of Strategic Planning*, New York: Free Press. See also John E. Barbuto Jr's (2001) overview: How is strategy formed in organizations? A multi-disciplinary taxonomy of strategy-making approaches. *Journal of Behavioral and Applied Management*, 3, 1 (Summer/Fall), pp. 64–73.

3 Mark Penn (2007), *Microtrends: The Small Forces behind Tomorrow's Big Changes*, New York: Hachette Book Group.

4 See the interesting study into strategy development in an organization's periphery as a highly inductive process by Patrick Regnér (2003), Strategy creation in the periphery: Inductive versus deductive strategy making. *Journal of Management Studies*, 40, 1, pp. 57–82.

5 Joseph L. Bower and Clark Gilbert (2007), How managers' everyday decisions create – or destroy – your company's strategy. *Harvard Business Review*, 85, 2.

6 Charles E. Lindblom (1968), *The Policy Making Process*, Englewood Cliffs, NJ: Prentice Hall.

7 D. Keuning and D.J. Eppink (2000), *Management en Organisatie. Theorie en Toepassing*, Groningen: Stenfert Kroese, p. 72.

8 David Maister (1993), *Managing the Professional Service Firm*, New York: Simon & Schuster, p. 226.

9 Ibid., p. 223. See also Jean-Louis Denis *et al.* (2001), The dynamics of collective leadership and strategic change in pluralistic organizations. *Academy of Management Journal*, 44, 4, pp. 809–37. Strategic changes in pluralist organizations require collective leadership with a large degree of internal variety.

10 Graeme Currie (2006), Reluctant but resourceful middle managers: The case of nurses in the NHS. *Journal of Nursing Management*, 14, 1, pp. 5–12.

11 Said Elbanna (2006), Strategic decision-making: Process perspectives. *International Journal of Management Reviews*, 8, 1, pp. 1–20.

12 Maister, op. cit., p. 223.

13 Roland Eshuis (2007), *Justice in Better Times. On the Effectiveness of Measures to Accelerate Civil Proceedings*, Rotterdam: Erasmus University.

14 Mintzberg, op. cit.

5

QUALITY MANAGEMENT

QUALITY MANAGEMENT AS A CONTRADICTION IN TERMS

Strategy is to many managers what quality is to the professional: a concept with a high feel-good factor. Quality is often seen as the opposite of quantifiable values such as productivity, speed and lead time. A scientist is not supposed to focus on the number of publications, but rather on their quality. A doctor shouldn't focus on how fast he can treat a patient, but on the quality and the attention he can devote to them. A manager who continually presses for shorter lead times of legal procedures can threaten the judicial quality. An often-heard complaint is that the professional, due to 'efficiency thinking' and 'stopwatch culture', has insufficient time to provide a high-quality service. Quality, in other words, is supposed to be *the* professional core value that is continually under pressure from other values. It is only a small step to interpreting this as a sharp contrast between management and professionals. Managers represent efficiency, productivity and speed, while professionals represent quality.

QUALITY SYSTEMS

There is yet another contrast between management and professionals. No one can deny the importance of quality, and therefore quality has increasingly become the management's domain. Quality, as is often assumed, can be improved through quality systems that may, for instance, describe work processes that are supposed to lead to a high-quality service delivery, or that prescribe a process of diagnosis and treatment. People who are somewhat familiar with this world may know one or more of these approaches: INK, Total Quality Management, ISO 9000, Deming's PDCA cycle (Plan, Do, Check, Act), the DMAIC cycle as part of the Six Sigma approach (Define, Measure, Analyze, Improve, Control) and the ProQA approach (PROject Quality Assurance).[1] And then there are countless benchmarks that are used to look for 'best practices' and 'evidence-based' professionalism.

The core of these and similar types of quality management is that quality can be codified: it can be caught in descriptions, procedures and protocols. If this is possible, the next step is to certify a professional organization, giving the outside world an idea of the organization's quality. It is even better if several levels of quality can be distinguished. A professional organization can continually strive for improvement – a higher level of quality – and the outside world can compare the quality levels of professional organizations. It is easy to criticize this approach: the essence of quality cannot be codified and framed in procedures or descriptions of work processes. A teacher who teaches different generations of students – with varying skills and interests – or a doctor who performs medical operations will have to rely on his professionalism and tacit knowledge. No two situations are the same, and therefore professional action cannot be codified. If this is done anyway, the consequences are evident. The codification will be of little use to a professional, because it is too generic, or because it applies specifically to situation A, and not to situations A' or A'' which are slightly different. Codification will result in a work process on paper that will differ from a work process in reality. When describing the work process no longer has any added value for the professional, quality management will soon become a kind of bureaucracy and hassle. It will be even worse if control systems are introduced and if the professional has to account for all of his actions. Which steps of the work process did or did he not follow? This will soon become a ritual: ticking off a few boxes on a form, without any added value. It will become even more problematic when quality systems do not only lead to bureaucracy and hassle, but also compromise professionalism. Quality systems will then drive out quality. Professionals will have their hands tied to such an extent that there is insufficient opportunity for innovation. Or professionals will take a risk-averse position and lose the courage to deviate from the work process in certain complex situations, even when this may be desired from a professional perspective. 'Forget the paperwork, take care of the patient', a surgeon once said about such systems. It sums up quite strongly the argument against this kind of quality management.[2]

When this criticism is valid, how could quality management be shaped? The answer to this question is a classic one, which can be found in all management books: through mutual professional control. When professionals perform complicated tasks, the only people who can evaluate these sensibly are their fellow professionals. Among themselves, professionals can reflect on the different components of quality, their optimal relative weight, other people's quality judgements, how to deal with these, and so on.

This mutual professional control will often be a tacit process. A person who aims to be a good teacher will undoubtedly learn most when he can cooperate with an excellent teacher for a few years. Just put them together and the mechanism of mutual professional control will do the work. On the other hand, an excellent teacher may also learn from young, beginning teachers. They are often closer to the new generation of students, and can teach their seniors about minor and major habits that may have been effective in earlier days, but have lost their impact on a younger generation. This is no different for other professionals.

This kind of quality care is not planned and is often not made explicit. As teachers spend time with one another and work together, quality management is shaped during their interaction. Interaction among professionals is the core of quality management and hardly requires any managerial effort. From a professional perspective, quality management may even be a contradiction in terms. Quality does not need to be managed, but originates from the interaction among professionals. How can a university develop a high-quality research group? Simply by providing a nice building, sparing scientists from all kinds of hassle, giving them adequate support, and attracting a number of reputable scientists. Quality will then emerge automatically in their daily work. The professionals keep one another on the edge, learn from one another, make their networks available to one another, create synergy, and so on. Quality is not managed. It just happens.

To sum up, the stopwatch culture can affect quality, quality can bureaucratize through the introduction of quality systems, and quality often emerges tacitly. But there is also another reality: reference to quality can also be a professional fallacy that can always be applied when a professional does not agree with a certain development. Mutual professional control does not always work. There is something we call the non-intervention principle (Chapter 3) – recall the example of the inadequate cooperation among the doctors at the cardiac surgery department of Radboud Medical Centre, which resulted in casualties. All in all, there is sufficient reason to explore the definition of quality, and whether or not it can be managed.

QUALITY AS AN AMBIGUOUS AND DYNAMIC CONCEPT

Quality is a concept that is comparable to 'freedom' or 'peace' or 'affluence'. These are called ideographs: they represent values that everyone should strive for, but that are also ambiguous: their meaning can vary between different contexts.[3] A situation that one person perceives as an aggressive military intervention that threatens peace and safety may be judged by someone else as a just war that will guarantee peace and safety. Quality is an ambiguous concept too, and any argument about quality should start from that premise. This ambiguity can be identified in three steps.

1. QUALITY IS AMBIGUOUS: THERE ARE CONFLICTING VALUES

A first observation should be that quality is always comprised of a number of values and that these can conflict. Let us look at values in the case of a judge and a teacher.

To a judge, quality is comprised of several components:

- A verdict has to be in line with laws and regulations and with jurisprudence. A judge whose verdicts are consistently rejected after appeal in a higher court usually does not deliver quality work. In this case it is about the *legal quality* of a professional's work.
- The *treatment* of the various parties in a lawsuit is an important component. Are all parties heard? Do they have sufficient opportunity to clarify their standpoints? Do they perceive the trial to be fair?
- Along similar lines, the *legal procedure* is an important aspect of quality. Is the judge able to manage the trial in a transparent and orderly manner?
- The *clarity* of the verdict is important. Is the verdict clear to all stakeholders, even those who have little or no legal background?
- The *speed* of the trial is an important component. A lead time that is too long can be harmful to the parties involved or it can stimulate them to turn to a mediator at a future occasion.

The same exercise can be done for a teacher. Quality of education also has a number of different components:

- The teacher is supposed to transfer the right knowledge and also master this knowledge himself. Education should have a sufficient *level of content*.
- A teacher should be able to identify with his student's everyday life, and to make his students enthusiastic. The *method of knowledge transfer and teaching* are important components of quality.
- A teacher's programme needs to correspond with the programme that students have followed already, for instance in previous years. There should be *knowledge accumulation*.
- The programme needs to be *feasible*: students should be able to master the substance within the given amount of time.
- The substance needs to be *applicable*: students should be able to connect it with reality.

It will be clear that quality is an ambiguous concept: it is comprised of various components, which may conflict. A perfect legal verdict can be unintelligible to the parties. Improving the legal quality of a verdict – for instance from an

80 to a 90 per cent score – could take so much time that too many sacrifices are made in the areas of speed and lead time. Similar tensions may arise in the case of the teacher. Thorough substantive analyses may not get through to the students. Education that is good in terms of substance but insufficient in terms of feasibility will hardly have any net effect. In short, quality is comprised of conflicting values and there is always a need for trade-offs between them.

2. AMBIGUITY: VARYING VIEWS ON THE RIGHT TRADE-OFF BETWEEN DIFFERENT VALUES

A second aspect of quality is the fact that different stakeholders may hold different views on what quality is and what the trade-offs should be. Let us take another look at the example of the judge. A judge does not reach his verdicts in isolation, but works in relationship with a large number of other players, such as court officers, the Public Prosecutor, and the parties who bring a case to court. These may be divided into 'repeat players' and 'one-shotters', or into winners and losers. A similar list can be made for the teacher: fellow teachers, parents, colleagues who teach other subjects, and students, who can be divided into good and mediocre students, and students with and without intellectual curiosity. Each of these stakeholders may hold different views on the optimum trade-off between the conflicting values. That makes the concept of 'quality' even more ambiguous. When verdicts are reached faster, one stakeholder may perceive this as a quality improvement, while another sees it as an example of a 'stopwatch mentality' that compromises the legal quality of the verdicts. One stakeholder may feel that the use of simulations and games in schools is an educational improvement, while another finds this just another example of the infantilization of education.

If different stakeholders can hold different views on what the optimum trade-off should be, this means that a stakeholder's judgement on quality is always subject to debate. What does it mean if students are highly enthusiastic about a teacher's programme? Nothing *per se*. It may mean that a teacher skips difficult components, lacks substantive background and invests too much effort in the educational method. It may also mean that the teacher has invested much effort in making complicated substance accessible, and is competent at clarifying the substance and making it relevant to the students' everyday life. The only way to get a representative impression is to ask not only for students' judgement, but also that of other stakeholders. Do these support the student's judgement or do they contradict it? In short, if quality is ambiguous, impressions of the quality of professional service are only valid if they are based on an exchange of views among different stakeholders. In some cases this will result in consensus, but in other cases it will not.

Different stakeholders may not only hold different views on the right trade-off between different values, but the dissensus can be more fundamental: there may be disagreement on each of the separate values. What is a good treatment? What one person may interpret as a right treatment of a suspect may be seen by someone else as an overly correct treatment that compromises the judge's authority. Take elderly care, which is shaped by the relationships among doctors, nurses, the elderly themselves, their partners and their children: each of these may hold different views on quality care, and on which actions are needed and which should be eliminated. There may be *uncertainty* about what sensible professional action implies. A care relationship may be full of dilemmas that are sometimes hard to answer unambiguously. In order to teach a lesson about responsibility, a professional in the care sector sometimes needs to tolerate irresponsible behaviour in order for the client to experience the consequences. This makes quality largely unmanageable: it cannot be framed in or controlled by behaviour protocols or quality systems.

3. QUALITY AS A DYNAMIC CONCEPT

A third aspect is the fact that the trade-offs between values are never static, but always dynamic. Due to all kinds of developments, certain components can gain importance at the expense of others. There may be new components: in education, the teaching method is becoming increasingly important, as is the degree to which the education is IT-supported. In court cases, dispensing justice in a foreign language may be a new component of quality.

In short, quality is an ambiguous concept that calls for trade-offs between the underlying values. There may be dissensus about these trade-offs and views on quality are always changing. Any kind of quality management should take this into account. Management is usually all about control, so there may be a risk that quality is used as an argument to focus on a certain aspect of quality, on a certain trade-off, or on a certain interpretation of a value.

PROTOCOLS ARE AN INSULT TO A PROFESSIONAL, AND HARM PROFESSIONALISM

What implications does this have for quality management? An important one seems to be the fact that codification of quality – the essence of many quality systems – is quite problematic. The surgeon cited pg. 68 – 'Forget the paperwork, take care of the patient' – seems to be right. This is increasingly so because many professions continue to specialize even further, which gives rise to super-specializations. The larger the need for specialized knowledge, the fewer the possibilities for codification. A doctor may have so many actions to perform that codification or protocollation would result in an extensive manual that is inaccessible. A few observations may clarify the problems surrounding codification:[4]

- In the *Annals of Thoracic Surgery*, a team of doctors describe a case of a three-year-old girl who falls into a pond in Austria, sinks to the bottom, and is found only after 30 minutes. At that point she has a 'core temperature' (the temperature inside the body) of 18.4°C and no heartbeat. An hour and a half later(!) she arrives at the hospital. Her heart is non-functional, her lungs are severely damaged and her brain has been affected. The chances of recovery are slim, but two weeks later she is released from the hospital and 20 months later she is fully recovered. This recovery had required a large number of medical interventions involving vital organs such as the heart, lungs and brain.[5] Which role could codification play in this case, in which different specialists have to act and cooperate under strong pressure? Does the choice and order of the interventions depend on this girl's condition in this situation, and could a future, similar situation call for other choices? Is the complex medical care that is needed here so strongly dependent on the competencies and experiences of these particular doctors? The question implies the answer, it seems.
- For another example of this complexity, let us look at a study into the number of actions taken per patient at an intensive care unit. An average patient requires a daily number of 178(!) different actions, such as administering medication, registering this or that, emptying the lungs to avoid pneumonia, brushing the teeth twice a day, inserting an intravenous catheter, doing exercises to avoid muscular atrophy, and so on. Mistakes are made in 1 per cent of these actions. This may seem like very little, but it amounts to two mistakes per patient per day. It should be noted that medical staff in an intensive care unit are working in an environment that is often chaotic. Those 178 actions need to be taken, 'despite some monitor's alarm going off, despite the patient in the next bed crashing, despite a nurse poking his head around the curtain to ask whether someone could help "get this lady's chest open"'.[6] Is it useful to codify all of these actions? If codification is indeed introduced, who will be able to recall all of these 178 actions, and act accordingly in an environment that is often chaotic and requires a lot of multitasking? Again, the question implies the answer.
- The variety of situations that a doctor can be faced with is enormous. A study among 41,000 trauma patients brought to light 1,224 different injury-related diagnoses. Of course several diagnoses can overlap: the

researchers counted 32,261 different combinations. How can the correct professional action be codified in this case? This seems to be impossible, particularly when we keep in mind that new medical possibilities only lead to more diagnoses and more combinations.[7]

Given this complexity it is hardly surprising that many professionals are critical towards quality systems. Acting professionally in such situations requires a large amount of tacit knowledge, local knowledge and what is called 'expert audacity' (the courage to make decisions) – rather than a protocol or a checklist or something of the kind.

A good professional being faced with the Austrian girl in the example above will act and improvise on the basis of his experience and knowledge, rather than on the basis of protocols. In fact, a professional who relies on protocols in such situations apparently lacks the necessary experience and knowledge. It is easy to make a comparison with a *chef de cuisine*. The chef cooks on the basis of experience, feeling, taste and smell. He has developed these over the course of the years. He makes decisions while cooking, and improvises depending on the way the dish in the pan is reacting to his cooking. It is the amateur chef, on the other hand, who nervously clings to the instructions of the cookbook. A chef who is forced to work according to a protocol will take this as an insult to his professionalism.

Imagine that the cooking instructions are codified, and other chefs start to follow this standard. This may harm their professionalism: if they meekly follow the instructions, the dish will be less tasteful than if they learn how to react to the way the dish in the pan is developing. There seems to be an inverse correlation between the complexity of a professional task and the potential for codification. The more complex a task is, the smaller the potential for codification.

HIGH QUALITY PROFESSIONAL SERVICES? PROTOCOLS ARE KEY

As stated on several occasions in this book, all of this is true, but it is only part of the truth, for simple as well as for complex professional actions.

SIMPLE PROFESSIONAL ACTIONS

To clarify this, let us take a look at a hospital intensive care unit (ICU). Many ICUs are faced with infections resulting from the insertion of catheters. It has been estimated that there are around 80,000 catheter-related infections in the US per year, resulting in 28,000 deaths. The average cost of an infection is estimated to be US$45,000.[8] The question arises, how many of these infections could be avoided? In order to look into this, a relatively simple action was codified in a few hospitals in the state of Michigan. The medical staff was given a checklist with five actions that everyone had to follow. If a doctor failed to do this, the nurse would be authorized to point this out to the doctor and to interrupt the medical actions. The checklist prescribed that doctors (1) wash their hands, (2) cover their hands and face as much as possible when inserting a catheter, (3) disinfect the patient's skin with a disinfectant, (4) avoid using patients' thighs, which research has shown to be prone to infections, and (5) remove unnecessary catheters. This checklist obviously contains five rather trivial points – almost disturbingly trivial. What doctor would not do these things? Who would fail to disinfect a patient's skin or to wear a mouth cap? Who would overlook an unnecessary catheter? It is like dictating to a *chef de cuisine* how to boil potatoes – the most basic action thinkable – and to tick a box every time he does this. 'Forget the paperwork, take care of the patient' – once again this seems to be the most sensible reaction in response to such a checklist.

But what was the result of the introduction of this checklist, which was used by 103 ICUs who performed a total of over 375,000 catheter-days? Before the introduction of the checklist, these ICUs were facing 2.7 infections per 1,000 catheter-days; three months later this number had decreased to zero. After 16–18 months there was still a strong reduction: the number of infections was 66 per cent lower.

Apparently harmful habits arise even in a complex and demanding environment in which a professional has to perform a countless number of actions, and even if these are relatively simple. Perhaps these two factors are in fact related: the more complex and demanding an environment, and the more professional attention is spent on this, the higher the chance that simple processes are neglected.

COMPLEX PROFESSIONAL ACTIONS

What is the situation relating to complex challenges, such as the case of the Austrian girl described above – cases in which different disciplines work together and every individual doctor is confronted with a very complicated task, tasks that are too complicated to be codified?

Codification of the actions to be performed by doctors seems to be impossible in this case. A medical intervention is much too complicated for that. But there is another thing that may add value to codification. The Austrian hospital was familiar with patients in similar situations to the girl – mostly skiers that had been caught in avalanches.[9] Their chances of survival depended on a large number of professionals: the helicopter rescue team, the trauma doctors, the anaesthesiologist, the cardiac surgeon, the pulmonary specialist, the bioengineering staff, the ICU support staff, and so on. The more professionals are involved in an activity, the more interfaces there are among these professionals, and it is particularly these interfaces that are risky. Interface problems can be avoided by codification of the process that needs to be followed in cases like that of the girl. Codification enables the professionals who are the first to arrive at a scene – and who are therefore involved early in the process – to quickly inform the professionals that are involved at a later stage, and to indicate which professionals need to be ready to start which actions. The doctor in charge of the girl's operation stated that such checklists have helped to save several comparable patients, while this had been impossible before.

The more complex an action, the more specializations are involved and the more interface problems can arise. In the case of the girl, these are particularly related to the loss of time caused by the many interfaces. Apparently the amount of complexity that a professional is faced with can be so high that standardization and codification become necessary. Another example: the aircraft industry developed in such a way that at any given moment, airplanes consisted of so many technical systems that a single expert (the pilot) was no longer able to operate the airplane: they were 'too much airplane for one man to fly'.[10] The solution consisted of standardized checklists that indicated how pilots should operate these systems, allowing them to deal with the multitude of systems and interfaces.

HOW CODIFICATION AND QUALITY CAN BE INTERRELATED: SIX DIFFERENT VISUALIZATIONS

As a result, the interpretations of the meaning of codification for the quality of the professional service are quite different. Codification can result in unnecessary paperwork because professional activities tend to be complex – like in the example of the *chef de cuisine*. Figure 5.1 is an illustration of this: in the case of simple service, codification may have an added value, but as the complexity increases, this added value decreases.

What's more, codification can even harm professionalism when it forces professionals to conform to a certain standard – again, refer to the example of the *chef de cuisine* who suddenly has to abide by a cookbook.

The Bathtub curve, as illustrated in Figure 5.2, implies that codification may be useful in the case of very simple tasks – infections at an ICU – but also in

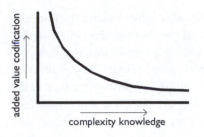

Figure 5.1
The Slide curve

Figure 5.2
The Bathtub curve

Figure 5.3
The Hockey Stick curve

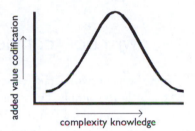

Figure 5.4
The Bell curve

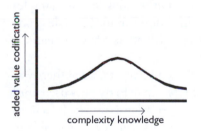

Figure 5.5
The Flattened Bell curve

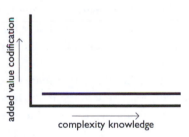

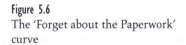

Figure 5.6
The 'Forget about the Paperwork'
curve

the case of very complex tasks, which involve a lot of interfaces among professionals – as in the case of the Austrian girl. But a Hockey Stick curve is also
a possibility (Figure 5.3). The example of the pilot illustrates that codification
has little added value in the case of relatively simple tasks, but as airplanes
become more complicated, the importance of codification increases – 'too much
airplane for one man to fly'. Another possibility is the Bell curve: codification

has no added value for simple tasks – as in the case of the chef and the potatoes – nor for complex tasks, which fully depend on the chef's professionalism and creativity. There may, however, be an added value for intermediate cases: see Figure 5.4. A Bell curve may also be less pronounced (Figure 5.5). Figure 5.6 shows a valuation of codification that appeals to many professionals: if tasks are simple, codification is not necessary; if they are complex, it is impossible. In addition, there are tasks that were initially very complex, but that have been standardized and codified in response to new medical developments, such as the introduction of so-called focused factories for cataract, hip and gallbladder operations. These medical interventions used to be extremely complex, but are currently subject to standardization.

WHY DOES CODIFICATION SOMETIMES WORK?

'Forget the paperwork, take care of the patient' – this statement turns out to be a little too simple. Even when professional tasks are complex, codification can have an added value. At the same time, codification can also result in bureaucracy and hassle. So when is codification a blessing for the profession, and when is it a disaster? When does it improve professional service and when does it impede a professional in using his tacit knowledge and audacity? It is the well-known 'tool for toy' question: when is codification a useful instrument to the professional, and when is it merely a toy for the manager or consultant?

In order to answer this question, let us take another look at the examples above. It can be noted that the effects of codification cannot be understood without knowledge of the underlying processes. I will name a few elements of these processes.

First, there was a high sense of urgency and a strong conviction that there was a problem. The statement 'too much airplane for one man to fly' was used until a very advanced airplane, which had raised high expectations, crashed. Infections at the ICU were high on the agenda. Austrian doctors had never been able to save the life of a patient such as the little girl. Second, codification turned out to be of added value to these professionals: no more crashes, fewer infections, and a life-saving intervention. Third, an important factor was the fact that there was *fast feedback*. In the Michigan hospitals, for example, there was monthly reporting on the number of infections. Showing the positive effect of a measure increases the support for it. Fourth, it was important that the idea of codification is not approached *in a dogmatic manner*. In Michigan a number of hospitals did not want to participate in the experiment, which was accepted right away. Successes are reached more easily when parties are willing to participate, and a proven success will multiply itself. Fifth, there was a *high level of professional involvement* – doctors and nurses were appointed as champions of the project. This involvement was also reflected in the codification itself. The codification in the Austrian hospital was owned by these doctors in this hospital. The checklist used in Michigan differed from the one used previously in other hospitals; there was an opportunity for *local codification*.

It will be obvious that these are all signs of a 'normal' process of change in professional organizations – see Chapter 9: a process in which professionals are involved in shaping the codification, and which can only succeed if the professionals see the added value of the codification. And there is room for different kinds of codification, but also for the possibility that there is apparently no added value in codification, and that the idea can therefore be abandoned. The *process of codification* has thus become as important as the codification itself. This process will create 'ownership' of the codification, and only then will it be effective. If there is no ownership, there is no room for codification. Codification, after all, is senseless if professionals do not see its added value even after having gone through such a process.[11] Managers can have an added value when they organize this process of codification, but under the condition that it needs to be of added value to professionals.

FROM CODIFICATION TO INTERACTION

So far we have identified two simplisms surrounding quality management:

- The first simplism is that codification and protocollation always contribute to better quality. They can also result in bureaucracy and hassle, and even compromise quality.
- The second simplism is that the meaning of quality management decreases when professional tasks become increasingly complex. Figures 5.1 through 5.5 show that there are many nuances to this relationship.

This situation, in short, calls for a nuanced approach. There are professional situations in which codification has an added value, and there are those in which they do not. Suppose the latter is the case; then how can quality management be shaped?

The answer was provided in the introduction to this chapter: through mutual professional control. When a young teacher is working alongside an older teacher, when senior medical students do their residencies, or when an inexperienced judge resides in a multiple court together with experienced judges, there is tacit quality care, the value of which can hardly be overestimated. It hardly calls for managerial interventions.

This tacit mutual professional control can in fact be made explicit. The essence of this is extremely simple: activities can be organized that stimulate professionals to reflect on their own work and that of their colleagues. Quality circles, peer groups, brainstorm sessions, training activities, and so on. These activities hardly call for managerial activities either. As a management guru once said at a conference that I attended: good quality management does not call for systems and managers, but for coffee and doughnuts. Let professionals meet, and tacit quality care will naturally emerge.

In short, the added value of management in the case of interaction seems to be limited. This is another paradox of managing professionals: when we approach the core of the professional activity – the essence of what is important in professional organizations – the added value of managers is extremely limited.

However, three observations need to be made here. The notion that quality care emerges spontaneously and is tacit rests on three assumptions (see also Chapter 3).

The first assumption is that the mechanism of mutual professional control works. This, however, remains to be seen – as explained in Chapter 3. A professional habitat depends on mutual professional control, but many professional organizations are also operating on the basis of the non-intervention principle. Professional A does not get involved with professional B if professional B does not get involved with professional A, which results in both of them having greater degrees of freedom.

The second assumption is that there is sufficient variety among professionals who control one another. If there is no variety, the mutual control will be less effective. This variety is not self-evident either. Professional communities can fall victim to 'groupthink'[12] or the 'principle of tenacity':[13] a group of professionals develops shared views on what constitutes good professional action, and these views are maintained tenaciously – perhaps tacitly as well, without the professionals realizing it. This is called cognitive fixation.[14] Cognitive fixations often emerge through social fixations: there is a group of professionals who share and create knowledge through interaction, but this group hardly changes in terms of composition and the patterns of interaction remain unchanged as well. When a judge, for instance, always resides with the same group of judges, the interactions will eventually become too predictable, which can hamper processes of mutual control. There may be, for example, an older judge who dominates the interaction, and the others therefore adopt a passive attitude. There is a risk that at a certain point, these professionals are no longer learning – and there is cognitive fixation – because of a lack of input of insights from other or new professionals.

In many professional organizations such cognitive fixations are all but unthinkable. Sometimes professional units are small, and many professionals prefer to stay in the same place, so they constantly run into one another.

Third, there is a difference between individual and collective quality. Individual quality refers to individual professional actions: the daily operational actions of individual professionals. The judge who administers justice, the television maker who makes programmes, the teacher who teaches – quality equals delivering good verdicts, good programmes and good education. Collective quality, on the other hand, refers to quality questions that transcend the individual level. It is about quality at the level of the professional organization, a professional sector or the branch as a whole. Even if an individual judge is doing his job properly, the result at the collective level can be that waiting times are too long. Even if a television maker produces fabulous programmes, the total programme package can be too limited, making the entire programming too limited. Professionals sometimes find themselves too much in 'smaller mind' rather than in 'larger mind' – as has been described in Chapter 3.

What to do if a professional unit is characterized by too little variety, a certain level of seclusion and groupthink, and many professionals who are in 'smaller mind'? What if there is a risk that the mutual professional control is working insufficiently? What role can the manager play? The dilemma is obvious: in such a situation, there is a need for an intervention, but the manager has insufficient expertise to intervene effectively. The way out, again, is extremely simple: if the manager cannot intervene *substantively*, due to his lack of expertise, he can intervene *procedurally*. He can organize the professional interaction by confronting professionals with other professionals, thus creating variety and breaking through groupthink, and drawing attention to collective quality. The easiest way to do this is by designing procedures that stimulate professionals to interact.

There are plenty of examples of such managerial interventions. Take a look at NASA, for instance: a prime example of a professional organization. Engineers from various disciplinary backgrounds work together on the construction of a space shuttle. There is often no proven technology available, and the technology is subject to constant development. NASA is a high-risk organization: if something goes wrong, the consequences can be disastrous. How can NASA's management make sure that the accident risk is as low as possible if there is no one who has sufficient expertise to oversee the entire process of designing and constructing a space shuttle, neither among the managers nor among the professionals?

The answer lies in organizing interaction among professionals.[15] NASA uses many 'check and double check' procedures. Designs and constructions are made by an engineering team, while another, competing team is tasked with examining these very critically, looking for mistakes and uncertainties. These constant challenging procedures make sure that engineers are followed critically by fellow professionals who only have one goal: tracing weaknesses in design and construction, and discussing these with the design and construction teams. This process continues until there is a closure in the technical debate: a choice is made for a construction and for an acceptable risk. Such a process can be organized and formalized, for instance by demanding a formal go/no-go for designs and constructions. Organizing this is a relatively simple managerial intervention that can prevent the non-intervention principle from being present among professionals.

This is an intern process to promote mutual professional control, but there is an external variation to this theme as well: external professionals are involved in the process of mutual professional control. The notion that managers can in fact organize the process of mutual professional control can be illustrated by the most famous example: an external review.

EXTERNAL REVIEWS: HOW THEY ARE USUALLY SHAPED

External reviews are a type of procedural intervention as well. The professional is reviewed by a fellow professional, and the manager intervenes through the design of the external review procedure. This procedure can usually be summarized as follows:

- A protocol is made for the external review: how are the external review committee's members selected, which criteria will they use, what are the formats for the various reports, who will be receiving these reports, and so on.
- The organization that is to be reviewed performs a self-assessment: it uses a particular format to describe its activities in the period that is to be reviewed, and which strengths and weaknesses it identifies for itself.
- The external review committee studies the self-assessment and visits the professional organization. During this visit, interviews are held with a number of professionals in the organization.
- The review committee writes a draft report that outlines its findings. This will be sent to the professional organization, which is allowed to provide feedback.
- The review committee concludes its final report.

External reviews that follow a procedure like this obviously have a strong focus on interaction, and the reviewee plays a very active role. Through the self-assessment, the reviewee can even set part of the review's agenda. During the committee's visit, which is a crucial element of the review, there is another chance to highlight the reviewee's performance. Even the process of concluding the final report is interactive, and offers the reviewee an opportunity to exert influence.

In a procedure like this, the reviewer operates at a distance from the reviewee on the one hand, but on the other hand the reviewer creates a strong connection with the reviewee. The advantages of this paradoxical attitude – being distant, yet connected – will be clear. There is an increased chance of a fair judgement because the reviewer works in close cooperation with the reviewee and will therefore be well informed on the reviewee. This cooperation makes it more difficult for the reviewee to shirk the reviewer's final judegment. Distance will prevent the reviewer from becoming the reviewee's captive and will also contribute to the authority of the final judgement.

MASCULINE AND FEMININE EXTERNAL REVIEWS

The next thing to note is that there are various types of external reviews. This variety can be summarized on the basis of a number of choices.

- Retrospective or prospective? A retrospective review focuses on the past performance of the professionals. It is assumed that a good past performance is the best indicator for future performance: a person who performed well in the past will do so in the future as well. A prospective review, on the other hand, focuses on the future. Which activities will the reviewee develop? What is the underlying vision? Do these activities fit into the developments within the profession and in society? The idea is that past performances cannot be changed, and that it is therefore more useful to look ahead, particularly when the profession is faced with a turbulent, ever-changing environment.
- Individual or comparative? It makes a difference whether the reviewee is an individual organization or a group of organizations that are not only judged separately, but also compared with one another. Comparison can be conducive to the quality of the review, because it offers the reviewer a larger amount of context. However, it may also hamper judgement when there are important differences among the reviewees that are to be compared.
- Quantitative or qualitative? A quantified judgement implies that a review committee will eventually grade the professional organization. In the Dutch system of university reviews, research is judged with four different grades: for quality, productivity, relevance and viability. Grading, however, is not a necessity. A reviewer can limit himself to passing qualitative judgement.

- Ranking or individual feedback? If a comparative review is opted for, including quantified judgements, the logical next step is to rank reviewees. The alternative is that there is no ranking, and every reviewee receives feedback individually.
- Closed or public? A closed external review implies that there is limited public reporting. The committee may, for instance, only publish a management summary of its findings. The underlying idea is that this creates a safer environment in which the reviewees will be more willing to discuss their weaknesses. The disadvantage, of course, is that the external review becomes harmless: it is easier for an underperforming, unwilling reviewee to dodge a closed external review than a public one.
- Judgement or feedback? Is the committee's conclusion a judgement that may have consequences for the reviewee? Or is it merely feedback, aimed at helping the reviewee to improve his performance?
- Reporting to the professionals or to the manager? The last question is who receives the report: the professional, in professional language? Or the managers, in managerial language?

Based upon these choices, one can distinguish two types of external reviews. I will call these the feminine and the masculine variants. The feminine variant places the external review committee and the reviewee in a horizontal relationship with each other, and learning and improving are key. In the most extreme case this is a prospective, qualitative, individual external review, which does not result in ranking, is not publicly reported, emphasizes learning, and does not involve the manager. The masculine external review is retrospective, is based on quantified scores, involves comparison and ranking, is publicly reported, and involves managers. The relationship between the reviewer and the reviewee is vertical.

With regard to feminine versus masculine external reviews, there is of course no right or wrong. Both variants involve certain risks. The most important risk of the feminine variant is that there is 'peer intimacy' – the reviewer and reviewee are so close to each other that the judgement cannot be fair, or that the reviewer becomes the captive of the reviewee. Suppose some professionals perform poorly and oppose change, for instance because they are over-content with their own performance. The risk of the feminine variant is that it does not challenge these professionals and that they get away with their underperformance. There are, after all, professionals who are able to charm others with their visions of the future and their ambitious plans that are supposed to conceal their past underperformance. Everyone is probably familiar with the professional who declares that his limited past performance is totally explicable – that it is actually a top performance, given the circumstances under which the work had to be done, that the local circumstances place specific demands on the profession's practice, or that the reviewer's criticism stems from a different paradigm and therefore lacks justification. All of this may be true, but they can also be professional fallacies. In a one-liner: the feminine approach codifies professional underperformance, and effectuates no modification whatsoever. This, however, is a risk rather than a given. The reality may also be that the reviewer or fellow professional is able to bring about a dramatic change because the review took place in a safe environment.

The most significant risk of the masculine variant is the fact that it can result in unfair judgements. After all, a review committee includes a limited number of individuals, who all have their professional peculiarities. I have seen a member of an external review committee, an internationally highly respected researcher, delivering a strong plea in his feedback to devote more attention to research into X. Many colleagues did not quite understand why, until it became clear that his chair was 'Philosophy, in particular X'. Members of external review committees – even philosophers – can also be in 'smaller mind'. The next question is what implicit or explicit criteria a committee uses. Then there are strict and compliant committees; committees whose members are much or little involved, with or without outspoken views on the profession, with chairs that have much or little influence on the reporting; committees with much or little tolerance towards local difference, and so on. Every judgement includes a certain amount of subjectivity, and every judgement results from the coincidental composition and working method of the committee.

In this case too, unfair judgements are a risk, not a given. Moreover, an unfair judgement is not the most horrible thing that can happen to a professional – everyone is judged unfairly at some point, and unfair judgements may provide valuable lessons. However, they become problematic when they have a high impact. Suppose that a university's board has a policy to terminate every research programme that scores less than 4.5 on a scale of 1 to 5. In that case the external review committee's judgement will have a high impact, and an unfair judgement does constitute a problem. Moreover, suppose that professionals are aware of the subjectivity and coincidence that play a role in the final judgement. This will be a strong incentive for strategic behaviour, such as intentional and unintentional attempts to mislead the external review committee. Box 5.1 lists 12 examples of such strategic behaviour.

Box 5.1 External reviews: how professionals can impress/ mislead external reviewers via strategic behaviour

1 Make sure that the paper reality is in perfect order. Criticism on missing plans, statistics and evaluations is the easiest thing for a reviewer. When the paper reality is in order, criticizing is a lot harder.

2 Be aware that reviewers are snowed under with information. It is often extremely difficult for them to pass judgement because they will be uncertain about the question whether or not they have an adequate overview of the organizations. Weaknesses mentioned in the self-assessment will almost certainly appear in the final report. Be chary in this regard – chances are that they will be magnified in the final report.

3 When something is dysfunctional, announce a reorganization of this aspect before the review. This forces the reviewer to conclude that something is dysfunctional, but a change for the better has already been initiated.

4 Even for fellow professionals in the review committee it is difficult to pass judgement on the activities in question. There are always specific and local circumstances that have to be taken into account and that the reviewer is less familiar with. Emphasize these circumstances.

5 Moreover, since passing substantive judgement is difficult, even fellow professionals will fall back on non-substantive issues, particularly governance issues. When professionals are able to give a good impression of the governance of their activities, many committee members will at least look tolerantly upon the substantive work.

6 Make sure you have a good strategic vision – meaningless though it may be. This has at least one advantage: the discussion moves from past performance to plans for the future. The latter is always easier.

7 Sometimes production statistics are required. Remember that these are what reviewers like to go by. When counting in fractions, the numerator is often a given (such as the number of verdicts, the number of scientific publications, the number of graduations). The denominator, however, can often be manipulated (such as the number of incoming cases, the number of full-time equivalents, the number of registered students). Play around with these numbers a bit. If the outcome remains poor, try to play with the numerator by using sensitivity analyses, or emphasize the unique nature of the organization, which made the outcome the way it is.

8 There are always external parties and external developments that influence the professional performance, such as an institution's board that does not cooperate, a ministry that imposes an increasing level of bureaucracy, and other professional organizations in a chain. Emphasize the important role that these parties play in determining the performance. With some luck the reviewer will take note of this – which is totally harmless for the professional.

9 When a reviewer is supposed to produce a quantitative judgement, keep in mind that he likes to present a range of numbers. Make sure that a weak unit is examined as well, which evokes a low score. This unit can be another professional organization, or a certain aspect of quality. When a professional organization has a low score in the area of 'building and facilities', the implications are often more severe for the managers than for the professionals.

10 Emphasize the enormous impact that the reviewer's judgement will have. The larger the impact, the more hesitant a reviewer will be to pass a hard judgement – and the more he will be blamed for not evaluating certain components correctly.

11 Remember that many members of the external review committee will – unknowingly – do the 'geranium test' or the 'fishbowl test' during their visit. The story goes that a classic school inspector sometimes noticed that the classroom geraniums had withered and the water in the fishbowl had partly dried up. Of course this did not say anything about the education, but it was nonetheless an indication that the teacher in question was a bit sloppy. A sloppy way of receiving external reviewers can influence their judgement.

12 Involve the committee members in the organization. Give them a future role, invite them to workshops, ask them for advice, and so on. This will create future relationships that are appealing to the committee members and may affect their judgement.

Is this the strategic behaviour of smart and shrewd professionals? Of professionals who balance on the thin line between smartness and deception of external review committees? No. Remember that much of this behaviour is unintentional. Why?

- Professionals know one another well, as do the people who perform the external review. Therefore numbers 8, 10 and 12 in Box 5.1 also emerge naturally.

- Professionals who start to prepare for an external review will discover certain weaknesses in the organization during the self-assessment. It is therefore self-evident that they will try to repair these weaknesses before the external review committee arrives. Therefore numbers 2 and 3 in Box 5.1 will emerge. It is often stated that the ex-ante effect of the external review (during the preparation, the professional already learns and improves the professional service) is more important than the ex-post effect (the influence of the analysis and the external review committee's judgement).

- What seems to be hard – such as production statistics – is often soft. One statistic can hide many different truths. Professionals are more aware of this than external parties. If they are still strongly judged on the basis of these statistics, it is only understandable that they will try to manipulate these (number 7 in Box 5.1). Chapter 8, which deals with performance management, will go deeper into this perversion of statistics.

- The paper reality that professional organizations are supposed to produce sometimes results from external review protocols that prescribe such paper realities. Therefore it is understandable that professionals who follow the protocol take good care of this paper reality (numbers 1 and 6).

No matter how understandable and tacit this behaviour is, it does complicate the external review committee's task. When such strategic behaviour is stimulated, the committee's judgement is hampered and there is no incentive for learning. The masculine approach may seem decisive, but will eventually result in the situation that no good judgement is passed, nor is there learning, because it stimulates the strategic behaviour described above. This is the mirror image of the low-impact feminine variant. As mentioned above, the risk associated with this variant is that is harmless and that it offers underperforming professionals a chance of getting off without a scratch.

A logical implication may seem to be that a masculine variant moves to quadrant III in Table 5.1, and a feminine to quadrant II. However, it is not that simple. If a masculine variant has been chosen, there is a strong incentive to attach a

Table 5.1
Risks associated with masculine and feminine external reviews

	Masculine	*Feminine*
High impact	I Strategic behaviour	II
Low impact	III	IV Harmless, not challenging

high impact to the external review. All aspects of this variant are suitable for this: there are grades and there is a ranking, which make it very tempting to use these. The feminine variant has a much higher tolerance towards ambiguous and nuanced judgements, which makes it more difficult to attach a high impact to it. In other words, the masculine variant almost always ends up in quadrant I, and the feminine variant in quadrant IV.

SUMMARY

So what does this teach us?

First, there are two main approaches towards quality management. The first one is codification of quality. Codification can contribute to better quality, but it can also result in increased bureaucracy and loss of professionalism. The second approach is professional interaction. This is usually spontaneous, but sometimes managerial interventions are needed to maintain this interaction.

Second, with regard to codification, it is impossible to establish an unambiguous relationship between the complexity of the professional service on one side and the added value of codification on the other side. Codification of relatively simple service provision can contribute to the quality of the service, but it can also result in bureaucracy and hassle. The same principle holds true for complex service provision, as shown in Figures 5.1 through 5.6.

Third, how can it be decided whether or not codification is useful in a certain situation, if this cannot be deduced from the complexity of the service? The answer: by involving professionals in the process of codification.

Fourth, it is often sufficient to rely on the tacit professional interaction and control when it comes to the quality of the professional service provision. This, however, can also be naïve: professionals can be defensive and secluded, and the non-intervention principle can play a role. How can interaction be initiated and maintained? By organizing processes that induce professional interaction, as illustrated by the NASA example and by the phenomenon of external review.

Fifth, are there any risks associated with these processes? Absolutely. Processes can turn into proceduralism and strategic behaviour. A manager is therefore always balancing between codification and interaction and between useful processes and unnecessary procedures.

NOTES

1 It is important to note that a strong institutionalization has taken place with regard to these instruments. There has not only been a rise of quality management methods, but also of processes of certification and accreditation. Organizations attach value to the fact that their primary processes have been certified, or they only want to cooperate with organizations that are also certified. Certification and accreditation call for regular updates. There are organizations that provide assessors, certifiers, accreditors and consultants to conform to the demands of quality management. The result has been the development of a quality industry – often stemming from producing organizations – that approaches the professional organization.

2 Cited from Atul Gawande (2007), The checklist: Intensive care can harm as well as heal, but there is a simple way of improving the odds. *New Yorker*, 10 December, pp. 86–95, quote on p. 93.

3 Rein de Wilde (2001, in Dutch), *De voorspellers. Een kritiek op de toekomstindustrie*, Amsterdam: De Balie, pp. 128–29

4 The statement in this paragraph is largely based on Gawande, op. cit. The references were found either in or through his work.

5 Markus Thalmann *et al.* (2001), Resuscitaton in near drowning with extracorporeal membrane oxygenation. *Annals of Thoracic Surgery*, 72, pp. 607–8.

6 Gawande, op. cit., p. 90.

7 Ibid.

8 Peter Pronovost *et al.* (2006), An intervention to decrease catheter-related bloodstream infections in the ICU. *New England Journal of Medicine*, 355, 26, pp. 2725–32.

9 Gawande, op. cit.

10 Ibid.

11 S. Newell *et al.* (2002), The importance of process knowledge for cross project learning: Evidence from a UK hospital. In: HICSS (2002), *Proceedings of the 35th Annual Hawaii International Conference on System Sciences*, Los Alimitos, CA: IEEE Computer Society Press, pp. 1019–28.

12 I.L. Janis (1982), *Groupthink: Psychological Studies of Policy Decisions and Fiascos*, Boston: Houghton Mifflin.

13 C.A. Sabel *et al.* (1999) Beyond backyard environmentalism: How communities are quietly refashioning environmental regulation. *Boston Review*, 24, 5, pp. 1–20.

14 Catrien J.A.M. Termeer and Brechtje Kessener (2007), Revitalizing stagnated policy processes: Using the configuration approach for research and interventions. *Journal of Applied Behavioral Science*, 43, pp. 256–72.

15 Dianne Vaughan (1996), *The Challenger Launch Decision: Risky Technology, Culture and Deviance at NASA*, Chicago: University of Chicago Press, pp. 88ff.

6

COORDINATION AND COOPERATION

THE PROFESSIONAL ORGANIZATION AND THE PROBLEM OF COOPERATION

A recurring theme in discussions about professionals is the lack of cooperation and coordination. A well-known complaint is that professionals are too isolated within their own specialization, showing an insufficient ability to connect with other professionals. This may negatively affect the quality of the professional service, as well as innovation.

Poor professional service delivery is a complaint often heard in youth care. Insufficient cooperation may result in adolescents receiving poor care, because good care requires cooperation among professionals with different disciplinary backgrounds. This was illustrated earlier by the case of the 'Rotterdam girl' and the Dutch Healthcare Inspection's criticism of care workers (Chapter 3). Due to their insufficient cooperation, the girl disappeared off the radar.

A lack of cooperation might also lead to a lack of innovation, an issue which is relevant, for instance, in the university context. Universities are divided into faculties, based on the traditional disciplines. Innovations often happen at the interface between different disciplines. When researchers isolate themselves within their own disciplines and are unwilling to make connections with other disciplines, opportunities for innovation are lost.

Professional organizations are too often too much of an 'archipelago', or a 'patchwork quilt' of autonomous units – a criticism that may be directed at organizations as well as at entire sectors.

Professional organizations are often over-fragmented. There are too many 'stovepipes' and 'silos': autonomous units that do not cooperate. A related criticism is that professional organizations sometimes look like a patchwork quilt, consisting of many units and lacking a clear and transparent structure. The same criticism applies to professional sectors: there are too many organizations which shield their autonomy instead of working together, giving rise to a structure that is sometimes arcane and patchwork-like. Youth care, for instance, is comprised of many institutions, university faculties, schools and research institutes, and many countries have a multitude of secret services with overlapping authorities. None of these organizations are prepared to sacrifice their own autonomy, and thus they maintain the patchwork quilt.

People who, in view of this problem, argue for more cooperation, better coordination or more exchange of information will easily receive support. This seems like a typical case in which managers are a solution – after all, when cooperation and coordination are left to professionals, the archipelago or patchwork quilt problem will not be solved because it is rooted in one of the core values of professionals: autonomy. Pleas for more cooperation therefore have a high feel-good factor. This, however, should make us suspicious as well. If cooperation is so self-evident, then why does it not happen? And if cooperation is not optimal, is management a solution? Or is the problem more complicated than that? If cooperation is not optimal, perhaps management is part of the problem? This chapter provides an analysis of coordination issues that will give a more complete picture of the problem of cooperation and coordination.

I. SPONTANEOUS COORDINATION: SWARMING BEHAVIOUR, TERMITE HILLS AND PROFESSIONALS

Despite the earlier-mentioned examples of insufficient cooperation, there are of course many cases in which cooperation is not a problem. A passionate professional has a network of other professionals, and will make an effort to perform as well as possible. If this requires cooperation with other professionals, he will use his network and seek contact with those other professionals. In a well-functioning professional habitat, coordination will largely be spontaneous – coordination and cooperation are tacit processes too, and this is another example of the fact that tacit processes require only minimal managerial intervention. Moreover, managerial interventions that aim to stimulate coordination can destroy tacit coordination, and therefore lose more than they gain.

Are there any professional communities that achieve cooperation without the intervention of a single manager, and even without one demonstrable leader? That do not have any formal coordination mechanisms? That are therefore completely self-guiding and self-coordinating? Yes, there are. This section will examine the conditions under which such communities can function.

OPEN SOURCE COMMUNITIES

The best-known example is the open source community. Large companies such as Amazon, IBM and the New York Stock Exchange are strongly IT-driven, and are therefore strongly dependent on the quality of their software. These companies have software at their disposal that is designed in open source communities: communities that may be comprised of thousands of developers who develop and maintain common software through the Internet, operating from all parts of the world. There are no formal coordination mechanisms; there is just spontaneous cooperation among professionals. How is this possible? How can it be explained that thousands of individual, headstrong professionals, often with rather different views on what constitutes good software, can achieve a major collective performance: the development of high-quality software that is used by multinationals and apparently can stand comparison with Microsoft products? How can this happen without any guidance from above, without any formal arrangements about how things should be coordinated, and without these headstrong professionals constantly being at conflict with one another?

COORDINATION WITHOUT MANAGERS: SWARMING BEHAVIOUR AND TERMITE HILLS

To answer these questions, let me use a metaphor that always works with professionals – just like the comparison with open source communities, by the way. In this case the comparison is with the swarming behaviour of birds.

Birds are able to swarm synchronously in groups of hundreds of individuals. There is no set formation (like in the case of bird migration, when birds fly in V-formation), nor a set pattern. The swarm suddenly moves upwards, downwards or sideways at seemingly random moments, and at various speeds.[1] The intriguing question is how birds are able to do this, without constant collisions. The original idea was that the swarm has a leader, but this idea is no longer valid. Another hypothesis was that the swarming behaviour can be compared to a Mexican wave among the audience in a sports stadium: one or several birds initiate a movement, and others follow. This suggests that there is something similar to leadership, but this is not the case either. The formidable collective patterns in the birds' swarming behaviour can be explained by the fact that every *individual* bird follows three simple rules:[2]

- every bird reacts only to the birds in its direct surroundings (called the *local sphere*);

- every bird adapts its own speed to that of the other birds in its direct surroundings; and
- every bird moves in the direction of the centre of the mass[3] of the group in its direct surroundings and thus prevents collisions in its local sphere.

Simulations show that birds that follow these three rules are able to swarm – without a leader and without any form of coordination.

Something similar is true in the case of termites. How are termites able to build their hills? They use pheromones (chemical signals). Termites take a bit of sand in their jaws, and every individual termite then follows three simple rules:[4]

- every termite starts by walking around randomly, and dropping the sand somewhere;
- every termite moves in the direction where the pheromones are strongest; and
- every termite drops the sand at the point at which the pheromone smell is strongest.

The termite is secreting a smell signal, so if termites follow these signals, they will eventually follow the same route. At places at which the signal is very strong, they drop the sand, making the signal even stronger at that place. As a result, other termites also drop their sand there, and after a while this will result in the formation of small towers. Some of these towers remain towers and do not grow, since they are not visited frequently. After all, the termites have various options when following chemical signals. Other towers are visited more frequently, which makes the signals stronger and leads to visits that are even more frequent, and eventually results in the formation of pillars.

At a certain moment there will be several pillars. Our hardworking termite, carrying sand in its jaws, is approaching an area with active pillars, and follows the rules above. Where will the smell be strongest? Suppose there are four pillars. The smell will be the strongest in the centre of the group of four pillars, because here the smells of the different pillars overlap. As a result, the termites will prefer to climb the pillars on the sides closest to the centre. This, in turn, will cause the pillars to lean over and touch, giving rise to a termite hill. An impressive construction – especially when taking into account the mental capabilities of a termite – that is made without any form of coordination. There is no leader, no architect, no supervisor, not even a labour distributor – let alone a department of Building and Housing Inspection.

These are beautiful case studies built upon very simple basic principles:

- collective performances result from actions by individuals;

- these individuals use a limited set of individual rules; and
- as a result, there is no need for formal coordination mechanisms.

COORDINATION WITHOUT MANAGERS: OPEN SOURCE COMMUNITIES

Let us move from birds and termites to professionals. How can thousands of software developers, who usually do not know one another personally, make highly advanced software without a leader, without an organizational structure, and without any formal coordination mechanisms?

Here, too, the answer is: because there are a number of individual rules – both implicit and explicit – that almost every developer abides by. These rules were first made explicit in the research carried out by Ruben van Wendel de Joode.[5] The software developers are like termites: they start out by walking around randomly, only on the Internet. Many software developers start to develop software in many different places. In the same way that termites leave behind their pheromones, which attract other termites, software developers leave behind *elegant* software. Elegant software is written in such a way that it is easily accessible to others. The more elegant the software, the greater the chance that other developers will visit the site with the software, and start contributing to its further development. The first individual rule is: develop software that is as elegant as possible, because elegant software attracts other developers.

At a certain moment, when a termite starts following another termite's chemical signal, this will become stronger and stronger, enticing even more termites to follow this signal. The same thing is true for developers. When many developers are attracted to a piece of elegant software, there will be a lot of activity within the community that develops this software: the sites will be visited frequently, many developers will contribute, developers will tell one another through mailing lists how interesting the community in question is. All of this will raise the interest of other developers. The more developers that become involved, the more expertise and thinking power are brought together, and the greater the chance that the result will be of high quality. The second rule is therefore: join communities with a high level of activity.

Among software developers, however – and this is where the comparison with termites ends – there can be a gradual build-up of substantive conflict. How to deal with this? A third individual rule is that developers avoid conflict as much as they can. If they disagree about how to proceed, they will go their separate ways. This is called *forking*. After the forking event, the software development will proceed in two parallel trajectories. There will be two communities that develop their software in different ways. The developers are not concerned:

either a community dies out because it proves to be unable to develop the software further, or the different communities remain active and will ultimately produce different kinds of software.

The idea of a self-guiding professional community, without any formal coordination mechanisms, will be appealing to many professionals. The essence of self-guidance in birds, termites and developers in open source communities is that they 'just' follow a set of individual rules and are thus able to achieve major collective performances. This approaches the classic idea that competent individual professionals should be granted all the space they need to follow their own judgement, and that it is in those cases that the organization as a whole will achieve an optimal performance.

FROM VIRTUAL COMMUNITIES TO NON-VIRTUAL ORGANIZATIONS

The idea of self-guidance through individual rules can also be applied to non-virtual organizations. Let us take a look at a university, which has a number of faculties. Suppose the cooperation among faculties offers many opportunities for innovation. Suppose individual professionals use three rules when deciding whether or not to cooperate – I will give as an example the rules that I detect in my own work:

- *Affection*: I cooperate with researchers whom I like personally.
- *Transaction costs*: I work together with other researchers if the transaction costs (costs of meetings, mutual arrangements, and so on) are low.
- *Overlap and added value:* I work together if there is an overlap between my work and that of the other researcher, which gives us something in common, but the other researchers also have something I lack.

When a large number of researchers use such rules, cooperation will emerge in several places within the university. It will be difficult to predict who will cooperate and in relation to which issues. After all, no one – particularly no manager at the top – will know how personal networks will develop, or where transaction costs are high and where they are low. Suppose a manager is convinced that there are plenty of opportunities for innovation at the interface of faculty X and faculty Y, and takes all kinds of measures to promote cooperation. Chances are that this cooperation will develop extremely slowly if the researchers from X are constantly annoyed by their colleagues from Y. The researchers from Y consistently request meetings, want to document all agreements in detail, make a fuss about money, are difficult to reach, and always see problems everywhere. In other words, the transaction costs are very high. When the researchers from

X use the rules mentioned above, there is a significant chance that the cooperation will fail, regardless of the structures and incentives developed by the higher management. On the other hand, cooperation may emerge in places where the manager does not expect it at all. The researchers from X may be able to get along with those from faculty Z, or with researchers from faculty Y at another university. Someone who only looks at the successes of planned cooperation will often be disappointed. Someone who also looks at cooperation that emerges spontaneously will get a picture that is much more positive.[6]

MANAGEMENT OF SWARMING BEHAVIOUR AND TERMITE HILLS: MANAGERS DESTROY SPONTANEOUS COORDINATION

What implications does this have for cooperation and for the role of managers?

A first implication: the added value of management is limited. Much of the coordination in professional organizations happens naturally. Someone who has no confidence in this, or who does not see this, will soon tend to create structures and procedures that dictate how things should be coordinated. This is a logical managerial action without any positive effect.

To stay with the termite example: it is easy for a manager who watches termites at work to see all kinds of problems. The termites move in a criss-cross way, especially when they have just started building their termite hill. This seems to be very inefficient, and there must be a way to improve this. There are unfinished towers: these too are inefficient and show room for improvement. Competencies and responsibilities are totally unclear. The manager will ask whether there is a 'Handbook for Building Termite Hills'. The current generation of termites, as the manager will note, knows how to build a termite hill. This has always been arranged more or less informally, and it has always worked. But in modern times these processes need to be described, in order for new termites to be able to learn the art of hill-building faster. Ideally these processes are also certified, so third parties will have more confidence in the termites and their hill.

At a reception, the manager meets his colleague from the bird world. Both note that their organizations are kind of messy. There is no 'Handbook for Swarming' either. No one, as the bird manager remarks indignantly, can explain to him who is responsible for the swarming pattern. Both conclude that times are changing, and that professional organizations are developing from sloppy, autonomous entities to well-structured, 'real' organizations. Back home the manager tells his termites that the bird world is developing in the same way as the termite world. Apparently this is a trend that is unavoidable, and therefore the termites need to adapt to the new reality.

Of course I am exaggerating. However, this goes to show what happens when spontaneous cooperation is formalized – a lot of hassle, little added value.

A second implication is the fact that tacit coordination can be destroyed by efforts to make it explicit. Formalization will have no added value for the professional – as explained above. But there is more. It will probably be impossible to codify the process of hill-building into a set of rules on paper. After all, the tacit nature of professional knowledge may imply that professionals themselves are unable to make it explicit. Ask a termite how it builds a hill, and it will not be able to give a sensible answer. There is a significant chance that the rules on paper differ from the ones that are used in reality. As a result, the termites will not abide by the rules on paper – which makes the effort to make them explicit senseless – or they do abide by them, which makes the building process more troublesome – in which case the efforts to make them explicit were harmful.

The worst case is if the manager starts to design *new* rules that are supposed to lead to a building process that is more efficient. He will conclude, for instance, that termites work efficiently on a hill when it is starting to take shape, but that their movements are too haphazard in the initial stages. All kinds of chemical signals fail to attract termites, and many different pillars will never grow into a hill. In the eyes of the managers, there must be a way to make this process more efficient. In reality, however, this seemingly inefficient initial phase may prove to be a prerequisite for faster building later in the process. As one of his efficiency measures, the manager may appoint coordinator termites. It will be fruitless: how many coordinators are needed to get thousands of termites to behave differently? Nevertheless, these coordinator termites may not be a short-lived phenomenon. After all, the result of their work is an apparent, visible efficiency, even though this results in an invisible inefficiency. Quadrant III in Table 2.1 (Chapter 2) shows that in the case of such visible efficiencies – which are in fact inefficient – there are often no incentives for change.

To recapitulate and to clarify: when tacit knowledge is an important characteristic of professionals, tacit efficiency and tacit inefficiency are also a reality. These are largely invisible to the manager and perhaps even to the professional himself. In addition, there is visible efficiency and inefficiency. When there is visible inefficiency, there is an incentive for change. This is not without risk when we are in quadrant number II (Table 6.1) and there are hidden, tacit efficiencies. These efficiencies might be destroyed.

When termites start out by walking around randomly, this seems to be inefficient: there is a visible inefficiency. The termites move in a criss-cross manner, their movements lack structure and there will be many towers that will never make it into pillars. In reality this is hidden efficiency. This apparent chaos allows for the development of signals that are stronger and those that are less strong, and this is a prerequisite for the construction of a termite hill.

Table 6.1
Visible and invisible efficiencies and inefficiencies, applied to the case of termites

	Hidden, tacit inefficiency	Hidden, tacit efficiency
Visible inefficiency		– Termites are walking around randomly – Many pillars do not make it into hills → Change the existing, desired situation
Visible efficiency	– Appointment of coordinating termites → Maintain the existing, undesired situation	

The manager of the coordinating termite that aims to eliminate this apparent inefficiency from the organization actually obstructs the building of a termite hill.

PROFESSIONALS ARE NOT TERMITES – AND THE COMPARISON WITH OPEN SOURCE COMMUNITIES OFTEN FAILS

Again, the example elaborated above is only half of the story. Analogies such as the birds' swarming behaviour and the termites' hill-building draw our attention to interesting phenomena, but they remain only analogies. Professionals are not termites – and nor are they birds. The open source community may approach these analogies, but it has a number of characteristics that most professional organizations do not have. When we compare open source communities with non-virtual organizations, a number of differences become apparent. As a consequence, mechanisms that allow the open source community to function cannot be transplanted to 'regular' professional organizations without further consideration.

Explorative versus focused professionals. In the examples of the open source community and that of university researchers, the professionals' activities are explorative rather than focused. The developers embark on the development of a software module without knowing in advance which modules will prove to be functional, and what their use will be. When they do not succeed in developing sufficiently elegant software, the developers will shift their course. When the number of developers interested in certain software is insufficient, a development will be aborted. Something similar is the situation for university researchers. They cooperate on the development of new knowledge without knowing which knowledge will be developed, thus leaving opportunities for cooperation with others – which may result in missed opportunities.

None of this is really a problem for developers and researchers. They are looking for innovation, and such search processes are never linear. But let us now take a look at professions that are much more focused. A youth care organization or a hospital is being confronted with clients and patients in need of care. When faculty staff are guided by the individual rules specified above (personal affection, low transaction costs, overlap, and added value) beautiful things may happen – even though there is no cooperation among other faculties. If the staff of these care institutions, however, are guided by such rules, beautiful things may happen as well – but there will be no cooperation among other care institutions. In a focused organization that is truly a problem: certain clients remain without care, and are left behind.

Does service follow capacity, or is it the other way around? In the open source communities, the capacity in terms of developers determines the amount of service: the more developers, the greater supply of software, and vice versa. Something similar is true in the case of a university's research capacity. The capacity determines the service supply. Inefficient habits, or what may prove to be disrupting conflicts, do not constitute a problem. They merely reduce the number of research results or the amount of software – that is the price that is being paid for this method of organizing. However, there are professions in which this principle would cause major problems. A college is faced with a question from students, youth care with a question from adolescents, the hospital with a question from patients. These professions cannot withdraw, taking the position that the service is limited simply because their capacity is limited – especially when it is the result of inefficiencies, conflicts or time spent on activities that no one is interested in anyway.

High or low tolerance for conflict. In an explorative environment, conflicts – the opposite of coordination – may be functional. Developers who disagree will each go their separate ways. The competition that arises between the two lines of development will determine which is the most fruitful. Conflicts between focused professionals are less functional. When two professionals disagree about the most appropriate treatment of a client they cannot decide to fork – in which case both professionals would follow their own course, confronting the client with two conflicting treatments. The tolerance is a lot lower than in the case of the open source community.

All in all we can conclude that a lot of coordination proceeds according to individual rules. It would be desirable for managers to develop some feeling for these rules. Someone who is unaware of them will not understand why some forms of cooperation are promising and others are not. Self-coordination is therefore a powerful mechanism in professional organizations. There is a constant risk that managerial interventions destroy this self-coordination. But at the same time, self-coordination has its limitations. After all, the individual rules in the open source community only have limited application to other, more focused professional organizations.

2. WHY PROFESSIONAL ORGANIZATIONS WILL ALWAYS HAVE A PATCHWORK-LIKE STRUCTURE – AND WHY THAT WORKS

Let us now focus on the criticism – often from managers – that professional organizations are like a patchwork quilt. There are two aspects to this criticism:

- Professional organizations are often a hopelessly tangled spaghetti of organizations and relationships: they are like an archipelago, with numerous units.
- This spaghetti lacks transparency to such a degree that clients lose their bearing: the care seeker is lost among organizations that keep referring clients to one another, and so on.

Before passing judgement on this criticism, we should first focus on the question of how such patchwork-like structures originate. Let us take a look at a university – a fictional example, but many insiders will recognize it immediately.

THE PROFESSIONAL ORGANIZATION AS A PATCHWORK QUILT

Let us look at a university that is comprised of eight faculties. Suppose a new manager arrives at this university and has a few days to familiarize himself with its organizational structure. Those readers who work at universities will easily recognize the following impressions.

Every faculty includes one or more disciplines. A faculty is led by a dean. So far the organization is transparent, but this is where the difficulties start. There are organizational units positioned between faculties that are called Research Centres (RCs). Every RC has its own research portfolio, and our manager identifies 15 of these, although no one seems to have the complete picture. The there are also Research Institutes (RIs) – which also involve researchers from different faculties. Sometimes RCs and RIs overlap, and sometimes their research portfolios are different. There are Educational Centres (ECs) that offer education, and these also involve cooperation among multiple faculties. Some of these ECs overlap with RCs or RIs, others do not.

Many staff members are not only part of a faculty, but also involved with an RC and/or an RI. Staff members' business cards often mention a variety of units that they are involved with. Some of these Centres or Institutes turn out to be powerful units, others are very small or only exist on paper. On paper, the competencies and responsibilities are well defined, but the reality is more complicated. An outsider may not always know who to turn to: the dean, or the director of a Centre, for instance. In one situation the dean may seem to be the right reference point, in another it seems that an arrangement with the dean lacks any value if the director of the relevant Centre or Institute has not been consulted. Some directors are clear in their statement that they are the ones in charge, rather than the dean, but this – as mentioned before – may be different for each Centre or Institute. The routine of dealing with finances, for instance, may differ between Centres and Institutes. Some have their own accounting department, others merge their financial affairs with those of a faculty. Even the legal natures of Centres and Institutes may show major differences. Some units are part of the university, others turn out to be an external foundation, and some may be a combination of both.

After a while, some Centres or Institutes may have reached the size of the smaller faculties. They are therefore granted the status of 'inter-faculty'. In other words, a patchwork quilt is born, and our manager tells his boss that he will be more than happy to provide the university with a 'clear and transparent structure'.

HOW DOES A PATCHWORK QUILT ORIGINATE?

How is it possible that such patchwork-like structures arise? Let us follow this process, and begin with an initial situation in which everything is still simple: there is a board of directors, and there are a number of faculties. The organization chart is relatively clear. The next step is societal demand for knowledge. The air traffic sector, for instance, is planning to invest in sustainable air traffic; it is in need of knowledge and it has funds available. The expertise that is needed to achieve this is embedded in at least three faculties: aerospace engineering, materials science (for instance in relation to lightweight materials), and applied physics (which can provide energy expertise). The air traffic sector complains about the degree of fragmentation of the expertise across the university. Is it useful to merge the three faculties? Of course not, because there are many other stakeholders with a demand for knowledge.

The sector of public works also reports to the university with a request for research. This calls for cooperation among civil engineering, technology and management, and – again – materials science. This sector too complains about the research fragmentation, which would call for these three faculties to merge.

How would a university deal with this? A logical next step would be to design a separate organizational structure for the most important stakeholders that are in need of knowledge. The division into faculties is maintained, but RCs are established for the main stakeholders, in which faculties cooperate, thus forming one front towards the stakeholders. This gives rise to a 'Sustainable Air Traffic' RC and a 'Management of Major Infrastructures' RC – and many more.

In this case, the driving force was the societal demand for research. In addition, there is a National Science Foundation outside of the university, which may, for instance, distribute funds for fundamental, multidisciplinary research. In order to raise these funds, faculties need to cooperate. Sometimes these alliances will equal those in the RCs, sometimes they concern new combinations. Suppose these alliances are referred to as RIs. They are added to the existing organization. These RIs allow the universities to show their sponsors their combined, more fundamental research; they increase the chances of third-party funding; and they also stimulate actual cooperation among scientists.

The universities also provide education. Much of this will take place within the faculties, but there may also be an interest in inter-faculty education. Some students like to take a minor at the interface of civil engineering and management. In addition, there appears to be a societal demand for inter-faculty education geared at practitioners. An educational programme at the interface of physics and medical sciences appears to attract many international students. The consequence is clear: new elements appear in the patchwork quilt: the inter-faculty education programmes, which are grouped into ECs.

In practice, these RCs, RIs and ECs will partly overlap. Individuals may, for instance, work both at a Centre and at an Institute, and sometimes it is not entirely clear in which department new research should take place. An RC could be asked to organize a class, which might actually be an EC's domain. This overlap is often functional for professionals. Overlap between fundamental and applied research is often a source of innovation. The same is true for the overlap between research and education. The manager, however, is increasingly under the impression that the organization is an unstructured patchwork quilt.

Similar processes may take place within other professional organizations. There is a certain organization, and certain societal or substantive developments take place that call for cooperation among existing specializations, and therefore new units are created for this purpose.

WHY A PATCHWORK QUILT ORIGINATES: THROUGH ENTREPRENEURIAL BEHAVIOUR IN A MULTIPLE ENVIRONMENT

Then why does a patchwork quilt originate? First, because professionals are entrepreneurial by nature. They identify opportunities, or they feel responsible for their clients, and therefore they form connections with one another, in the interest of their clients.

Second, because professionals are forced to function in a multiple environment. Researchers are active within their discipline (faculty), in society (research centre) and in multidisciplinary fields (research institute), as well as in inter-faculty education. Each of these environments requires a different structure in relation to the organization and to the cooperation with others. The idea that a patchwork quilt is undesired is therefore based on the simple – all-too-simple – notion that organizations can be classified unambiguously. In a multiple environment, however, unambiguous classification is impossible by definition.

There is a third reason. Patchwork quilts and archipelagos are characterized by a large amount of overlap among the organization members. From a managerial point of view, this is not always appreciated – at the managerial level, people often advocate a clear division of tasks and competencies, and overlap is regarded as duplication of effort. Some overlap, however, can be functional. When organization A is spending some of its time on organization B, and organization B on A, this may simplify their mutual cooperation. Besides, overlap is often a consequence of cooperation. When organizations C and D are entering into a cooperation, organization C will develop some expertise regarding D, and vice versa. Overlap is a prerequisite as well as a consequence of cooperation, and therefore it deserves to be cherished rather than suppressed.

Finally, there is the argument of redundancy.[7] Organizing redundancy (in other words: creating overlap) is always a sensible thing to do to limit an organization's vulnerability. It leads to variety, and can therefore be a source of innovation. Suppose an organization has several professionals taking the same position. Since each position only requires one person, the others are always watching from the sideline at crucial moments. The disadvantages are immediately clear. The costs of this double staffing are enormous. There is always a base for conflict among those people, and sometimes conflict actually arises. Some employees are highly frustrated because they hamper one another. Something is wrong with the structure (double staffing) and therefore with the processes (conflicts) and the individuals (frustration).

But suppose this organization is the main soccer team of FC Barcelona. The double staffing of all positions in the organization is suddenly the strength of the organization. It is less vulnerable to injuries. Redundancy can be a source of innovation: players who compete for a playing position in the team keep one another alert, and top players learn from one another. Redundancy makes the team adaptive. It allows for a variety of structures and playing systems, depending on the strength and tactics of the opponent. The single fact that an organization does not have clearly defined roles or competencies does not mean anything. It can be functional as well as dysfunctional. Some tolerance towards seemingly chaotic structures can be justified. Something that may be obvious for FC Barcelona may be obvious to professional organizations as well. A faculty that participates in many RCs, RIs and ECs is probably less vulnerable and has more opportunity for learning and innovation than a faculty that does not.

These four explanations suddenly give the patchwork quilt a positive connotation: it is the result of behaviour that should be valued positively, and it is inevitable in a multiple environment. One may criticize the fact that the patchwork quilt lacks a 'clear and unambiguous structure' (which is typical managers' talk, by the way), but clear and unambiguous structures simply do not exist in multiple environments. An organization that does have a structure like that might be the result of a lack of entrepreneurship and sense of responsibility.

Does the patchwork quilt have disadvantages? Of course it does. To the outside world, it can be difficult to fully understand. Someone who joins the organization – a new manager, for instance – may easily get lost in the organization. The more different units an organization has, the larger the tension between the formal and informal structures, which increases the chances of getting lost. At a certain moment, the patchwork quilt can become so intricately composed that even the people whom it was originally designed for – the clients – no longer understand it. Reality, in other words, is more nuanced: a patchwork quilt is inevitable, it is functional, but when it comes to our tolerance for quilts and archipelagos there is a line we dare not cross: they can result in lack of clarity, and totally fragmented organizations.

If one limits oneself to the simple observation that an organization is a patchwork quilt, one soon feels the need to re-organize. Structuring and simplifying the quilt are a precondition for better cooperation, and simple and clear models are quite appealing in this regard. The quilt, however, is the result of the daily practice of professionals who act intelligently. A manager who ignores this is always busy – after all, the patchwork quilt is a given and will always manifest itself. He will often have to conclude that the results of such simplifications are ultimately quite disappointing.[8]

TWO NICE METAPHORS: THE TAPESTRY AND THE CHINESE ENCYCLOPAEDIA

In conclusion, let us look at two powerful metaphors that illustrate the function of patchwork quilts.

The first, often-used metaphor is that of a tapestry or embroidery. One person may look at the front side, seeing an understandable and well-structured pattern. Someone else may look at the back, and see an ugly, chaotic pattern with many loose ends. Lesson number one: apparently there are two different ways of looking at the same reality: something that may seem like a chaotic patchwork quilt to one person may be an adaptive organization to someone else. Lesson number two: the chaotic pattern is a prerequisite for understandability and order: the patchwork quilt makes an organization adaptive and allows it to function well. Lesson number three: tolerate the fact that something that appears as ordered from a professional perspective will always, to some agree, be perceived as chaotic from a managerial perspective.

The second metaphor is Jorge Luis Borges' Chinese encyclopaedia. In 'El idioma analítico' (1952), Borges describes a categorization of animals that is derived from an old Chinese encyclopaedia. Animals are divided into:

1 those that belong to the Emperor,
2 embalmed ones,
3 those that are trained,
4 suckling pigs,
5 mermaids,
6 fabulous ones,
7 stray dogs,
8 those included in the present classification,
9 those that tremble as if they were mad,
10 innumerable ones,
11 those drawn with a very fine camelhair brush,
12 others,
13 those that have just broken a flower vase,
14 those that from a long way off look like flies.

Someone who reads this from a modern, Western perspective may see this as a completely senseless, inconsistent and illogical categorization. But apparently it wasn't to the person who made it at the time. He looked at reality in an entirely different way. The same thing is sometimes the case for managers and professionals. Something that a manager may perceive to be a patchwork quilt, with a lot of overlap, may be an ideal habitat for a professional. But, again, there is a line we dare not cross. The three lessons above are valid here as well, but there is a fourth one: if too many players in and around the organization – not just managers, but also clients and fellow professionals – are more inclined to see the disadvantages in the patchwork quilt than the advantages, there is a need for simplification. At a certain point the organization can be so non-transparent, and the categorization criteria so incomprehensible, that adjustment is needed. Even if we totally understood the Chinese categorizer, his line of reasoning would not fit into today's society. We can simply not apply it.

3. COOPERATION HERE WILL ALWAYS RESULT IN FRAGMENTATION THERE

The complaint that professional organizations are like archipelagos often results in a plea for cooperation: 'integrated approaches', 'joined-up' organizations, 'spanning silos'. However, do fully joined-up organizations exist? Is there such a thing as an integrated approach to problems in a multiple environment, which can always be structured in different and competing ways? The answer is no, and the illustration below may help in understanding this. Here is some background information:

- There is an organization with 16 units; each unit has two tasks. One task is represented by a colour, the other one by a symbol (Figure 6.1).
- Figure 6.1.1 shows a fragmented organization, and the question is how to change it into an integrated, 'joined-up' organization. Which categorization would be intrinsically logical for an integrated organization like this?
- Each of the following three figures shows another categorization of the units; each of them is intrinsically logical.

Figure 6.1.2 shows a categorization according to symbol, 6.1.3 according to colour. Someone who is of the opinion that the categorization should be based on colour rather than symbol will regard the second figure as a completely fragmented organization. Figure 6.1.3 has an integrated structure with a logical order of tasks. However, those who support Figure 6.1.2 will perceive this as a fragmented organization. The same thing is true for Figure 6.1.4: its supporters will regard this figure as a neat structure, and everybody else will call it total fragmentation. These are three visions of an integrated, joined-up organization, which each led to a completely different way of categorization. Something that appears integrated to one person may seem like a patchwork-like structure to someone else.

The bottom line of all of this is the fact that integration and joined-up cooperation are multiple terms: they have different meanings to different players,

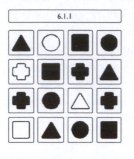

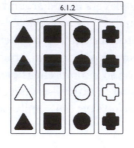

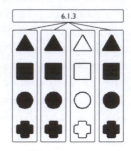

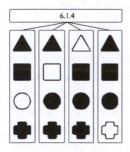

Figure 6.1
A Patchwork Quilt Organization

and these meanings may be in conflict with one another. A doctor and a nurse will value the same cooperation in a very different way.[9] In youth care, children and their families may have conflicting goals and interests – and therefore integration means something different to each of them.[10] When someone calls for 'integration' or 'a joined-up approach', one should always ask which side is being taken: 'integration' and 'a joined-up approach' are needed from whose perspective? Often the conclusion will be that an integrated approach from one stakeholder's perspective may lead to fragmentation from another's. Cooperation here, in other words, creates fragmentation there. Conquering silos and patchwork-like structures is an ongoing process: it creates new silos and patchwork quilts, which in time we will want to solve through coordination, which will create fragmentation elsewhere.

Figure 6.1 shows something else as well. For these 16 units, there is no such thing as one preferable structure. The question should therefore not be: what is the best structure? Multiple structures are possible, and each of them has its own, intrinsic logic. Another question becomes important. If a certain structure is chosen, does a unit have enough flexibility to be able to function in varying alliances? Sometimes a unit will have to cooperate with another unit in the same column, at other times with another unit in the same row, and sometimes with a unit in another row *and* column.

If this is the correct question, we reach a striking conclusion: units should be sufficiently adaptive to be able to function in varying alliances. When are they sufficiently adaptive? If they have sufficient autonomy, and if they are not linked too much to other units. In other words, perhaps Figure 6.1.1 (which seemed like a problem a little while ago) may present the solution to the problem of cooperation. Perhaps the autonomy of units should be strengthened. Powerful units that are loosely coupled with one another are able to function in alliances that constantly change. Units that are forced into a certain structure will lose their flexibility. Remember the English fleet that consisted of many smaller ships, and was much more adaptive and ready for action than the Spanish Armada with its large ships.

4. COORDINATION AS THE MAGIC FORMULA AGAINST PROFESSIONAL SHORTCOMING

Let us conclude by looking at a fourth problem associated with the ambition to achieve coordination. Professionals perform complex tasks, which means that it is often unclear which way of acting would be best. When a client enters the healthcare system, it is very possible that one professional will diagnose him with a socio-psychiatric disorder, and another professional with a psychotherapeutic disorder. Parents who have a child with behavioural problems may feel that the problem lies with the child, while the care worker mostly identifies problems in the relationship between the parents. Sometimes care workers do not know the answer either, and their only option is to just try a certain therapy. Clients may not cooperate and try to withdraw from the treatment. For other clients, the care workers see no solution, and they have to abort the treatment.

There is the simple fact that professionals make mistakes. The psychiatrist of the father of the 'Rotterdam girl' (Chapter 3) diagnosed him with ADHD and prescribed medication. The diagnosis was wrong, and the medication had an opposite effect: the mental problems became worse.[11] Of course it would be wrong to say that the father would not have killed his daughter without this diagnosis, but in any case it is clear that professionals make mistakes: a wrong diagnosis, wrong medication, wrong treatment, and a client who disappears off the radar.

All of this can be characterized as the inherent professional shortcoming: sometimes professionals don't know the right answers, and professionals make mistakes. If something goes wrong, it is very tempting to attribute this to insufficient cooperation. Disagreement about the diagnosis might have been prevented if the cooperation had been better. The wrong diagnosis by therapist A could have been prevented if he had cooperated better with therapist B. All of this can be true, but such pleas for increased cooperation can also serve to hide the inevitable professional shortcoming and feed the notion that better coordination can eliminate this shortcoming. In that sense, coordination is a hollow term. Almost any kind of human failure can elicit the statement that it could have been prevented, had there been better coordination. Think about Eve, for instance, who was seduced by the snake to eat the forbidden fruit, and who then involved Adam in her fall. The story is about human shortcoming, but a manager could perceive it as a question of cooperation. If Adam and Eve had cooperated better at an earlier stage, perhaps their problem could have been avoided. Adam could have warned Eve, they could have developed a strategy to deal with snakes making indecent proposals.

Someone who denies the concept of professional shortcoming and takes measures to improve coordination – by changing structures and strengthening cooperation procedures – increases the risk that such measures result in a lot of hassle while having little added value.

WHAT CAN MANAGERS DO?

So far so good. In conclusion, there are four important points in the discussion about coordination in professional organizations:

1 Cooperation and coordination often proceed naturally. A manager who aims to improve coordination has to be aware of the risk that well-intended and visible 'improvements' might destroy the spontaneous and tacit coordination. The managers of the birds and the termites do more wrong than good. Visible inefficiencies, too, need to be weighed against the invisible intelligence of processional action – remember the termites that are efficient despite the fact that some of their pillars will never become a termite hill. But this is just part of the story. Professionals are neither birds nor termites. Coordination does not always proceed naturally, and it may in fact require managerial action.

2 The professional organization as a patchwork quilt is not only a problem, but often also a solution for the multiple environment in which the professional is operating. A manager who aims to structure or 'clean up' the patchwork quilt can be compared to someone who admires the back side of the Bayeux Tapestry. The apparent chaos calls for re-organization, but as soon as the back side is neatly structured, the front side – which was the original aim of the project – may be a complete mess. The patchwork quilt

is often the solution rather than the problem. There is, however, a line we dare not cross. If a patchwork quilt is as inaccessible as the categorization of animals in the Chinese encyclopaedia, there is a need for change – which will not always originate from the profession itself.

3　A professional organization is often an archipelago, and that too seems like a reason for managerial action: there is a need for a more integrated approach. However, in a multiple environment there is not a single, all-encompassing integrated approach. Coordination here will always create fragmentation there. As a result, the quest for coordination is a continuous process: there is a focus on coordination, which creates fragmentation elsewhere, and at any time this fragmentation can become professionally or socially unacceptable, so another kind of coordination is created, which again causes fragmentation elsewhere.

4　There is such a thing as professional shortcoming. A plea for increased coordination can be a denial of this professional shortcoming. 'Increased coordination' becomes a magic spell: good cooperation can offset professional shortcoming. It is possible, but sometimes this shortcoming is a given that we just have to learn to live with.

What implications do these have for the role of managers?

TOLERANCE FOR PATCHWORK QUILTS, ARCHIPELAGOS AND FRAGMENTATION – THE PIGEON SQUARE

The observation may be slightly self-evident, but good management starts with managers being aware of these four mechanisms, and thus having a reasonable level of tolerance towards seemingly chaotic structures.[12] Such managers are also aware of the fact that an apparent improvement of coordination may destroy tacit, spontaneous coordination. Coordination problems should therefore be approached with a certain level of reserve. There is no such thing as optimal coordination – coordination is always sub-optimal.

This is not self-evident. The managerial language that is used to justify interventions is always quite powerful. Someone who sets out to combat silos, stovepipes and patchwork quilts, and who advocates a clear and unambiguous division of tasks and clear lines of accountability, is often met with more understanding than someone who claims that patchwork quilts and even silos can be effective. In this regard there is a useful metaphor: the pigeon square. The structure of a pigeon square is always somewhat chaotic: the pigeons move about in a random and chaotic manner. A manager who wants to re-organize the square is like someone who loudly claps his hands. The pigeons take off, fly around a little bit, and resettle after a little while. The old, chaotic structure is re-established immediately. Why? Because the pigeons (read: the professionals) had no problem with walking around randomly in the square. To them, this situation is not chaotic at all.

However, there is a line we dare not cross. A professional organization may be too fragmented, or the units may have too much autonomy. A doctor who is a loner; the care provider who does not coordinate with his colleagues; the faculties that do not innovate because they do not develop any cooperation with other faculties – all of these may benefit from managerial action.

HOW TO ORGANIZE COOPERATION – PLAY WITH STRUCTURE, PROCESS AND INDIVIDUALS

How can this be? When it comes to coordination, there are three possible solutions for a manager to choose from. He can address:

1 the structure of the organization;
2 the processes of cooperation; or
3 the values and unvalues of the individual professional.

Let's take the problem of organizing youth care. In almost all Western countries, there is a multitude of organizations that are involved in youth care. These include, but are not limited to: schools, health organizations, mental health organizations, the police, the probation service, juvenile justice, child welfare organizations, care of drug addicts, and so on. This may result in inadequate and patchy services and young people not being able to access the services they need.[13] Suppose the cooperation among these organizations is sub-optimal. What are the possibilities for improving cooperation? To deliver high-quality, multi-agency services?

A first possibility is changing the *structure* of youth care. Examples include: mergers between organizations; the appointment of one central figure who has hierarchical authority and who can therefore force others into action; the introduction of an 'under one roof' model;[14] and the creation of partnerships with 'front-line officers',[15] which should make these services more easily accessible and should contribute to better cooperation.

A second possibility is accepting the current structure and changing the *processes* of cooperation among the various youth care professionals. Design protocols and procedures that indicate how organizations should cooperate, and who should consult with which other organization at which point in time. Procedures create a common language for commissioning multi-agency services and makes organizations aware of the fact that they are all links in a chain of care.[16] Another process improvement is to design pathways clients should follow across the multi-agency field. A pre-structured pathway will help clients to find their way, and agencies to improve their cooperation.

A third possibility is investing in *individual professionals*. If structure and process cannot make the necessary change, it is up to the individual youth care professionals. Just like birds and termites make collective performances because individuals follow certain individual rules, so can professionals achieve better cooperation when they follow certain rules or learn certain values. A few examples:

- Suppose that schools are annoyed by the fact that it is hard for them to come into contact with a mental health organization. People at this mental health organization are difficult to reach, they fail to return phone calls at all, or within a reasonable time. As a result, healthcare is delayed – after all, information provision by the mental healthcare institution is vital. If the mental health organization realizes this, it can introduce a new value that can easily be translated into a rule: staff members should always return phone calls from other organizations within 24 hours.
- Any type of organizing will result in some clients being left behind. A rule or value could be that individual care workers who attend to adolescents and who notice that they cannot help them further should feel responsible for these adolescents until another professional has taken over their case.
- Sometimes 'multi-problem families' have so many healthcare workers around the house that the quality of their care is compromised. A rule could be that an individual professional who notices this is supposed to discuss this with fellow professionals, and to make arrangements on how to deal with this problem.
- When healthcare strongly depends on the quality of cooperation it is sensible if care workers continually seek contact with fellow care workers. Someone once described the message that she gave her colleagues as 'calling, calling, calling' – in other words, someone who continually seeks contact with fellow professionals reduces the risk of overlooking certain information.

The solution, in other words, is not sought in structures or processes, but in the development and empowerment of individual professionals.[17] The more empowered they are, the better cooperation will proceed as a tacit process.

THE POWER OF 'STOP-GAP SOLUTIONS' TO THE PROBLEM OF COOPERATION

It is absolutely key for a manager to understand that in a multiple environment, each of these three possibilities has a limited problem-solving power. After all, practically every choice for optimal coordination here will lead to fragmentation there, whether it concerns structure, process, or the attitude of the individual professional. To list the three possibilities again:

- *Structure*. Introducing hierarchy only offers limited opportunities. Someone who centralizes in a fragmented field makes the person with the central authority strongly dependent on the others. These others, after all, have the information that is needed to implement the authority adequately. This is what we call the centralization paradox: centralization creates dependencies of decentralized units. A front-line officer offers a limited problem-solving ability as well. Who is able to oversee all situations that can arise in a multi-agency field, and to coordinate them? In a worst-case scenario, the front-line officer is an extra player who only aggravates the fragmentation. 'Under one roof' might help, but there is always the risk that the former inter-organizational fragmentation is transformed into intra-organizational fragmentation. Once again, fragmentation is a fact of life, and therefore it cannot be addressed by structural measures alone. Structural measures have a limited problem-solving ability.
- *Processes*. Process arrangements contribute to cooperation, but they are never sufficient to allow cooperation to proceed smoothly. They can grow into bureaucracy and proceduralism because the process arrangements do not fit properly into the professional practice. Processes that work in general will not always work in specific situations – and the more fragmented a field is, the more specific situations there are. Using procedures and pathways might be very time-consuming, especially when from a professional perspective a shortcut should be preferred. Inherent to a fragmented field is that not all professionals will agree with the new procedures or the pathways across the multi-agency field. In all these situations, the professional ownership of these procedures and pathways is problematic, and when processes are not owned by those who have to implement them, they will not work. In short, process arrangements contribute to cooperation, but their problem-solving ability is limited.
- *The Individual*. The fact that individual professionals familiarize themselves with certain values or rules may improve the cooperation, but its problem-solving ability is limited. Some professionals may not naturally be inclined towards this kind of behaviour. This can result in high interaction

costs. Applying these values subserviently – something that termites do when it comes to individual rules – may be meaningless as well. Something that works in one context, may not work in another context, or may result in hassle.

What implications do these observations have for the manager? There are no cure-all solutions for improving coordination. For a manager, improving cooperation is a creative combination of structure, process and empowerment of the individual professional. A change in structure might work, until it becomes clear that structural measures may cause coordination here to lead to too much fragmentation there. Process or empowerment of individuals may perhaps offset the shortcomings of the new structure: they are the glue and strings needed to make the new structure work – the 'stop-gap solution'. New processes might work, until it becomes clear once again that coordination here results in too much fragmentation there. In case process arrangements no longer have a problem-solving potential, the solution may lie in investing in empowerment of the individual professional, or in new structures.

Empowerment and structure are the 'stop-gap solution' to the limits of the process approach. The opposite is possible as well: the manager invests a lot of effort in the empowerment of the individual professional until there is no longer a net gain. In that case he may turn to processes and structures. It is all a matter of a creative process: there is no cure-all solution. 'Stop-gap solutions' will always be necessary to make something new successful. 'Stop-gap solutions' might have a rather negative connotation, but are inevitable in a multiple environment, where by definition there is no single kind of coordination that is perfect.

DISTRUST MODELS WITH GRAND DESIGNS

In view of the above, the manager has to be highly sensitive to what works and what doesn't. He has to be able to look through the connotations of patchwork quilts and fragmentation, and form an opinion on whether these are functional or dysfunctional. If action is needed, it can be helpful to adjust structures, processes or values, but the manager has to be aware of the shortcomings of each adjustment. Promoting cooperation is a continuous learning process, and there is no such thing as a simple solution in a multiple environment. A model in which cooperation is framed perfectly only exists on paper.

Why is it important to emphasize this? First, because this kind of model can be quite tempting. Table 6.2 indicates why there are always incentives to radically change the existing situation.

Table 6.2
Model and reality in change processes

	Model	*Reality*
Existing		Patchwork quilt; overlap; silos; stovepipes; 'stop-gap solutions'; Chinese encyclopaedia; chaotic organization with many loose ends; random assembly of structure, process and individual
New	Clear structure, clear authorities and responsibilities, unambiguous process management	

The table shows an often-made mistake. We are familiar with a sub-optimal, existing reality and compare this reality with a new model. The new model has not yet been tested against reality, and there is clear and unambiguous model talk – 'clear division of tasks', 'straightforward management', 'integrated approach'. Models, in this case, leave no room for patchwork quilts, silos and 'stop-gap solutions'. This unfair comparison always creates incentives for change: after all, according to these models, there is room for improvement. Of course a different comparison is needed if one aims to be fair. Either we compare the new model to the model that once was the basis for the existing reality – and that no doubt was wonderful too, on paper – or we perform some kind of ex-ante evaluation to examine the reality to which the new model will lead. In both cases, the incentive for change is probably not nearly as strong.

Second, it is important to observe some restraint when it comes to radical changes on the basis of new models. An incremental strategy of change – a step-wise, continuous improvement of the existing cooperation – is better suited in an environment that is somewhat patchy and 'stop-gap'-like by definition. If the final result is always the somewhat 'stop-gap'-like situation, the introduction of a completely new model always implies the implementation of a radical change that will then fail in a number of ways, which in turn creates 'stop-gap'-like constructions to counteract this failure. Moreover, the new model may seriously disrupt the existing cooperation that is owned by the professional in question.

In short, the transformation costs related to change are high, especially when taking into consideration that the old situation is partly restored. That is another disadvantage that becomes clear in Table 6.2: we often compare old to new while neglecting the transformation costs, which may be astronomical.

NEW WAYS OF COOPERATION SHOULD BE OWNED BY THE PROFESSIONALS

This will be the case if professionals are involved with their development, and if they are enabled to participate in shaping it. Chapter 9 will deal with the question of how such a process of change can develop, but the following points will provide a preview of such a process:[18]

- A certain *openness* on the manager's side when it comes to the question of who is involved in the process of change. Openness also with regard to the solution that the manager has in mind. A manager who enters a trajectory of change with a fully defined solution takes three risks: he is unable to learn, he is unable to adapt to local or unforeseen circumstances, and he alienates professionals from the process.
- A certain sensitivity to what it is that professionals regard as their *professional core values*. If a new type of cooperation is an infraction on these core values, resistance will be significant, and the chances of successful implementation are slim.
- The prospect of a *gain* for both the manager and the professional. If this is lacking, there is no incentive for them to participate in the change process. This gain may impact other issues besides the new cooperation – as is illustrated by the multi-issue strategy that will be described in detail in Chapter 9.

New structures and processes only work if they are owned by the professional in question. Radical, model-based changes are less easy to internalize than incremental changes. Does this mean that radical changes are impossible? No. An incremental process can eventually result in a radical change. After a while, the organization and the entire sector may look entirely different because of the total effect of the changes. Changing in an incremental manner is often regarded as muddling through, and choosing the path of least resistance. But is this true? It is rather a question of constantly being aware of the developments with regard to change, constantly noticing shortcomings, and constantly evaluating what helps: a bit of structure, a bit of process, a bit of values and unvalues. It requires an understanding of a professional organization or sector. This may place more demands on a manager than designing a completely new model, implementing it, and then, as soon as the old situation is restored, complaining that professionals are actually quite stubborn.

NOTES

1 Some stunning images of this can be seen on the DVD *Planet Earth* (BBC, 2007).

2 Philip Ball (2005), *Critical Mass: How One Thing Leads to Another*, London: Arrow Books, pp. 152–53.

3 The centre of gravity: comparable to a dancer who makes a pirouette and seeks the point in his or her body that will allow for perfect balance, usually somewhere in the lower abdomen.

4 J. Kennedy and R. Eberhart (2001), *Swarm Intelligence*, San Francisco: Morgan Kaufmann Publishers; Mitchel Resnick (1994), *Turtles, Termites, and Traffic Jams*, Cambridge, MA: MIT Press.

5 Ruben van Wendel de Joode (2005), *Understanding Open Source Communities: An Organizational Perspective*, Delft: Delft University of Technology.

6 See also Donald Chisholm (1992), *Coordination without Hierarchy: Informal Structures in Multiorganizational Systems*, Berkeley: University of California Press; and the many publications on network guidance that I strongly rely on in this chapter: Tanja A. Börzel (1998), Organizing Babylon – on the different conceptions of policy networks. *Public Administration*, 76, 2, pp. 253–73; Joop Koppenjan and Erik-Hans Klijn (2004), *Managing Uncertainties in Networks*, London: Routledge; Charles E. Lindblom (1968), *The Intelligence of Democracy: Decision-making through Mutual Adjustment*, Englewood Cliffs NJ, Prentice Hall; B. Guy Peters (1998), Managing horizontal government: The politics of co-ordination. *Public Administration*, 76, 2, pp. 295–311.

7 J.B. Bendor (1985), *Parallel Systems: Redundancy in Government*, Berkeley: University of California Press.

8 Jaap Boonstra (2005, in Dutch), Veranderen en adviseren. Tussen beklemming en passie. In: Gabriël van den Brink *et al.* (eds) (2005), *Beroepszeer. Waarom Nederland niet goed werkt*, Meppel: Boom, pp. 145–67.

9 Unni Krogstad *et al.* (2004), Doctor and nurse perception of inter-professional co-operation in hospitals. *International Journal for Quality in Health Care*, 16, 6, pp. 491–97.

10 Jo Warin (2007), Joined-up services for young children and their families: Papering over the cracks or re-constructing the foundations? *Children and Society*, 21, 2, pp. 87–97.

11 As shown in the Dutch Pieter Baan Centre's report; see Adri Vermaat (2007, in Dutch), Zodra het over Gessica gaat: diepe stilte. *Trouw*, 26 November, De Verdieping, pp. 2–3.

12 Charles Glisson and Anthony Hemmelgarn, The Effects of Organizational Climate and Interorganizational Coordination on the Quality and Outcomes of Children's Service Systems. *Child Abuse and Neglect*, 22, 5, pp. 401–21.

13 Breaking down the barriers key findings. Available online at: http://www.youthaccess.org.uk/publications/bdb-key.cfm

14 CAMHS.

15 As illustrated by the many well-documented initiatives on the Children's Mental Health Partnership in Illinois, USA.

16 Department of Health (2008), *Final Report of the National CAMHS Review*, London: UK Department of Health, chapter 6.

17 Ibid.

18 Hans de Bruijn *et al.* (2002), *Process Management*, Dordrecht: Kluwer Academic Publishers.

7

KNOWLEDGE MANAGEMENT AND INNOVATION

KNOWLEDGE IS THE ESSENCE OF THE PROFESSIONAL ORGANIZATION ...

Knowledge and innovation are themes that are closely related to quality. Many of the concepts that have been dealt with in Chapter 5 can also be applied to the management of knowledge and innovation. In this case, too, there is for instance an approach based on codification and one based on interaction. I will therefore address these issues a bit more briefly here than I did in Chapter 5 (on quality management), and will occasionally refer to that chapter. Readers who skipped directly to this chapter are therefore advised to read Chapter 5 as well.

It all starts with the well-known difference among data, information and knowledge.[1] Data means numbers, or words, or symbols, for instance 900, 1138, 222. When data is supplemented with a meaning, the result is information. If we connect these numbers to London Euston, Preston and Edinburgh Waverley, respectively, people will soon realize that they are looking at a railway timetable. Knowledge is a deeper understanding of this information, based on experiences or other learning processes. Knowledge can imply, for instance, that I am aware of the fact that the train arriving at Preston at 11.38 am is always full on Thursdays when the weather is bad, while there is plenty of room in the train arriving an hour earlier. Knowledge is making meaning of information. Knowledge is often local: someone who often boards the train at Preston will know most about the trains that leave Preston that morning.

While data and information can exist independently of professionals, for instance in data banks, handbooks or systems, knowledge is nearly always strongly dependent upon a professional. A question such as 'Where is the information?' sounds more logical than 'Where is the knowledge?'. The first question refers to documents and systems, while knowledge is connected to people. The professionals are the knowledge bearers. They possess tacit and local knowledge, and knowledge management therefore touches upon the core of the professional organization.

No one will deny the usefulness of making data and information accessible. Through data banks, judges have access to jurisprudence, doctors to handbooks, and nuclear reactor technicians to manuals on how to act in any situation imaginable. This chapter will focus on knowledge – the knowledge of a judge who has much experience with complex cases, of the doctor who is specialized in complex surgical operations, of the technician who has been working with nuclear reactors for a sufficiently long time to know the reactor inside out. Do these situations leave room for knowledge management, in addition to data and information management?

Knowledge management, as is often assumed, can be shaped in different ways. Knowledge can be codified, which is what happens in the case of data and information storage. Knowledge management can imply that information sharing is stimulated. If there is codification and sharing, this implies by definition that new knowledge is created. And knowledge creation is of course closely related to innovation. As a result, knowledge management and innovation are inseparable concepts.

... WHICH THEREFORE LEAVES ONLY FEW OPPORTUNITIES FOR MANAGERS

A seemingly logical line of reasoning about knowledge management starts with the observation that knowledge is a crucial asset in professional organizations, which, after all, are knowledge-intensive by definition. Another observation is that managers pay only very little attention to this crucial asset. Managers are attentive to the traditional management functions – such as money, planning, coordination – but not to the concept that can be regarded as the essence of the professional organization: knowledge. The conclusion is inevitable: knowledge management is crucial, and should be added to the traditional management functions.

This line of reasoning, however, calls for a certain degree of caution. After all, as has been noted in this book before, the essence of the profession can hardly be influenced by managers. To make this point clear, I will start with the simple question of how knowledge will be shared in the absence of something like knowledge management. What if things happen the way they usually happen in professional organizations, with managers not interfering with knowledge codification, sharing and creation? The answer will be self-evident by now: knowledge will be shared tacitly, through professional interaction. Examples abound: the technicians in the control room of the nuclear reactor, the researchers in a faculty, the doctor and the resident, the judges on a bench: they learn from one another in their daily work, during the daily professional interaction.

Sometimes this happens in a way that is difficult for a manager to understand.

This is nicely illustrated by Julian Orr's famous ethnographic study into service technicians of copy machines.[2] The technicians tell one another stories – 'war stories' – about their experiences. These stories circulate within their professional community. They are retold and adjusted when new, similar situations arise. The stories make the experiences reproducible and reusable. Stories are particularly important if the problems faced by the technicians are complicated, and if it is difficult to come to a diagnosis. These stories are characterized by the fact that outsiders can hardly understand them. Many elements that would make a story understandable to an outsider are omitted, because the stories are carefully adjusted to the professionals at whom they are directed. The amount of detail and content is tuned to these professionals, and it would be a waste of time for the storytellers to compose a story that is well structured and understandable to everyone.[3] In short, knowledge transfer happens (1) in the interaction among professionals; these interactions are (2) fragmented and ill-structured to outsiders, including managers; however, (3) they are sufficient for professionals to transfer knowledge. The story may be useless to a manager, while it is very meaningful to a professional.

If all of this is true, then what is the essence of knowledge management? The answer is the same as in the case of quality management: make sure that the interaction among the professionals is sustained. From this perspective, there is a major risk that there is too little interaction among professionals – for instance because there is a strong reduction in the number of cases for which a full bench is created, as a result of which judges rule by themselves more frequently. Or because the technicians are so busy that there is insufficient time for informal exchange of experiences and storytelling.

However, there are also certain risks that apply to quality management as well:

1 Phenomena such as groupthink might arise: a group of professionals develops shared views about which actions are useful, and these shared views are maintained stubbornly, leaving no room for new knowledge.

2 There is insufficient variety, which reduces the chances that new knowledge is introduced.

3 The non-intervention principle is operational. An individual professional is simply more occupied with himself than with his professional environment. University research groups, for instance, may be completely fragmented: professionals are hardly present at the university, everyone minds their own business, and there is hardly any mutual professional control. In short, there are cognitive fixations – the same ones that we encountered in Chapter 5.

How to deal with this? A well-known rule of thumb is: if there is *cognitive* fixation, make a *social* intervention: introduce new or other professionals.[4] Make sure the resident sees several doctors at work, make sure to regularly change the composition of the full court or the nuclear reactor control room. This will reduce the chance of unwanted cognitive fixations by changing the configuration of the professionals – in other words, through a social intervention. Knowledge management, in that case, implies that

- there is faith in the professional interaction;
- this will lead to spontaneous knowledge sharing and creation;
- where these spontaneous processes do not emerge, there is an intervention;
- which is aimed either at sustaining interaction; or
- at breaking through phenomena such as groupthink.

The interventions that are needed to sustain the interaction among these knowledge bearers are usually minor and ordinary: changing work schedules, for instance, or organizing new meeting formats. Sometimes the interventions are a little more substantial: developing an HR policy that has a greater focus on job rotation, or asking outside professionals to take a critical look at what happens in the organization. These interactions are characterized by the fact that they are closely related to spontaneous processes of sharing and creating knowledge, and to an organization's existing daily routine. The striking thing is that while sharing and creating knowledge may be crucial to a professional organization, its management can be quite light-handed: without models and IT tools, and particularly without especially appointed knowledge managers. Let us look at the development of knowledge management while using these observations as a starting point.

THE CIRCULAR STORY OF KNOWLEDGE MANAGEMENT

As with many other management themes, knowledge management has been a major fad. It can be traced back to the second half of the 1990s. This period displays all the characteristics of hype. Almost simultaneously, several management gurus published books about knowledge management.[5] The theme is *sticky*, it appears on the agendas of many organizations, and there is an increasing call for models and strategies for knowledge management. Management consultants develop such models and strategies, and knowledge managers are appointed within professional organizations, or certain existing staff departments are charged with knowledge management. There is also a special role for IT managers who develop information systems that are supposed to contribute to better knowledge management, simply because knowledge is more easily accessible. As is often the case with hype, this results in a few valuable things, but also in many senseless things. The following reconstruction is a rough characterization of the development of knowledge management.

Suppose that the assumptions behind many of the pleas for knowledge management are true. There is a need for increased codification, sharing and creation of knowledge, and professionals will not automatically take action. This will result in high costs and a lack of innovation and quality. This observation may evoke the initial reaction that knowledge, data and information should be codified and then stored in systems. That can be done in a classic way, but also in a 'wiki-like' manner – comparable to the online encyclopaedia Wikipedia, which is created and maintained by millions of internet users and has a narrow error band. It is assumed that wiki communities can also be created within organizations, allowing for bottom-up knowledge codification.

THE FIRST STEP: CODIFICATION – AND ITS ASSOCIATED LIMITATIONS

There is of course an intrinsic tension within the concept of knowledge management-as-codification: tacit knowledge is usually characterized by the fact that it cannot be codified. What happens if codification is attempted nonetheless?

Let us look at an engineering organization that may find itself in the following situation. The manager notes that there are several different units that are working on similar projects. Every unit has its own specialization, but the specialists' knowledge is hardly shared and the wheel is continually being re-invented. This gives rise to the idea that the knowledge that is needed for these projects should be codified in modules. The project is logically divided into sub-projects and sub-sub-projects, resulting in a number of modules. The knowledge for each of these modules is codified. The main specialists for each module are asked to contribute to this codification; they have to make their tacit knowledge explicit. This results in an IT-supported knowledge management system (KMS). The professionals in the organization, including the newcomers, now have access to the most recent knowledge and there is no need to keep re-inventing the wheel.

This line of reasoning can easily be challenged. Apart from the fact that this can prove to be quite a burdensome task (or, put more elegantly, that the transition costs are very high), there are several significant obstacles to this kind of system:

- The KMS has to be totally reliable. When professionals note that there are major or minor faults in the system, the authority of the system as a whole may be affected. A no-error KMS is almost impossible.

- Codification calls for a clear terminology, which is much more complicated than it seems. The terminology in many professions is ambiguous: one concept may have different meanings in different contexts. Codification without a context is risky.
- Part of the knowledge will be ambiguous, based upon assumptions that may or may not be correct. It may contain uncertainties, have exceptions to the rules, and so on. These aspects of knowledge are difficult to codify.
- The knowledge has to be described at a reasonable level of abstraction. It cannot be too general, thus becoming empty, but not too specific either, in which case it would contain too many details. Every user, however, may have a different view on what is too abstract or too detailed – after all, this depends on the user's knowledge level and on the concrete questions among users.
- Keeping a KMS up to date is crucial for its authority. If it is outdated, it will be distrusted after a while. The less maintenance is needed, the better.

The example of the service technicians of copy machines is applicable here as well. The technicians have manuals – a type of codified knowledge. It turns out that they do use these manuals, but only to a limited extent. Why? Apparently the manuals do not or cannot contain all possible types of machine failure. The repair procedures are described in detail, but often the technicians have easier ways to repair a machine. Some technicians have the experience that the procedures are inadequate, and they no longer trust them. The significance of codified knowledge is therefore limited. Keep in mind that this example refers to knowledge of copying machines, which is relatively easy to codify compared with other types of professional knowledge. And there is an important human factor as well: the real professional, of course, feels that he is too much of a professional to need the manuals: 'technicians like to think that they have more on the ball than just following directions'.[6] This is sometimes called the 'IKEA Syndrome'. A professional handyman will be too proud to use the IKEA manuals – he can assemble his new wardrobe himself.

The five obstacles to codification listed above are reasonable, yet difficult, and they can compromise the codification of tacit knowledge, and even turn it into a mission impossible. If codification is attempted anyway, the result may be an inadequate system that remains unused by managers. There may be another risk as well: the demands may become so dominant that large chunks of tacit knowledge become very difficult to codify. It might be very hard to make the terminology unambiguous, or it turns out that it is difficult to formulate all knowledge at the same level of abstraction. There may be disagreement about what exactly constitutes the intelligence of the professional action, and thus about what exactly needs to be codified. If the process of codification is continued nonetheless, the result is obvious: eventually all that is codified is the explicit and proven knowledge, because this is the type of knowledge that can meet all demands. This can be useful – just like manuals and references can be useful – but it can also render a system uninteresting for professionals. The system is flawless and unambiguous, but uninteresting exactly for that reason, and therefore it will not be used.

SHORT INTERMEZZO: IS WIKI AN OPTION?

Is the situation any different if things happen in a wiki-like manner? We know that Wikipedia has a high level of reliability. Would an organization be able to build a knowledge system like that based on the wiki principles? This would imply that professionals (1) are able to enter their knowledge into a system on a voluntary basis, that they (2) can correct or complete one another's entries and that (3) there is space for professionals to codify only the things they find interesting. I will not deal with this question in detail here, but there are at least five considerations that one should take into account when contemplating a wiki-like approach.

The first is that professionals' tacit and local knowledge is often more ambiguous than the information in Wikipedia. It is therefore less easy to codify, even in a wiki-like manner.

The second, there is a traditional version of Wikipedia: regular encyclopaedias and other codified information that users can always fall back on if they want to verify that the information is correct. Moreover, the people who enter a contribution may also use these written sources.

The third is that Wikipedia can only exist by virtue of the willingness of large numbers of people to make a contribution and to check entries. A wiki approach therefore requires large numbers of knowledge suppliers, and it is questionable whether an organization is willing to allot this time to its employees.

The fourth is that Wikipedia has a high tolerance for inefficiency. Someone can spend a lot of time on an entry and submit it while it contains many factual mistakes, which calls for subsequent corrections by others. Eventually this may result in a good entry, but the transaction costs are high. This is not a problem in the case of Wikipedia, because it is made by anonymous people, but in an organization the situation is different.

The fifth is that the quality of Wikipedia depends on more than just the entries. Staff members continuously supervise the entries, which makes Wikipedia less bottom-up than is sometimes suggested – something that can also be noted for open source communities.

THE SECOND STEP: FROM 'WHAT' TO 'WHO' – MAKING AN INVENTORY OF KNOWLEDGE OWNERS

If knowledge management-as-codification is unsuccessful, a much-observed reaction is a new attempt towards codification – albeit not of knowledge, but of the owners of knowledge. The idea is simple: this KMS does not contain substantive information – no information about 'what' – but information about the knowledge owners: who are the experts with regard to which subjects? Every professional is included in this system, with a reference to his expertise.

In this case, the same thing is true: the system can either be useful or meaningless. When a professional is asked to indicate what his expertise is, many different answers are possible. They depend, for instance, on the level of abstraction (to what level of detail do I describe my individual areas of expertise?), the target group (colleagues, versus professionals in another area of expertise), or the degree to which there are clearly definable areas of expertise within a profession. Many university professionals have multiple CVs. The first is directed at colleagues, the second at potential clients – while for each type of client there may be different CVs – and the third at professionals in other fields that the person often cooperates with – in which case there may also be different CVs for each professional field. The manner of exhibiting expertise strongly depends on the target audience. This may result in a problem: the more professionals are using a system – in other words, the larger and more varied the target audience – the more difficult it is to file professionals' expertise.

A second problem is the fact that professionals can, just like everyone else, over- or underestimate themselves. An excellent professional may be too modest when elaborating on his areas of expertise. Others may list a whole range of areas of expertise, but as soon as a fellow professional contacts them through the system, their expertise turns out to be disappointing. And there is the typically human phenomenon: someone who advertises himself as a major expert in many different areas may receive many requests for advice, while professionals – perhaps particularly the major experts – are characterized by their lack of time.

A third problem relates to the added value of this type of system. Why would a professional need a system when he has his own network of professionals to turn to? Keeping in mind that every world citizen is only five handshakes away from the President of the United States, we can conclude that it is often more useful for a professional to activate his own networks when looking for a colleague with a particular expertise.

When professionals have doubts about the added value of a system, the mechanisms above are activated: it happens too often that the information is too rich, too unreliable, too outdated, and therefore the KMS is distrusted and remains unused.

This system approach – codifying what or who, and storing this information in a KMS – can easily be criticized, but the attractiveness of this approach should not be underestimated. The greater the distance between managers and the profession, the greater the temptation to resort to systems. When knowledge management is made the responsibility of a staff department that lacks access to professionals and is offered a ready-made knowledge-storing system by an IT consultant, it is more difficult to resist the temptation to purchase and introduce this system. Moreover, when it 'only' concerns information – jurisprudence for the judge, nuclear reactor data for the technician, sample quotes for the consultants or sample pleas for the lawyer – such systems may be useful. Useful systems always evoke a thirst for more, and the distinction between useful codification of information and useless codification of knowledge is not always clear.

THE THIRD STEP: BACK TO THE BASICS – FACILITATING INTERACTION

The next reaction to these observations is that the attention shifts from knowledge management as codification to knowledge management as interaction. The important thing is to connect professionals, and to allow them to share knowledge face to face. Tacit knowledge, after all, cannot be codified, but is – often implicitly – transferred in the interaction among professionals. Knowledge management, in this case, is aimed at facilitating this interaction, for instance by establishing communities of practice (CoP): groups of professionals who regularly confer about the questions, dilemmas, problems and solutions that they come across.[7] This evokes the question of how to make such a CoP attractive to professionals. What instruments are needed to keep them vivid, how can the created knowledge be dispersed across the organization?

This completes the circle: knowledge management is back to its tacit character. If there is no such thing as knowledge management, knowledge sharing and creation happen spontaneously, perhaps after some minor managerial interventions. If there is no added value in codification of knowledge and of knowledge bearers, knowledge management will imply that the interaction among knowledge bearers is promoted, for instance through the establishment of a CoP. That brings knowledge management back to its original starting point: as an activity among professionals, which is subject to minor managerial facilitation.

CODIFICATION CAN BE USEFUL – IF PROFESSIONALS PERCEIVE IT THAT WAY

Does this mean that codification is useless? That there is never any added value in a system that provides insight into who possesses which expertise? Of course not. It is also too simple to assume that knowledge can never be codified. The rule of thumb here is simple: codification is useful when professionals think it is useful. In Chapter 2 I used the example of language as tacit knowledge. Our native language is tacit knowledge: we speak it flawlessly, and yet we are not aware of the underlying grammar. Someone who has been speaking his native language all his life will fail to see the added value in learning the underlying grammar, perceiving this as a hassle. The same thing is often true for codification: for professionals it is a lot of hassle with very little added value.

In which cases is this different? When is there added value in codification?

- When professional interaction is too time-consuming. Someone who tries to learn from the interaction with professionals without any form of codified knowledge may not learn as fast as someone who has already learned the codified knowledge. This can be compared to learning a foreign language: someone who moves abroad will learn the language through interaction with native speakers, and will eventually be better at speaking the language than someone who learns the language from books. But someone who moves abroad with some background knowledge from books will probably learn faster than someone without any codified knowledge. The question is not 'codification or interaction', but how much codified knowledge is needed to accelerate and improve learning through interaction.

- When professionals find that they are starting to lose a certain skill or knowledge. Professionals learn through interaction, but in the absence of interaction these learned things can be lost. There is also the constant risk that in their interaction, professionals teach one another the wrong things, just like language is sometimes eroded when people in a certain community keep making the same mistakes.

- When new, innovative knowledge is sufficiently developed, and ready for standardization. Codifying such knowledge in a kind of body of knowledge prevents the wheel from being re-invented. At the least this is efficient, and an organization that deals efficiently with its people and resources creates room for the search for new innovations. Let us take another look at the example of language. A language is dynamic. Dictionaries are continually updated, and every language is regularly enriched with new words and phrases. These originate in the interaction among the language users, and are eventually codified: they are assigned a specific meaning. This paves the way for such words and phrases to be used in official documents and in language education. What would happen if nothing was codified? At any moment there would be many words and phrases that are not part of the official language. This would enlarge the gap between daily speech and the language used in documents and education. The resulting hassle would be inefficient at the least. It is therefore not a question of 'codification or interaction', but of which knowledge, born through professional interaction processes, is a likely candidate for codification.

- When risky activities are involved. There is a low tolerance of failure towards activities that entail a high risk of damage. When there is a possibility to codify how these activities should be conducted in order to minimize the risk of damage, it is self-evident that codification is preferred to interaction. The risk that the wheel is re-invented, and sometimes not re-invented, is too large. Returning to the language example, an American who learns a foreign language will make some standard mistakes in meetings, negotiations or dinner speeches. 'I believe' and 'I think', for instance, can often be used interchangeably in English while in many other languages they cannot. This may be not only hilarious, but also harmful. Codification of such common mistakes can be more sensible than learning through experience.
- When there is a net loss of expert professionals. An organization with an ageing body of professionals who are retiring over a short period of time may benefit from codification. A language such as Retoroman, spoken in north-eastern Italy and south-eastern Switzerland, with very few speakers, may die out if it is not codified.

There are probably many other conditions under which codification is useful. When keeping in mind two statements – codification can be useful, but it can also become highly bureaucratic – it will be clear that the line between useful codification and codification-as-bureaucracy can be very thin. A manager who aims to address knowledge management will therefore have to be very sensitive: when does codification contribute to learning processes, and when is it trivial and without any added value? The answers to these questions will largely have to come from the professionals. When there are not enough professionals who recognize the added value of codification, it will be of little use, and it will probably fail. If the professionals do find codification useful, the barriers described above will persist, but a common attempt to overcome these will always be more likely to succeed than an attempt by a manager who is dealing with unmotivated professionals.

KNOWLEDGE MANAGEMENT IS A PROCESS

What implications does this have for knowledge management?

1 Knowledge management is about interaction processes among professionals. These need to be maintained in order for knowledge to be shared and created.

2 In many cases, this is a spontaneous process, and knowledge management is a tacit process that does not require any managerial interventions.

3 There are two risks associated with sharing and creating knowledge spontaneously: there is insufficient development of spontaneous interaction, or there are cognitive fixations. The interventions needed to prevent this are often light-handed and aimed at promoting interaction and preventing social fixations.

4 Codification of tacit knowledge has limited added value for professionals and can become a bureaucratic hassle. However, it can also be useful. The answer to the question when is codification helpful and when is it not calls for a high level of sensitivity on the manager's side. Moreover, it calls for ownership among professionals. If they do not see any added value, there isn't any. In this sense too, knowledge management is a process: involve professionals in the questions whether and how is codification useful.

5 Knowledge management is never a must, but always a trade-off. The added value of knowledge management will always depend on a large number of contextual factors. Which type of knowledge is being addressed? Is much of this knowledge new, or is it well-developed? What is the composition of the professional body? Are there many young, inexperienced professionals, or are many of them seniors with a lot of experience? Does local knowledge, which originated in interaction, result in undesired effects at the macro level? Which tacit types of knowledge management does the organization have? An organization that invests much in the coaching of young professionals – residencies in a hospital, young judges participating in full-bench decisions – may have less need for knowledge management than an organization that doesn't.

6 Knowledge management is about the *content* of professional expertise, but it is usually shaped by *process*-based interventions. The manager does not get involved with the substantive side of knowledge, but brings professionals together. He organizes the entire interaction process, aiming for the development of substantive learning processes.

7 What if something like knowledge management is needed, according to a manager, but the professionals fail to recognize the added value? What if, for instance, professionals are internally focused, highly content with themselves, yet incompetent? Suppose that professionals are deceived by their sense for language, and they keep making the same mistakes in their sentence structure. The manager – let us compare him to the non-native speaker – will have little success in explaining to the native speakers (the professionals) what the right construction is. It is also quite useless to bring these professionals together to make their tacit knowledge explicit: they will confirm one another in the correctness of the wrong sentence

constructions. The earlier-mentioned strategy is applicable here as well: it is possible to break through cognitive fixations through a social intervention. In other words, add other professionals/native speakers who make correct sentence constructions to a group of professionals/native speakers who make mistakes in their sentence constructions. Be confident that there will be learning through the newly developed interaction processes. In this case, too, the manager performs a non-substantive intervention. This intervention will give rise to new interactions and new learning processes. Everyone who has some experience in professional organizations will know that it will be hardly successful to challenge professionals in what they see as the core of the profession – and that this costs a great deal of energy. Non-substantive interventions cost a lot less energy, and often have a better result. How did a national language originate in nineteenth-century France, even though there were many different dialects that didn't have many similarities? Not because Paris prescribed a national language (a substantive intervention) but because roads and railroads were constructed, and a national military service was introduced.[8] Infrastructural measures led to more interaction among the dialects and to the development of a national language. In managerial terms: interaction promotes knowledge creation, and therefore it is important to support interaction.

8   If codification is useful, according to professionals, it can be shaped in different ways. For instance, in a system, or partly in a system and partly through interaction, or partly in a system and partly in the minds of 'knowledge officers'. The exact method of codification is of less importance than whether or not the system is owned by the professionals, and whether or not they recognize its added value. If there are enough incentives for professionals to maintain and use a system, its exact make-up is often of secondary importance. The rule is that the system follows the professional, rather than the other way around.

Based upon these interpretations of knowledge management, it is interesting to note two more things about managerial lines of reasoning that are common in discussions surrounding knowledge management: first, that professionals often suffer from the 'not invented here' syndrome, and prefer to keep re-inventing the wheel, and second, that knowledge management greatly profits from benchmarking.

THE WHEEL IS RE-INVENTED TIME AND AGAIN – AND THAT IS OFTEN NOT A PROBLEM AT ALL

An often-heard managerial complaint is the fact that many professionals suffer from the 'not invented here' syndrome. They keep re-inventing the wheel, which is rather inefficient. This supports the plea for knowledge sharing.

Is this true? Why is it not necessarily bad if professionals keep re-inventing the wheel?

- Someone who re-invents the wheel will have gone through the process of inventing, will know everything about wheels, and will internalize knowledge about wheels a lot faster than someone who copies another person's wheel. During the process, he will develop his tacit knowledge of wheels, and someone who possesses tacit knowledge can deal with future wheel problems in a way that is much more efficient.
- Someone who re-invents the wheel, owns a wheel. That is probably a better guarantee for future use of this knowledge than copying someone else's wheel. Future innovations are easier to accomplish if the innovator owns the wheel.
- There are different types of wheels. A manager may see the same wheel everywhere, while a professional sees a lot more variety: in functions, in diameters, in materials, and so on.
- When professionals are given a chance to re-invent the wheel, this does not imply that they will not use the existing wheels. They will probably use some of the existing knowledge and build upon this knowledge, which might lead to an innovation. Copying wheels will never lead to innovation.

'A professional keeps wanting to re-invent the wheel' – it can be a costly waste of professional energy, but it can also be a much too simple reproach from a manager who is blind to the hidden efficiency of 're-inventing the wheel'.

BENCHMARKING CAN BECOME KARAOKE – A BAD COPY OF REALITY

The alternative to re-inventing the wheel and to 'not invented here' is benchmarking: compare organizations, identify best practices, and adopt these best practices as much as possible. This may be a useful exercise, but benchmarking can also become mindless imitation behaviour: the assumed best practices are simply transplanted from organization A to organization B, while it remains unclear what exactly *is* the best practice, and whether or not it is transplantable at all.

Suppose organization A is worried about the amount of support staff: the HR and finance departments seem large, and the staff-to-line ratio seems high: there is a relatively high number of staff. The organization uses a benchmark to establish the staff-to-line ratio in other organizations. One of these, organization B, turns out to have a relatively low ratio. This organization is asked for an explanation of this. It turns out that organization B has decentralized its staff. This best practice is then transplanted to organization A. There are a few significant risks associated with this process:

- *The codification of the best practice is questionable.* The first question concerns the reality behind organization B's small staff. How are staff and line workers counted? How are they defined? Which tasks are performed by staff and which by line workers? What kinds of support do line workers need? Does the organization have a culture in which line workers receive maximum support, or in which line workers are supposed to be self-sufficient? There are plenty of other questions to ask as well, which show one thing: the ratio is a number that hides a much more complex reality. A codification of best practice is always a construction of reality, and in many cases this construction might have been different. If organization B had used slightly different definitions of staff and line, its ratio might have been much higher.
- *The rationalization of the explanation is questionable.* The second question is whether or not the explanation for the low ratio is correct. Is it really the decentralized staffing that explains this ratio? Or are there other explanations? There may be additional or even alternative explanations: the high level of the staff workers, their physical location, the make-up of the primary processes, the rotation of staff members. Perhaps the decentralized staffing has a disastrous impact on the service, but is it thanks to the line workers that the level of service is maintained through all kinds of temporary measures. Perhaps the decentralization only partly explains the low ratio. Or perhaps organization B would have an even lower ratio if its staffing had been centralized. The explanation for the small size of the staff departments is therefore always a rationalization of the complex reality, which is questionable by definition. Someone who codifies the explanation suggests that this rationalization is not open to question, but rather an objective observation.
- *The best practice is badly copied.* The third question is whether or not organization A is able to adopt the best practice. What, in fact, is the best practice? Is it decentralization? Of what specifically? Or is it decentralization plus a high level of the staff members? Or is it decentralization plus a high level of the staff members plus a specific make-up of the primary

processes? Often the best practice adopted by organization A is a bad copy of organization B's reality.

- *Best practice cannot always be transplanted.* The fourth question is whether or not organization B's best practice fits into the structure and culture of organization A. In medical terms: will organization A accept the transplantation of organization B's best practice, or will it reject it? If organization A has a centralized culture, it is questionable whether decentralization of staff departments is favourable.

When benchmarking becomes mindless copying of best practices from elsewhere, these problems may arise. In that case, the adoption of best practices is bound to be a failure. As Ridderstrale and Nordström put it: 'Benchmarking never gets you to the top'. They compare benchmarking to karaoke: a bad copy of reality.[9] Alternatively, in knowledge management and innovation terms: much professional knowledge is tacit, local and embedded. It has meaning to *these* professionals in *this* organization. The tacit, local and embedded nature of knowledge makes it difficult to codify and then transplant. Much knowledge is suitable to this particular unit, but it can easily lose its meaning when it is transplanted to another professional unit.

Does this mean that benchmarks have no value at all? No, but there is always the risk of karaoke. The manager as well as the professional will have to evaluate whether the best practice represents a more or less objective codification of reality, or just a challengeable construction. They will also have to evaluate whether or not this best practice can be transplanted. Depending on these questions, benchmarking can be useful in three different ways:

1 *The content of the best practice is generally applicable.* Let us look at a simple example. An emergency doctor who sees a patient with an ankle injury has to decide whether or not he orders an X-ray. This is only needed in the case of a fracture. To determine whether an X-ray is necessary, so-called prediction rules have been developed that can exclude the possibility of a fracture. North American doctors use the Ottawa Ankle Rules, which have a very narrow error band. Can these rules be transplanted to other hospitals, outside of North America? Research shows that this is often the case. Apparently the rules have been formulated so well and in such a practical manned that they yield the same narrow error band in other hospitals. The substance of this best practice – the set of prediction rules – can be transplanted.

2 *Perhaps the content of best practice is not generally applicable, but the process of its development can be transplanted.* Someone who aims to use best practices may not transplant the content of the best practice, but rather

the underlying process that resulted in this best practice. 'Underlying process' implies, for instance, questions such as who was involved in developing the best practice, how they were involved, how the implementation was organized.[10] So perhaps a hospital did not implement the Ankle Rules, but instead it may have implemented the process used to make these rules. This process will perhaps result in similar Ankle Rules or in different Ankle Rules that fit the local situation.

3 *Perhaps neither the content, nor the process can be adopted, but the best practice can serve as a source of inspiration.* The prediction rules mentioned above are often transplantable, but not always. In some hospitals, the composition of the patient population is too different from that of the Ottawa hospital, or the threshold for reporting to the emergency room is higher or lower, or there may be more language barriers between doctors and patients. Even in these cases, the Ottawa example can inspire, and lead to the development of local prediction rules. The observation is that the Ottawa Ankle Rules are functional, and this is a reason to develop an own set of rules. Someone looking for good Ankle Rules should not mindlessly copy the codified rules, but learn from them by staying alert.

INNOVATION

Let us take a closer look at innovation, an issue that is closely related to knowledge. Here, too, I will focus on the bottom line of literature on innovation.

TWO OPPOSING VIEWS ON INNOVATION – WHICH ARE BOTH TRUE

Innovating is no different from sharing and creating information: innovations often originate without managerial interventions. Nevertheless, some professional organizations are innovative while others are not. When we take a manager's perspective, and ask what a manager can do to promote innovation, we come across two views that seem to be mutually exclusive.

The first view – which will mainly be supported by professionals – is that innovations cannot or can hardly be planned. Innovations 'just happen', they develop emergently. Studies into the development of innovation always show that innovation processes are unpredictable and unstructured. They resemble a meandering river rather than a straight canal. Something that may seem like an unimportant side-stream today may turn out to be tomorrow's innovative breakthrough, and the meandering river starts to flow in an entirely unexpected direction. Woe betide the person who attempts to canalize this process, because he might have closed off the side-stream in question and have chosen another direction, which seemed promising at the time but turns out not to be.

The organizational implication will be clear. This view goes hand in hand with a certain aversion to model talk: aversion to the idea that innovations can be planned, or that the use of managerial instruments can lead to innovation. Professionals should be granted enough space to pursue activities within the organization that seemingly do not contribute towards the mission and that lack any kind of focus. Another observation from this perspective is the fact that innovations often happen in the periphery or on the fringes of the organization. They happen in the periphery because managerial attention to the periphery is limited, which allows for interesting developments to take place under the radar, and on the fringes, because this is where relationships are more easily formed with other disciplines, and the interface between disciplines often results in innovation. By allowing space, and cherishing the periphery and the fringes, one can force luck: the sudden innovation, the unforeseen breakthrough, the side-stream that becomes the main stream, the by-catch that becomes the main catch, the accident that turns out to be a happy accident, serendipity.

Innovation, after all, implies that existing frameworks and lines of thought are challenged, and this is only possible if there is enough space to venture away from the beaten path. Only when professionals are allowed space will the Einsteins and the Edisons have a chance to come up with innovations. Someone who denies professionals this space will limit innovation to what is called incremental innovation: a gradual improvement of the existing situation – 'tweaking the parameters' – which will never result in radical innovation. Management, standardization, protocollation, the stopwatch culture, a sole focus on increased efficiency – they will all result in the destruction of creativity and deliver a fatal blow to budding innovation. An organization that allows its professionals space will have to tolerate variety, failure and randomness – the organization might take a direction that seems to be random – but allows its employees space to explore and to use their right-brain hemisphere.

A second view – which is probably more popular among managers – is characterized by values that are entirely different: standardization rather than space, consistency rather than variety, a low tolerance towards failure, exploitation versus exploration, analysis versus intuition. After all, space for professionals can result in sloppiness, loss of focus, pursuit of side-streams that have dried up, too little attention to streams that are promising, and in the possibility of speeding up parts of the river by canalizing them. Space does not create Einsteins and Edisons, but Gyro Gearlooses – characters who spend all their lives searching for an innovation that will never happen, and that everyone knows will never happen. There are two advantages to standardizing and streamlining professional activities: they lead to increased efficiency and to innovations. Even if they 'only' result in increased efficiency, this will allow financial space for innovation.

Streamlining can also contribute to the faster market introduction of innovations that become available, even if this is an unforeseen process in a side-stream of the meandering river. Canalization can result in the formation of rapids. Moreover, the distinction between incremental, step-wise innovations on one hand and radical, leap-wise innovations on the other hand is much too simple. The sum of the small changes can constitute a large change. In the world dominated by the right-brain hemisphere, creativity is a central value, while the world of the left-brain hemisphere relies on all kinds of tools that can help in streamlining the profession: DMAIC, PDCA, business process re-engineering, and so on.

A nice and often-used example of an organization that has been faced with both approaches is 3M.[11] 3M has always been recognized as an organization with a rich innovation history. It invented, for instance, adhesive tape and the Post-it note. The Post-it note is a classic example of serendipity – in other words, a happy accident. In the late 1960s a 3M employee invented glue that was reusable and had a low degree of stickiness. The invention was retailed within 3M, but no application was found until another employee, Arthur Fry, made a connection between this invention and his main frustration: loose sheet music that would swirl to the floor during his church choir's concerts. Apparently the glue could in fact serve a purpose. 3M has a bootlegging policy, which means that there is space to develop ideas without official approval, and sometimes even without the management being aware of it. Fry used this space to further explore his idea. Eventually this led to the very successful introduction of the Post-it in the early 1980s – nearly ten years after the original invention.

Up until 2000, 3M was a company that met all the criteria of the first view explained above. When a new CEO was appointed, James McNerney, the second view became dominant. The organization became much more disciplined. All kinds of management tools were introduced, aimed at efficiency improvement and reduction of the number of operational mistakes. While the R&D budget was maintained at its original level, R&D was approached more systematically, and regular reviews were performed to analyse the added value of research projects. The aim was to accelerate the innovation process. There was in fact a reason for this operation: before 2000, 3M had practically stopped growing, and it had become very inefficient and bloated. That is the risk associated with an organization in which the bootlegging mechanism prevails: there are major inefficiencies, market opportunities are missed, ideas are incubated much longer than needed, insufficient attention is paid to innovations, the good will be the enemy of the best, and so on.

The new regime put the emphasis on incremental innovation and took away the space for 'blue sky work'. Arthur Fry has put the difference between the two approaches nicely into words: innovation is 'a numbers game. You have to go through 5000 to 6000 raw ideas to find one successful business'. McNerney's focus on increased discipline was aimed at accelerating this kind of process.

This emphasis on incremental innovation paid off: for many years, 3M was able to present impressive figures, and without this transformation the company may well have been doomed. The risk was obvious as well: insufficient space for serendipity, happy accidents and the kind of innovation that calls for a longer incubation time. Under McNerney's regime, the glue would probably have been aborted as a project long before the idea of the Post-it had been born. In an overly disciplined organization, there is little room for today's side-stream, which may be tomorrow's mainstream. So James McNerney was eventually replaced by a new CEO, with the ambition of re-activating the old, innovative culture.

NEVER THE TWAIN SHALL MEET ...

If all of this is true, the tension between the first – professional – and the second – managerial – view constitutes a dilemma, and there is no right or wrong. A professional who advocates more space, tolerance towards failure, and exploration of what seems to be fruitless, may in fact be right. However, space, failure and exploration can eventually be like flogging a dead horse. It can result in high costs that inhibit innovation elsewhere or in slow decision making, which slows down the implementation of the innovation. When a management question has the structure of a dilemma, chances are that the following dynamics can be observed:

- An organization is characterized by space and tolerance towards failure. This results in innovation, but after a while the disadvantages will become apparent as well: high costs, slow decision making, too many professionals who spend too much time working on their hobby horses without any success, space becoming an excuse for inactivity, and so on.
- A logical reaction is that these negative effects are addressed. There is a stronger focus on efficiency, tools are introduced to establish the added value of the hobby horses, trajectories that have remained unsuccessful for a long time are phased out, attention shifts from occasional leap-wise innovations to a continuous process of step-wise innovations.
- After a while, the disadvantages of this system become visible as well. There is insufficient space for leap-wise innovations and there are no opportunities for further efficiency improvement in the organization. Step-wise

innovations have fully optimized the service delivery and further innovation is impossible.

- A logical reaction to this is that these negative effects are addressed. Professionals are granted more space, a bootlegging policy is developed, there is more space for experiments, professionals are freed from review procedures that are too strict, and so on. This brings us back to the initial situation, and the process can start all over again.

After a while, the disadvantages become visible again, and there is a breeding ground for a return to a more control-focused culture. The result is a perpetual movement between the two extremes in this dilemma. This movement is made even stronger when it coincides with a change in management. Many managers want to introduce changes, or want to leave a certain legacy – which is a worrying character trait – and when there is a dilemma behind a management question, there are always arguments for change. This is the exact development that took place at 3M. The company was innovative, but seemed to be unable to translate this into commercial successes, and therefore it attracted a CEO who disciplined the company until innovations dried up and a new CEO was appointed who cancelled many of these disciplinary measures and who tried to recreate a culture of tolerance towards failure.[12]

These two styles tend to alternate in time, and this development is more or less autonomous: it just takes its course. Perhaps this development is positive: after one style has been prevailing for some time, it may be time for the other style. The risks of this alternation will also be clear: high transaction costs. On one hand, someone who disciplines destroys creativity. Once creativity is destroyed – and a culture has been born in which no risks are taken, good and creative professionals have left, and incubating ideas have disappeared from the institutional memory – it is hard to revitalize it. In short, the transaction costs are high. On the other hand, someone who offers space will create sloppiness. Once an organization has become sloppy – people find it normal that hobby horses are endlessly pursued, there is no cost awareness whatsoever, no one is alert to the question whether or not things can be done faster and cheaper, it is a sign of professionalism not to be interested in time and money – it is difficult to restore some degree of order. Remember 3M's attempts to restore some discipline: the entire organization was turned around – and the transaction costs were high.

Alternating, in other words, means that an organization continually tries to escape from the past. Is there an alternative for this? For the transaction costs involved in this alternation? Is it possible to incorporate the best of both worlds in one organization, and thus create a hybrid organization? We know beforehand that this is not simple. In hybrid organizations – organizations that incorporate two opposite cultures – there is always a risk that the opposite cultures will displace each other. Exploration displaces exploitation, or the other way around.

… EXCEPT IN AMBIDEXTROUS ORGANIZATIONS

The American researchers Charles O'Reilly and Michael Tushman have performed an interesting study into this issue. They introduced the concept of an *ambidextrous organization*:[13] a double-faced organization that both explores and exploits. They postulate that this kind of organizational structure is common in innovation organizations, and that they have the following characteristics.

First, there is a sharp distinction between units that explore and those that exploit, units that tolerate chaos and creativity and units that are well-organized and streamlined. These units may differ strongly with regard to their internal structure, culture and work processes. The focused, efficiency-oriented units are in balance with units that include Einsteins, Edisons and Gyro Gearlooses. In their study, O'Reilly and Tushman name some other differences between the two types of units: one includes older and experienced professionals, the other young professionals; one features mainly insiders, the other outsiders as well; there are different compensation systems, different support staffs, and so on. In other words, fragmentation is purposely created. Fragmentation prevents contamination between the two cultures: innovation is not displaced by 'business as usual', and 'business as usual' is not disrupted by continuous innovation.

Second, these units may be separate, but at the top they are strongly integrated. The senior managers at the top are acutely aware of the need for this fragmentation. They allow the units to have their own culture, but at the same time they are always looking for useful connections. They constantly search for potential for cooperation and for using one another's knowledge and expertise, and professionals are stimulated to cooperate with the other unit, while the strict organizational separation is maintained. The innovators can thus make use of the knowledge (about the market, clients, work processes) of 'business as usual', while 'business as usual' maintains a feeling for and insight into emerging innovations.

Third, the idea of the ambidextrous organization is openly advocated. After all, underneath this organizational structure there is a dilemma, and when professionals fail to see this dilemma there will be fruitless discussions. One person will say that the organization is much too fragmented, while in fact fragmentation is the strength of the organization. Another will state that there is too little uniformity in the organization, while in fact variety – even in management – is the strength of the organization. A third person will hold that incentives for cooperation distract from the core activities of a unit (whether it is business as usual or innovation) but this too is the strength of the model.

The crucial thing is that innovation calls for space for both approaches – exploration and exploitation – in an organization. The organization is structured in such a way that both worlds are separated, but at the same time the connection between these worlds is also organized.

WHAT CAN MANAGERS DO?

First, accept that innovations often happen naturally when professionals are granted space. Accept that innovation processes are rarely linear, and that this calls for a reasonable tolerance towards seemingly chaotic processes and structures.

Second, be aware of the fact that this is only part of the story. Space for meandering processes can also be an excuse for major inefficiencies, missed market opportunities, professional hobby horses that are past their expiration date, insufficient focus on commercialization, the good becoming the enemy of the best, and so on. Discipline and an emphasis on exploitation may also promote innovation.

Third, when there are two entirely different ways to accomplish innovation, namely space and exploration versus discipline and exploitation, there is always a risk that one of these styles will become dominant. If this is the case, the result will almost always be a counter-reaction. In an ambidextrous organization, both worlds are brought together, albeit strictly separated, with a connection between the two worlds. Both worlds are disconnected in the organizational structure, but at the same time they are connected through a number of key players. Disconnection prevents the two worlds from infecting each other. Connection means that both worlds can learn from each other.

NOTES

1   J. Roberts (2000), From know-how to show-how? Questioning the role of information and communication technologies in knowledge transfer. *Technology Analysis and Strategic Management*, 12, pp. 429–43.

2   Julian Orr (1996), *Talking about Machines*, New York: Cornell University Press.

3   Ibid., pp. 125–26.

4   Catrien J.A.M. Termeer and Brechtje Kessener (2007), Revitalizing stagnated policy processes: using the configuration approach for research and interventions. *Journal of Applied Behavioral Science*, 43, pp. 256–72.

5   Well-known publications: Thomas H. Davenport and Laurence Prusak (2000), *How*

Organizations Manage What They Know, Harvard Business School Press. I. Nonaka and H. Takeuchi (1995), *The Knowledge-creating Company*, Oxford: Oxford University Press. See also *Harvard Business Review on Knowledge Management*, Cambridge, MA: Harvard Business School Press, 1998.

6 Orr, op. cit., pp. 110–13.

7 Etienne Wenger and William M. Snyder (2000), *Communities of Practice: The Organizational Frontier*, Cambridge, MA: Harvard Business School Press.

8 Geert Mak (2007), *In Europe: Travels through the Twentieth Century*, London: Harvill Secker.

9 J. Ridderstrale and K. Nordström, *Karaoke Capitalism*, Harlow: Pearson Education.

10 S. Newell *et al.* (2002), The importance of process knowledge for cross project learning: Evidence from a UK hospital. In: HICSS (2002), *Proceedings of the 35th Annual Hawaii International Conference on System Sciences*, Los Alimitos, CA: IEEE Computer Society Press, pp. 1019–28.

11 Bruce Nussbaum (2007), Inside innovation: At 3M, a struggle between efficiency and creativity. *Business Week*, June, pp. 3–26.

12 Ibid., pp. 8–14.

13 Charles O'Reilly III and Michael Tushman (2004), The ambidextrous organization. *Harvard Business Review*, April, pp. 74–81. This is a way of thinking that can also be seen in R.E. Quinn and J. Rohrbaugh (1983), A spatial model of effectiveness criteria: Towards a competing values approach to organizational analysis. *Management Science*, 32, 5, pp. 539–53.

8

PERFORMANCE MANAGEMENT

PERFORMANCE MANAGEMENT: SPREADSHEET MANAGEMENT OR RESPECT FOR THE PROFESSION?

A development common to almost all professional organizations is the increasing use of performance measurement systems (PMSs): the evaluation of professionals, based upon quantification of their performance. Judges are evaluated based on the number of verdicts, scientists on the number of publications, doctors on the number of interventions, and schools on their test scores. If performance can be quantified, professionals or professional organizations can also be ranked. Sometimes these rankings are only disclosed to the professionals in question, but it happens more and more often that they are openly accessible. By now, we are all familiar with national rankings, for instance of hospitals and schools, and with the international ranking of universities in the *The Times Higher Education Supplement.*

No other issue shows the tension between manager and professional more clearly than performance measurement. One may argue that performance measurement does not say anything at all about the actual professional performance. Take a university professor. What does the number of published articles say about the quality of these articles? And about whether or not the research is innovative? What does a high test score say about a school's performance if the measurement does not take into account the type of students, or whether or not the parents are stimulating their children? Or if the school does only one thing: teaching to the tests? Looking only at quantified performance does no justice to the profession. It is merely spreadsheet management. The complexity of the profession is reduced to a spreadsheet of figures, which often hide more than they expose.

Others may argue that performance management can fit into the specific characteristics of a professional organization – and there are two arguments that support this. First, professionals deserve autonomy and this autonomy is respected by performance management. The manager is only interested in the researcher's scientific publications. It is up to the professional to decide how these publications come about, whether it is through hard work, long walks on the beach, or participation in many conferences. The second argument is that performance management is often focused on the essence of the profession. A judge may be expected to pass verdicts. Why should these not be counted, especially when it becomes clear that one court passes more verdicts per judge than another? Why should this not be discussed? A professional who is willing to account for his performance will earn quite a few degrees of freedom. Of course these figures are a limited representation of reality – adversaries are right about this point – but they are sufficient. This too is an advantage of performance management: it does not require extensive reports – a fact sheet is sufficient. An intelligent professional will not spend his energy on resisting performance management, but rather on conforming to this reality and thus buying freedom and limiting bureaucracy.

This chapter will start out by making clear that both these arguments are too simple. Performance management *can* contribute to better professional service delivery – in opposition to the first argument. Performance management *can* lead to decreased professionalism and increased bureaucracy – in opposition to the second argument. The interesting question is under which conditions professionalism will decrease or increase.

THE ABC OF PERFORMANCE MANAGEMENT: POSITIVE AND PERVERSE EFFECTS

Let us start by taking a look at the ABC of performance management. The principle is simple: performance measurement can have positive as well as negative effects. The main positive effects are described below.

Performance measurement is an important incentive for performance. It results in a focus on activities that are apparently important in an organization. The scientist's task is to do research and to publish about that research. A study conducted at my own university shows that the introduction of a PMS resulted in more publications.[1] When the Dutch Healthcare Inspection registered and published figures on bedsores, hospitals were stimulated to pay attention to this issue – and the incidence of bedsores decreased.[2] 'What gets measured, gets done' is the well-known adage.[3] Performance measurement can also lead to a decreased level of bureaucracy in an organization: the professional is simply evaluated on the basis of his actions. There is no need for plans, policies, and complicated accountability strategies. Moreover, the focus on production will decrease the amount of attention being paid to activities that have no added value for the organization.

Performance measurement increases transparency and is an elegant way of accounting. The often complex performance of a professional organization can be reduced to a limited amount of figures. Figures are usually a powerful communication tool. A police organization's legitimacy can be increased if the figures are positive – the crime-solving rate goes up, the amount of robberies goes down. If the figures are negative – a city is ranked last in a nationwide poll on safety, for instance – people's and politicians' problem awareness can be increased, and this may induce necessary changes.

Performance measurement can improve an organization's intelligence. If an organization evaluates some of its performance figures over a longer period of time, it can use the resulting information for further improvement of its performance. The extensive figures produced by the New York Police Department (NYPD) are a good example.[4] Not only do these give an impression of the performance of the various districts, they are also used to analyse the development of crime and how crime spreads through the city.

Performance measurement stimulates learning processes. Figures can be compared, and notable differences among police departments, for instance, can be a reason to examine them closer. Why does one department perform better than the other? Can the experiences of the well-performing departments be used in ill-performing departments? The experiences of the NYPD are an interesting example here as well. Police officers use performance figures to question one another critically during specially organized meetings. They address the way in which crime develops, as well as possible explanations, the actions to take if crime rates increase, and the effectiveness of these actions. This peer questioning is sometimes tough: the police officer 'is peppered with questions'.[5] As a result, professionals learn and can improve their performance.

There are some disadvantages too. In jargon, these are referred to as 'perverse effects'. The essence of perverse effects is quite simple: performance measurement focuses on figures and takes attention away from quality. This can be made explicit as follows.

Performance measurement always results in incentives for strategic behaviour or 'game playing'. How can the waiting lists for the emergency room be reduced on paper? By letting patients wait outside the waiting room, so they are not included in the figures.[6] What does it mean if a hospital reports a sharp decrease in the incidence of decubitus? Better professional service, or tweaking definitions? Perhaps the term decubitus is differently defined and registered.[7] How can a school improve its test scores? By excluding underperforming students from the test.[8] This is called strategic behaviour. There is production on paper, but this has nothing to do with the professional's actual performance. If there is strategic behaviour, performance figures can no longer be used for the intelligence function; after all, they do not say anything about the underlying reality.

Performance measurement leads to pseudo-transparency. Performance measurement does not necessarily lead to transparency. Production figures are always a sub-optimal representation of reality. What do mortality figures, for instance, really say about the performance of a hospital? The answer to this question, and similar questions, should always be: 'nothing'. Mortality figures do not say anything as long as they are not related to people's illnesses. Likewise, satisfied clients do not imply anything about the quality of the professional service. It is difficult to capture quality in one or more numbers, and if this is done anyway, the score strongly depends on the chosen definitions. Figure 8.1 below illustrates this.

Figure 8.1 represents the scores of Dutch hospitals. There are two methodologies for scoring and ranking hospitals.[9] The dots represent individual hospitals. If both methodologies use similar definitions of quality and similar measurement criteria, all of the hospitals should be on one straight line. The 'Starry Sky' of hospitals indicates that some hospitals are ranked high on the basis of one methodology, and low on the basis of the other. Then where is transparency? Which hospital is good and which one is not? Apparently, performance measurement creates pseudo-transparency.

Performance measurement results in decreased professionalism. Strategic behaviour is often – though not always – harmless, sometimes even funny. It is more serious when performance measurement actually decreases the level of professionalism. This can be the case when the incentives that result from a measurement system displace professional considerations. If a police officer

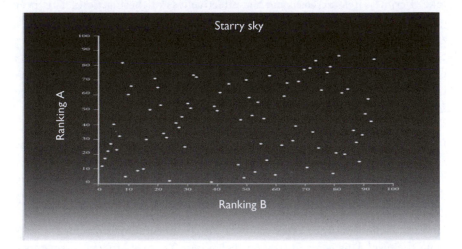

Figure 8.1
The Starry Sky
Source: Maarse and van Velden 2004.

deals with an incident in an informal way, this may be more sensible than a sanction, from a professional point of view, but it does not lead to measurable production in the system. So there might be an incentive for a police officer to impose a formal sanction, even if, from a professional perspective, this seems counter-productive. Incidents that cause societal unrest but that do not result in tangible scores in a measurement system may receive less attention than incidents that do result in production but that hardly have any societal added value. When the police force's production is rewarded, preventive tasks may be less interesting even though they are in fact important from a professional perspective.

Performance measurement obstructs ambitions. Ambitious professionals will always be motivated to perform better. It is questionable whether measurement systems will be stimulating to them. Sometimes this is not the case. Mediocrity can become the norm: when someone is judged on the basis of a certain level of production, there is a risk that he or she will regard this as a sufficient or adequate performance. Another risk is that input is optimized in order to arrive at a desired output. The violence rate against prison staff (output) can be reduced by arranging a quick transfer for troublemakers (optimizing input). It is more ambitious if the prison staff make an effort to prevent prisoners from becoming violent, but performance measurement might obstruct ambitions like these.

Performance measurement obstructs innovations. Innovation is a risky activity: it can fail, and thus not deliver the desired results. If there is a PMS, this risk may be a stimulus *not* to innovate. The existing standards and routines, after all, will yield a predictable production, while innovation can have a negative impact on the production. Performance measurement may be an 'idea killer'.[10]

Performance measurement leads to an increase of bureaucracy. PMSs may entail a heavy bureaucratic burden. Activities such as gathering and maintaining data, the continuous battle for comparable and consistent product definitions, reporting, designing supplements to product definitions, and rules for reporting all result in certain bureaucratic costs.

The advantages and disadvantages are partly contradictory. Performance measurement can promote performance, but obstruct ambitions. It can improve an organization's intelligence, but also result in strategic behaviour and therefore in non-information. It can induce learning processes, but also be an 'idea killer'. It can reduce as well as increase bureaucracy.

This picture becomes even more ambivalent when we realize that it isn't always easy to determine whether performance management will have a positive or a perverse effect. When a researcher is publishing about the same issue over and over again and therefore achieves a high score on the spreadsheets, this appears to be indicative of a type of perverse incentive: innovations are being obstructed. However, the effect may be positive as well: the performance measurement stimulates the researcher to disseminate his knowledge and expertise, and he realizes that one or a few articles may not be sufficient to achieve this.

It is important to keep in mind this ambivalent picture for a while. Apparently, performance management can lead to good and bad things. The interesting question is not whether this is good or bad, but *under which conditions* performance measurement works, and under which conditions the perverse effects become dominant.

THE LAW OF DIMINISHING EFFECTIVENESS: THE MORE IMPACT PERFORMANCE MANAGEMENT HAS, THE MORE THE INFORMATION WILL BE PERVERTED

The crucial variable in this case is the *impact* of performance figures. A high impact means that these figures have direct and severe consequences for a professional or a professional organization. Examples of high impact include:

- Financial sanctions. The performance figures will result in a high positive or negative financial sanction. The future budget, for instance, will be made largely dependent on the performance figures. An organization that underperforms will get a sanction, while the one that over-performs will get a reward.
- Naming and shaming. The performance figures are published and organizations are ranked, which makes it clear to the public which organizations deliver the best and the worst performance. The impact is high, because a low ranking may affect an organization's image, the confidence that clients have in an organization, or the choice behaviour of future personnel who would rather work for an organization with a higher ranking.
- Managerial interventions. Organizations that underperform run the risk of being subject to a managerial intervention: there may be more managerial involvement in the daily routine, a change of structure, increased supervision, and so on. This is not attractive, as it affects an organization's degrees of freedom. A score that is higher than average, by the way, may also be unattractive, for instance because it may result in even higher product targets in the next year.

A high impact will result in perverse incentives: professionals will be tempted to game the numbers. A manager who makes a financial reward dependent on figures may create an incentive for perverse behaviour. Schools will ask ill-performing students to stay home on the day of the test and invigilators will give certain signals to their students to save them from making mistakes.[11] Publication of bedsore figures per hospital may be an incentive for certain hospitals to tweak the definitions, hoping that this will have a positive effect on the figures. This is what is called the Law of Diminishing Effectiveness: the higher the perceived impact of a measurement system, the stronger the incentive for perverse behaviour, and the less effective a system will be. This is illustrated in Figure 8.2.[12]

It should be emphasized that professionals often feel that it is legitimate to arrive at perverse effects. Many services of professional organizations are in essence unsuitable for quantified performance measurements, because:

- Quality is an ambiguous term with multiple and mutually conflicting dimensions. Performance measurement is aimed at only one of these dimensions, and ignores the others.
- Many professionals' performance is relational: it is achieved through cooperation with others. The throughput time in legal procedures in a court is partly dependent on the attitude of the defendant's attorney; a school's performance is partly dependent on the attitudes of the parents.
- There isn't always a causal relationship between effort and result. The activities of a probation officer that are aimed at preventing relapse constitute

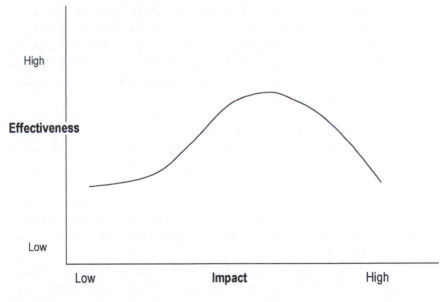

Figure 8.2
The Law of Diminishing Effectiveness
Source: de Bruijn 2006.

only one of the factors that influence whether or not relapse will occur – and therefore it is difficult to relate relapse figures to these activities.

- Output cannot be understood without knowledge of input. A hospital with top surgeons that attracts patients who have been rejected elsewhere will have a high mortality rate by definition. If a ranking is made and published on the basis of mortality figures, this hospital will score very poorly.

When a PMS is used for such services despite these factors, and when the impact is high, professionals may perceive this to be highly unfair. The PMS ignores the invisible aspects of quality, or the role of third parties, or the impact of other factors, or the impact of an organization's input. That is unfair; someone who is treated unfairly will see legitimacy in perverting the system.

THE LAW OF MUSHROOMING: THE MORE PERVERSE EFFECTS, THE LARGER AND MORE BUREAUCRATIC THE SYSTEM

As soon as the Law of Diminishing Effectiveness is activated, another phenomenon is born: mushrooming.[13] The more perverse effects become manifest, the stronger the stimulus to repair the PMS. New and more detailed production definitions are developed, reporting rules are tightened, there will be closer control, additional indicators are introduced, and so on. This expansion – 'mushrooming' – may strip a PMS of its elegance. Let me give a simple example from my own organization. My university, like many other universities, finances research partly on the basis of production figures. One type of 'product' is an 'international scientific book'. Everyone knows what is meant by this, yet this 'product' evokes some questions:

- Should this book have a minimum size?
- Are English books the only ones that are international, or can the same be said about books in Spanish or in Mandarin? And how about French or German?
- Does a second edition count as an international scientific book? If not, does a second, fully revised edition count as an international scientific book?
- And what about books that consist of a number of articles that have already been published?
- What is the factor that determines the scientific nature of the book? Should the publisher work with a peer review system? Or should a book be published by a scientific publisher? But what exactly is a scientific publisher? Can a book that is written for education purposes be scientific?
- What about a book that is published in the national language, and then in

English and then in Spanish? Does this count as three international books?
- And what about books that are published digitally, and that are available through a 'print on demand' system?

Given the high impact of production figures, and given these loopholes, one might expect some strategic behaviour on the part of the professionals. If a PMS like this is introduced, these kinds of questions will have to be answered sooner or later, and the answers will need to be included in some kind of protocol. This will cause the system to expand.

PMSs expand not just because of efforts to combat strategic behaviour. There are other incentives as well. It is often concluded after a while that a system is a limited representation of reality. An emergency department with long waiting times will find that these waiting-time figures do not give a fair picture of its performance. It may for instance be the only emergency department in the region, the region may be attractive to tourists, the region's inhabitants may be more likely to go to an emergency department than those in other regions, and so on. A hospital with an emergency room that scores poorly could likely push for additional indicators. There should not only be an indicator for waiting times, but also a ratio that indicates the number of emergency rooms per thousand inhabitants. Alternatively, the number of treated inhabitants should be supplemented with figures about the number of treated tourists and the number of visits to general practitioners. Figures are a limited representation of reality, so additional figures are needed to make this representation more truthful. One figure calls for another, and this will cause the system to expand.

Expanding PMSs may become so complicated that they can no longer be communicated – to the outside world or to the professionals. This is when they lose their effectiveness. The strength of performance measurement should be its simplicity or elegance: the performance of an organization can be reduced to a limited number of indicators. 'What gets measured gets done' is no longer true when the definition of 'what gets measured' is accompanied by all kinds of nuances and exceptions. The result is an incomprehensible, bureaucratic system, and moreover, a bureaucracy of control is needed to keep the system active.

WHY PERVERTED SYSTEMS CONTINUE TO EXIST

PMSs can create perverse incentives, the systems expand and become more bureaucratic. The logical consequence seems to be that these systems need to be phased out at a certain moment. They have achieved what they were supposed to achieve, the positive effects are now offset by the perverse effects, and therefore it is time to introduce another kind of management. This development, however, is not self-evident. Perverted systems appear to be resistant to change. When a system has become embedded in an organization, its abolishment or phase-out is not always easy. How can this be explained? Why are perverted systems resistant?

The first answer to this question can be found by asking who owns the PMSs. Of course the main owners are the managers and professionals in question: they are the ones who work with this system. But there are third-party owners as well: parties that do not work with the system, but that work with the system's information. These can be the parties that use the data for rankings – of schools, hospitals, safe and unsafe neighbourhoods, child-friendly and child-unfriendly neighbourhoods, universities, and so on. Since 2004, *The Times Higher Education Supplement* has published a ranking of universities in which citations and the staff-student ratio play an important role. 'Fascination with international comparisons is undiminished' and 'the search for the world's leading universities is surely unstoppable'.[14] This third-party involvement may be a strong incentive to keep systems in the air: keep the system in order to provide the publication with the right data – regardless of what the perverse effects of this kind of system may be within the universities. The result may also be a domino effect. Other parties – ministries, financers, other universities, future staff of the organization – can find these rankings useful. They seem to be a representation of quality, or at least of reputation, and this may have an impact on all kinds of decisions.

There are many other third parties who have an interest in resistant PMSs: audit officers, civil servants at government departments, Members of Parliament, interest groups, and staff departments of planning and control that manage the systems within the organization. An entire economy may be born around these instruments. Consultants who develop new instruments, for instance, which always carry the promise of improving the performance of the professional organization. Or institutes function as the external guards of these kinds of systems, and build data banks based on these systems and sell these data. Such an economy will lead to the continued existence of PMSs, even if they no longer have a positive effect within professional organizations.

The second answer to the question why are perverted systems resistant is that third parties are not the only ones to benefit from the continued existence of perverted systems. Managers and professionals can benefit too. Systems can ritualize: everyone uses them, but their nature is purely ritualistic and they have nothing to do with reality or with what is really important. The complaint that performance measurement is a ritual is often heard;[15] organizations invest a lot in PMSs, but these are used in a very limited way.[16]

How does this ritualizing process develop? First, PMSs lose their effectiveness. The perverse effects displace the beneficial effects. Professionals carry out their own activities, according to their own professional values, and they have learned to feed the PMS with the figures and information required by their management, which satisfies the managerial echelon.

When a university research group is able to show a large number of publications per researcher, it is hard for the board of directors or for an evaluation commission to be critical towards this research group.

Higher up in the organization are the managers, who have their own world of planning cycles, annual reports, planning and control figures, strategic papers, and so on. Ritualizing means that the professional echelon does not embark on a mission against the managerial world and its paper reality, but maintains it and even feeds it. Feed the system with a sufficient number of publications and everybody will be happy: the board because there are sufficient publications per researcher, the researcher because a satisfied board will probably respect his autonomy.

As long as both these worlds exist alongside each other, with professionals using the PMSs to dodge managerial interventions, performance measurement is not threatening to them. It is a ritual that ensures a peaceful coexistence between managers and professionals. To the professionals, this situation is comfortable: the professional has enough of a degree of freedom to shape the primary process according to his own views. The ritual is comfortable for the management as well: the desired figures become available, and these are usually an indication of the desired trends. The system thus feeds the notion that everything is under control.

WHAT CAN MANAGERS DO?

The paragraphs above offer an ambiguous picture of performance measurement. Performance management can have positive as well as perverse effects. Sometimes a single phenomenon can be regarded as a perverse effect as well as a positive effect. The more pressure managers put on professionals to improve their performance, the larger the chance that there will be perverse effects, and, similarly, that a system expands and becomes more bureaucratic. These processes of becoming perverse and bureaucratic are sometimes quite visible, but the system is maintained anyway – by third parties, and sometimes even by professionals and managers themselves.

Then what is the sensible way to approach performance measurement? To prevent the system from become perverted? To make sure that the PMS is meaningful both to professional and manager? The remainder of this chapter will provide some answers to these questions.

The essence is that performance measurement is used in a moderate and predictable manner. Moderate and predictable use is possible when managers and professionals abide by certain rules. These rules address:

1 The impact of performance measurement, which should be limited.
2 The design and use of performance measurement; which requires interaction between manager and professional.
3 The coupling of centralized and decentralized PMSs; loosely coupled systems are often more effective than tightly coupled systems;
4 The product definitions within PMSs, which require a certain tolerance for variety.
5 The interpretation and meaning assigned to figures, which also needs to result from interaction between manager and professional.

These five topics are discussed in-depth below.

1. LIMITED IMPACT: DON'T JUDGE ONLY ON THE BASIS OF FIGURES

Limit financial rewards

The first and most important rule is self-evident: the impact of performance measurement should always be limited. When it is a large proportion of a professional organization's budget, and reputation or degrees of freedom are dependent on performance figures, the system will become perverted (see the above discussion on the Law of Diminishing Effectiveness). This may seem logical when taking into account the previous paragraphs, but for managers it may be counter-intuitive. 'Rewarding performance' sounds effective, but is actually *deceptive* – after a while, the manager will only receive perverted information.

The question immediately arises: what is a high impact? Should 40, 20 or 5 per cent of the budget be dependent on output? Of course there is no right answer. The issue requires an assessment by managers and professionals – as will be illustrated by the following section on the importance of interaction.

Limit functions and platforms

Impact is also limited when managers and professionals reach agreement on the *functions* of the figures and about the *platforms* for which they are intended.[17] Agreements about the functions relate to what the performance figures are used for. Are they used to create transparency? Are they connected to a financial reward? Or are they used for benchmarking? Agreements about platforms have to do with *who* will see these figures, and be allowed to use them. Are the figures used for internal use only? Or may other parties outside of the organization use them as well? Will they be published or do they remain confidential?

Without such agreements, there is a significant chance that the system will become perverted. The professional may develop a lack of trust regarding the way in which the performance measurement will be used. The professional will turn his figures over to his manager without knowing who will get to see them, and how and for which purposes they will be used. Will the figures regarding a group's number of published articles be used only by the group and its manager? Or will they be published? And will they be used as a basis for allocating funds? Will they be used for rankings? Will they play a role in the assessment of individuals? The more functions a figure has and the more platforms are allowed to use it, the greater the perverse incentives.

2. INTERACTION: PERFORMANCE MEASUREMENT RESULTS FROM INTERACTION WITH THE PROFESSIONAL

There are many decisive moments during the development and use of PMSs. How will the products be defined? Which indicators are chosen? What agreements are reached about the production that is to be achieved? What will be the consequences if this production is or is not achieved? How will the production figures be monitored?

A PMS can only be owned by both the manager and the professional when they formulate a common answer to these questions. This implies that the design and use of PMSs should always be the result of an interaction process between manager and professional. If the system is a shared system that can also be of use to the professional, there is a smaller chance of the system becoming perverted.

A well-known example of this is professionals and managers negotiating about production agreements – the professional can indicate what he wishes to focus on. Another simple example is the monitoring of production figures. At my own university, every faculty reports on its scientific output on a yearly basis. Since budgets are dependent on these outputs, the output is monitored through the involvement of several professionals from different faculties. The advantages are plenty. First, professionals see through reported publications much easier than non-professionals do. They are often better suited to identify strategic behaviour. Put in a less diplomatic way: employ poachers if you want to catch poachers. Second, if there is any doubt, there will be a negotiation among professionals themselves. Professional involvement may result in a common opinion among the professionals about what is and what is not allowable, in which respects the system works, and in which it doesn't. If only managers were involved in the monitoring, discussions about the output achieved would soon become discussions between managers and professionals, which might have a less satisfactory outcome.

3. ROOM FOR DECENTRALIZED DEVIATION – NO INTEGRAL AND CONSISTENT SYSTEM

The roll-out of PMSs often involves multiple managerial echelons. Education is a good example: a ministry rewards universities on the basis of performance, universities reward faculties, faculties reward departments, departments reward research groups, and research groups reward individual researchers, all on the basis of performance.

The question is whether the centralized PMS should be copied to the decentralized levels, or whether these decentralized levels should be allowed to develop their own systems. Copying the central system seems to be the best option. In the university example there are six echelons, which may result in five different PMSs. When these systems provide conflicting incentives, the impact of performance measurement will be lost.

However, from the point of view of a faculty executive, for example, there may be valid arguments to deviate from the national- or university-level system. The system, for instance, has lost its effect within the faculty and only results in perverse effects. Alternatively, the professionals perform well even without a system of incentives, or there is a need for innovation, and the university-level incentive system does not manage to achieve this. Or activities that are crucial to the faculty score badly in the PMS and run the risk of being undervalued. Or there appear to be major differences among the different research groups within a faculty, and the central system cannot deal with these differences. Developing a specific faculty-level incentive system may do justice to the special circumstances under which a faculty operates.

At every echelon there are special, local circumstances that are known only to the local managers and professionals. If these local circumstances are disregarded, there is a major chance that the PMS will not work. Moreover, even within a single university with its variety of disciplines, it is unthinkable that a university-wide system will be effective in all faculties. Allowing deviations from the PMS at the level of the decentralized echelons will create room, and room is always a condition for aligning a central system to a decentralized reality.

This may sound logical, but in fact this implies that a PMS should never be integral (i.e. applicable to everything and everybody) nor consistent (i.e. being the same at all levels). Managerial model talk, however, does include these terms. The sentence 'a system of performance measurement should be integral and consistent' has a high feel-good level, while integrality and consistency are actually a problem in a world that is characterized by variety.

4. TOLERANCE FOR VARIETY – CONFLICTING DEFINITIONS AND CONFLICTING SYSTEMS SHOULD BE ALLOWABLE

This brings us to the next recommendation: tolerate variety. An important aspect of a professional's performance is that it cannot be captured in a simple figure or set of figures. Professionals often have to meet various and conflicting criteria, as has been described in Chapter 5 (on quality management). A judge has to pass verdicts quickly, but he also has to meet certain legal quality demands, and he has to treat the various parties well. These criteria may be in conflict with one another. Registering only the number of verdicts and their lead times does not do justice to the profession. Moreover, the definition of professional's 'products' is always disputable. What exactly is a verdict? What is a scientific publication? Definitions always result from a choice that may be questioned. A professional who is evaluated on the basis of performance figures may therefore be treated unfairly in two respects. The chosen definition does not do justice to the multi-value nature of his work, and the performance figure disregards other, potentially important aspects of his work. How to deal with this?

A first answer is: tolerate the fact that performance can be evaluated in different ways, using different definitions and measurement methods. The Starry Sky in Figure 8.1 above illustrates how performance measurement may create pseudo-transparency. The Starry Sky, however, can also be interpreted in positive ways:

- The service delivery of hospitals cannot be reduced to a limited number of products and indicators.
- Every chosen product definition and indicator is questionable.
- Choosing only one set of product definitions and indicators therefore never does justice to the profession.
- Using different, perhaps even conflicting product definitions and indicators may bring us closer to reality.
- If a professional organization scores well according to two different sets of product definitions and indicators, there is a major chance that the organization is really performing well.
- If a professional organization scores poorly according to both systems, the performance is probably inadequate.
- If an organization scores well according to one system, and poorly according to the other, the impression is ambiguous and it would be wise to use some caution when formulating the final judgement.

The Starry Sky, which initially seemed to illustrate pseudo-transparency, suddenly illustrates transparency as well. An organization in the top left-hand corner of Figure 8.1 performs badly, an organization in the top right-hand corner performs well, and for the others the picture is not so clear.

A second answer is: tolerate other evaluation mechanisms alongside performance measurement. These may include judgements by clients, fellow professionals or external peers. Fellow professionals and external peers will be particularly able to pass a qualitative judgement in addition to a quantitative judgement. Here, too, there is a Starry Sky effect: sometimes quantitative and qualitative judgements will be in agreement with each other, sometimes they will be in conflict. This is illustrated in Table 8.1.

A first example is a professional who shows high productivity, and performs well from a qualitative perspective as well. This could be a researcher who publishes a lot and who is innovative as well; a hospital that performs many interventions according to professional standards; or a judge who passes many verdicts that stand when appealed. In sports terms: this would be the soccer player who does not only score many goals, but also plays beautifully, feels responsible for the team, participates in the defence, and stimulates others to play better.

A second example is a professional who performs badly from a productivity perspective. A researcher hardly publishes any articles; a surgeon is associated with a high mortality rate; or a judge hardly passes any verdicts. The professional judgement, however, may be positive. The researcher is an inspiring leader to a group of young and talented researchers with an international reputation. He stimulates others to excel. The surgeon is of such a high quality that he treats many patients that were rejected by other hospitals. The judge is assigned many major, complicated cases on the basis of his competencies.

These professionals can be compared to wing players in soccer. The forward player who plays on the wings and seeks out the lines of the field hardly scores any goals himself, even though he plays in the front line. His tactics, however, create room for others – the centre forward, the offensive midfielders – and allows them to score, just like the researcher whose quality it is to turn others into good researchers.

A third example is that of the 'bean counter': the professional who makes every effort to score well in the PMS, but whose performance is poor from a

Table 8.1
Four types of judgement about performance

	Productivity: high	*Productivity: low*
Peer judgement: good quality	Star player	Wing player
Peer judgement: bad quality	'Bean counter'	Candidate for degradation

Source: de Bruijn 2006.

quality perspective. The researcher publishes a lot, but manages to do so by continuous reproduction of existing knowledge. The surgeon is able to achieve wonderful productivity figures, but leaves the difficult cases to colleagues. The judge passes a large number of verdicts, but has a bad reputation because of the ill treatment of the parties involved and the little time he spends on each case. The lazy centre forward fits into this category: he is only interested in scoring goals, does not participate in the defence and therefore shares the blame for goals scored by the opposing team and for the loss of a game; he fails to recover the ball from the midfield, and does not inspire his fellow players but rather irritates them with his superstar attitude.

Finally, a judgement can be bad from both productivity and professional perspectives. Productivity is low, while the performance is also judged badly professionally. In soccer terms, this professional would be a candidate for degradation.

Table 8.1 shows that both judgements – the professional judgement based on a process approach and the productivity judgement based on the PMS – are needed to get an adequate impression of a professional's functioning.

Again, tolerance for variety is often not reflected in managerial model talk. After all, it will result in inconsistencies – different product definitions exist alongside one another – and in a limited applicability of the performance measurement. A person who scores well in the system – a bean counter – can still be an ill-performing professional. This inconsistency and limited applicability, however, also represent the strength of the system: they have a moderating effect on the perverse incentives.[18] After all, the professionals always have some room: there is some variety of product definitions, and there are other systems alongside PMSs which may measure other aspects of the professional's performance.

5. MEANING MAKING AND INTERPRETING ARE PROCESSES – TOLERATE CONFLICTING INTERPRETATIONS

Every performance figure hides a reality that is only partly represented by the figure. An important question with regard to performance measurement is therefore *which* interpretation and meaning should be assigned to the figures and – similarly – *who* will do that. The outcome of these questions is significant. The consequences may be serious if an incorrect meaning is internalized. Managers may be deceived. Professionals may become less likely to take risks. If mortality rates are published, for instance, and they are interpreted incorrectly, cardiologists may not be willing to perform risky operations anymore.[19]

Mortality rates

In many Western countries, it is common practice to publish mortality rates of hospitals. The number of patients who died at the hospital may be expressed in various ratios, for instance as a percentage of the total number of patients, or of the total number of medical interventions.

The meaning of such a figure is highly limited. It cannot be interpreted without any knowledge of the reality behind the figure.[20] Consider the following:

- Mortality rates in rural Scotland are higher than those in England. This can be explained by the fact that Scottish patients need to travel a longer distance to the hospital, and therefore arrive in a worse condition.
- Low mortality rates can be the result of a reduction of the length of the hospital stay. Patients are dismissed, may die at home, and are not included in the figures.
- The nature of some treatments, for instance oncological interventions, has changed drastically. Patients are treated at the hospital, they can go home, and then return for a new treatment. In other words, there is not one single treatment period. If a patient dies, it may be random whether this happens at the hospital or at home. In the former case, the patient is included in the mortality figure, and in the latter case he is not.
- As medical knowledge increases, patients are admitted who would previously have been regarded as beyond help. The mortality rate among these patients is higher than among regular patients almost by definition.
- Some hospitals closely cooperate with hospices, where patients receive palliative care. Such cooperation reduces the hospital's mortality rate.

The bottom line of these examples is that mortality rates are influenced by a multitude of factors, and not just by the quality of the medical interventions. If a meaning is assigned solely on the basis of the figures, this meaning will most likely be poor or even incorrect. Since different, partly conflicting interpretations of mortality rates are possible, it is important that meaning making is a process in which both managers and professionals participate. What can be the results of such a process?

- The process might result in consensus on the interpretation of the figures. Perhaps this final interpretation is richer than the initial interpretation, prior to the start of the process. An interpretation that results from a process of interaction will have more authority than an individual party's interpretation.
- If managers and professionals disagree about the meaning of a figure, this may be a reason for further investigation – which may be very helpful, and

may contribute to learning processes for managers as well as professionals.

- If managers and professionals fail to arrive at a shared meaning, and their meanings are mutually conflicting, that is an important given as well. It may give rise to caution when formulating a policy that is in conflict with one of the meanings, and that would have irrevocable consequences.
- In this case, too, giving the manager as well as the professional an opportunity to assign their own meaning to the figures will give them space – after all, determining a product figure and assigning meaning to it are two different activities – and this will reduce the risk of perverse behaviour.

A NUANCED PICTURE

Let us take a look at the resulting overall picture of performance measurement – a managerial instrument that beats all others when it comes to instigating conflict between managers and professionals.

First, the idea that performance measurement is unable to improve professional service delivery is incorrect. Performance measurement calls for a nuanced approach: it can contribute to improving the profession, but it can also create perverse incentives.

Second, perverse incentives will arise when performance measurement has a high impact on professionals. A high impact – such as significant financial consequences, naming and shaming, managerial interventions – will create perverse incentives.

Third, there is therefore a need to use the system in a moderate way. Unmoderated use, for instance, is judgement based on performance without any reserve: a manager develops product definitions unilaterally and judges professionals on the basis of these. Unmoderated use will result in a system that *has* to be integral and consistent – there is no room for conflicting systems, and meaning automatically follows from the production figures. Moderate use, on the other hand, implies that the figures only have a limited impact. PMSs are developed via interaction. Systems are not integral, but show decentralized deviations. Professional organizations always have a high degree of variety; therefore there should be room for conflicting product definitions and systems. The professionals are involved in the process of assigning meaning to the results.

Performance measurement is based on the idea that professional organizations deliver products that can be counted. Moderate use means that performance measurement is turned into a process in which managers and professionals cooperate to define performance, and reach agreement about impact and meaning.

NOTES

1 Delft University of Technology (2000, in Dutch), *Evaluatie toepassing allocatiemodel 1996–1999*, Delft: Delft University of Technology.

2 Dutch Healthcare Inspection (Inspectie voor de Gezondheidszorg) (2007, in Dutch), *Het resultaat telt 2006. Prestatie-indicatoren als onafhankelijke graadmeter voor de kwaliteit van in ziekenhuizen verleende zorg*. The Hague: Inspectie voor de Gezondheidszorg.

3 David Osborne and Ted Gaebler (1992), *Reinventing Government*, Reading, MA: Addison-Wesley, pp. 138–39.

4 The figures are available online at: http://www.nyc.gov/html/nypd/html/pct/cspdf.html (last consulted 26 March 2010).

5 M.H. Moore and A.A. Braga (2003), Measuring and improving police performance: The lessons of Compstat and its progeny. *Policing: An International Journal of Police Strategies and Management*, 26, 3, pp. 439–53, p. 447.

6 This kind of behaviour is illustrated in M. Goddard (2000), Enhancing Performance in Health Care. *Health Economics*, 9, pp. 95–107.

7 R.H. Houwing *et al.* (2007, in Dutch), Vochtigheidsletsel is 'gewone' decubitus. *Medisch Contact*, 62, 3, pp. 103–5.

8 As research by A. Visser shows. See Hans de Bruijn (2007), *Managing Performance in the Public Sector*, London: Routledge, pp. 34–38.

9 H. Maarse and M. van Velden (2004, in Dutch), Nutteloze informatie. *Medisch Contact*, 59, 44, pp. 1722–24.

10 A convincing argument about the risks associated with benchmarking can be found in J. Ridderstrale and K. Nordström (2004), *Karaoke Capitalism*, Harlow: Pearson Education.

11 As research by A. Visser shows. See de Bruijn, op. cit., pp. 34–38.

12 de Bruijn, op. cit.

13 Ibid.

14 John O'Leary (2005), Determined challengers keep heat on the elite. *The Times Higher Education Supplement*, 28 October.

15 R.J. in 't Veld (2001), *Relations between the State and Higher Education*, The Hague: Kluwer Law.

16 Aimee Franklin (1999), Managing for results in Arizona: A fifth-year report card. *Public Productivity and Management Review*, pp. 194–209, p. 205.

17 A.G.J. Haselbekke *et al.* (1990, in Dutch), *Prestatie tellen. Kengetallen als instrument voor een bedrijfsmatig(er) bestuur en beheer van decentrale eenheden*, The Hague: VNG, pp. 131–32.

18 Carol Propper and Deborah Wilson (2003), The Use and Usefulness of Performance Measures in the Public Sector. *CMPO Working Paper Series*, No. 03/073, Bristol: Centre for Market and Public Organisation, p. 14.

19 Bobbie Jacobson (2003), Hospital Mortality League Tables. *British Journal of Medicine*, 326, pp. 777–78.

20 See, for instance, Jacobson, op. cit.

9

CHANGE MANAGEMENT

CHANGE AS MUDDLING THROUGH

An often-heard complaint about change in professional organizations is that it can be really slow. The processes are often unwieldy, erratic, sluggish and sometimes even chaotic. It seems like muddling through is the standard. Today's hard-and-fast agreement may be forgotten tomorrow. Command and control hardly ever work. The question addressed in this chapter is as simple as it is important: how to organize a process of change in a professional organization?[1]

CHANGE IN THE PREVIOUS CHAPTERS OF THIS BOOK

Change, like many other processes discussed in this book, often happens naturally in professional organizations. Change is a tacit process that often doesn't require any managerial intervention. This chapter, however, will not address such tacit change. Rather, it will focus on situations in which change does not happen spontaneously, and is still needed. Such situations have played a role in each of the previous chapters. Change connects with the themes of previous chapters in the following ways:

- Change and strategic management. Strategy development is often an emergent process. Emergent processes, however, may also have highly undesired outcomes (such as waiting lists in healthcare). Management may therefore have to take a strategic direction which deviates from, or even counteracts, these emergent processes or the views of professionals.
- Change and quality management. Protocollation may have an added value, while being criticized by professionals nonetheless. After all, they may regard it as paperwork – which it often is – but it can also be meaningful.
- Change, coordination and cooperation. Although change may be necessary, it may not come from the professionals themselves. As a result, managers

may be asked to formulate work routines that are to change existing routines.

- Change, knowledge management and innovation. Professionals will often be reluctant to employ codification and make knowledge explicit. There may, however, be situations in which these can be helpful, for instance if an organization is envisioning a significant exodus of staff, and consequently a large amount of knowledge may be lost.

- Change and performance management. Few professionals will happily embrace the introduction of a performance measurement system. These systems, however, may be useful. They can unveil, for example, a poor professional performance, as illustrated by the mortality rates of Radboud Medical Centre in Nijmegen, the Netherlands, discussed in Chapter 3. The surgeons felt that their performance was in accordance with professional standards, while the mortality figures unveiled that there was something seriously wrong. The change issue: how should a performance measurement system be introduced when professionals see it as nothing but bureaucracy, and a sign of decreasing professionalism?

It may be clear: each of the functions discussed has a change-related aspect. This chapter can therefore be regarded as cutting through Chapters 4 through 8. In each of these chapters, after all, one may ask how the necessary change can be achieved.

WHY CHANGE IS (ALMOST) ALWAYS SLUGGISH

The reason is not very difficult. First, the relationship between managers and professionals is characterized by interdependence. Professionals need managers and managers need professionals. After all, professionals have quite a lot of *make and break power*. Usually they do not have the primary power sources (money, authority), but they do have the somewhat more diffuse, secondary power sources: power of expertise, of reputation, of relationships. The first refers to the professional's knowledge and expertise. The second implies that others attach a lot of value to the professional's view – imagine, for instance, a professional who is highly respected by his colleagues or by society. The third relates to the question, how many other people can a certain professional activate in his fight against the manager? These latter two categories of power should not be underestimated, even though they may not appear as impressive as 'hard' sources of power, such as formal authority or money. 'How many divisions does the Pope have?', a Soviet leader once asked his staff in a derogatory way. None, and yet it was a Polish pope who quickened the fall of the Soviet Union.

Without a certain amount of support by professionals, many change processes are bound to fail. Professional organizations are sometimes described as network organizations: they consist of networks of interdependencies. Someone who manages such a network on the basis of *command and control* will evoke resistance.

Second, many professional organizations are characterized by variety – the hospital disciplines, the court sectors, the school departments. Variety makes change more difficult, because an intended change that may be suitable for departments A and B may, for that same reason, be unsuitable for departments C and D. As a result, C and D will resist the change.

Third, the professional is autonomous, and therefore it often remains unclear whether he really implements the change initiated by a manager. In the end, the professional delivers the service. The teacher in the classroom has to shape the change of didactic methods initiated by a school's management. A professional needs autonomy to deliver this service; this autonomy gives him the room to implement changes-on-paper as he pleases. Our teacher might decide that he will implement the change half-heartedly – he might have good professional reasons for that – and thus frustrate the process of change.

HOW DECISIVE MANAGERS CREATE SLUGGISH PROCESSES

Change is therefore all but simple if the manager needs the professional to implement it, while the professional might fail to see its added value. A logical consequence is therefore that change processes are likely to become sluggish.

There is, however, another point. Many change processes are defined as a project, and therefore implemented in a project-oriented manner. Entire organizations are enrolled in project management courses – but project management often actually represents the problem when it comes to change processes. A project-oriented approach has three characteristics.

First, there is a well-defined number of steps that have to be taken – for instance, starting at problem formulation, and then moving via information gathering to decision making, implementation and evaluation. These steps have an intrinsically logical order: there is no decision before there is information, there is no implementation before there is a decision, and so on.

Second, in each of these steps values such as 'focus', 'accuracy' and 'precision' are very important. An effective process of change requires a precise problem formulation, focused goals, accurate information, and so on. The assumption is that clarity about problems, goals and decisions is conducive to an adequate change process.

Third, time is an important theme. The change process is divided into several phases, which requires planning in which each of these phases is accompanied by a deadline. It makes the change process predictable and transparent for everyone involved.

Project management works under one condition: everyone agrees, everyone is on the same page – but people in professional organizations rarely are. What happens when change is addressed like a project in a network-like organization in which managers strongly depend on professionals? In which managers and professionals have different opinions on what should happen? The more precisely and accurately goals are formulated, the greater the chance that some people will disagree, and the greater the chance of resistance – and therefore of a sluggish change process. Someone who formulates a very precise goal has less chance of support than someone who formulates it more broadly. Phased deadlines often are an incentive for resistance. Suppose a professional does not agree with a change and there is a set of deadlines, imposed by the manager. Who has a problem when the deadline has passed and the process is lagging behind? The manager. So who has an incentive to delay the process? The professional. Perhaps it is opportune to ask the manager for favours just before the deadline – after all, the manager strongly depends on the professional's support. Phased deadlines may evoke resistance, and are therefore an explanation for muddling through.

FROM PROJECT TO PROCESS

If projects are an incentive for resistance, the consequence is self-evident. Rather than to impose a *project*-oriented approach upon professionals, it is important to go through the *process* together with them. This is what we call process management. If change is an interaction process between the manager and the major professional stakeholders, attention shifts from *project plans* to *process-oriented strategies* to entice these professionals. Such a process-oriented approach is based upon three assumptions:

1 The manager needs the support of the people whose behaviour he intends to change. Change is only likely to be successful if professionals are involved in the process of change, and if they are granted the space to help shape this process.
2 The professionals whose support the managers need will always – intentionally or unintentionally – ask: 'What's in it for me?' Some may argue that this question disregards common interest and is therefore slightly vulgar, but this is often not the case. Each problem or solution can be approached from different perspectives. One person may feel that the establishment of a shared service centre (SSC) could make the professional

service more effective and efficient, while another may perceive a risk of increased bureaucracy and standardization. A third person may hold that some activities do not fit within such a centre. All of this may be true, and therefore there is no such thing as a prior common interest. Of course in the course of a process, managers and professionals may arrive at shared views on the common interest, but this is not a prior given, but rather the result of a process.

3 These professionals behave strategically. Strategic behaviour implies that parties do not only have a *substantive* point of view, but they also play the *game* of decision making. Intentionally or unintentionally, they behave in a way that allows them to act according to their own viewpoints as much as possible. Party A would like a certain change, and asks party B to participate. Perhaps party B does not think the change is a bad idea, but sometimes it might pay off to adopt a 'wait-and-see' strategy, in other words to not agree with the proposed change just yet. This would mean that A needs to put in a little extra to gain B's support. Or suppose that a unit within an organization would really like to develop a new initiative. It could follow the formal decision-making procedure and submit its proposal to the board. This, however, takes time, and carries the risk of the board rejecting the proposal. The unit could also just start on a small scale, let the initiative develop, and only submit it for decision making when all the board has to do is to give its approval.

The three assumptions also show that a process is not always the most suitable strategy for change. If resistance is absent or limited, there may be nothing wrong with a project strategy. If a process is organized while a project would be better suited, this creates unnecessary bureaucracy and sluggishness.

WHAT CAN A MANAGER DO?

How can a manager succeed in starting a process of change? How will he stimulate professionals to participate in a process towards the desired change together with him? There are five central elements to the process approach, which can be compared with a project approach:

1. MAKE THE PROBLEM BROADER

A first observation with regard to a project approach is that there is a problem. A substantive analysis can be used to define this problem further. Once it is properly defined, it will guide the method of problem solving. Many project managers will recognize this: if the problem is not clear, project implementation is impossible.

This is entirely different in a process approach. A manager who defines a problem will have to be aware of the fact that there is 'only' a *perceived* problem. The problem perception of others, particularly the professionals, may be entirely different. Attention thus shifts from a substantive problem analysis to strategies to influence the problem perception of others.

In a process, a precise problem definition may be dysfunctional. After all, the more precisely a problem is defined, the smaller the chance that the problem definition will receive support. In many cases it is more sensible to formulate the problem broadly. The advantage of such a broad problem definition is that it may be easier for professionals to identify themselves with this problem.

Let us take a look at a professional organization with decentralized support staff. Every unit has its own departments of HRM, Finance, Facility Management, and so on. This may be appealing to professionals: the support staff can easily be contacted and have a large amount of local knowledge. The board, however, decides to transfer all support staff to an SSC. Professionals may easily perceive this as a kind of centralization. Suppose the board presents a problem analysis which shows that the decentralized support is inefficient. Such a precise analysis is often an incentive for resistance. There are plenty of arguments to be made in favour of the notion that centralization will lead to inefficiency. The board may also formulate the problem more broadly: the support service should be made more efficient; this will create extra funds that can be re-invested in the organization's professional units.

Such a broad definition is more than just not stating what the problem is. First, defining the problem broadly will allow professionals to offer their views on what they perceive to be the best way to organize the support service. Second, a precise problem definition will create an incentive for resistance. A broad problem definition, however, will be a stimulus to cooperate with the board. Third, a broad definition increases the chance of a positive answer to the question 'What's in it for me?'.

The same thing can be said about goals. A manager who supports a project approach will prefer clear goals – which will not work in a process. A manager who has committed himself to a clear goal has little flexibility, and deprives himself of the space that is needed to be effective in a process. A precise goal formulated in advance also obstructs learning processes: suppose that it becomes evident during the process that an SSC for one of the functions, for instance for HRM, does not lead to the desired efficiency? And that the professionals who opposed the SSC appear to be right at this point? A manager who has defined his goals with much aplomb can turn back a lot less easily than a manager who has allowed himself some space. Just like problems, goals should be defined broadly in order for them to be sufficiently recognizable to the other parties.

2. DESIGN MULTI-ISSUE PROCESSES

This example hides a second important strategy. The board in question will not only put support on the agenda but also extra funds for the primary process. It could also put other issues on the agenda. A project manager is focused and will therefore concentrate on a single issue: the desired change. Someone who is more process-oriented will know that a one-issue focus often generates conflicts. When the one and only issue on the agenda is the organization of the support staff, there is the risk of an either/or discussion. Either you support the idea of an SSC, or you oppose it. The alternative strategy is to add other issues to the agenda. This is called a multi-issue strategy.

Imagine that a board intends to introduce an IT system in a professional organization. Many units show some resistance to this system. It is too costly, it fails to do what it is supposed to do, or it affects the core of the profession by standardizing certain tasks. The board wants to introduce the system anyway, but this is of course risky given the amount of resistance. If the system is perceived to be nothing but a toy for the board, the units will use every opportunity to emphasize every technical problem in the implementation process. What can be done to stimulate ownership of the system among the units? To make sure that they do not wish to emphasize technical problems, but rather solve them?

Strategy No. 1 is command and control: imposing the system upon the units. Of course this will seem to be decisive, but it entails a significant risk. Strategy No. 2 is management by expertise: hire an expert, ask him what the best solution is and explain this to your rank and file. The board will explain once again and in substantive terms how adequate the system is and how skilfully it will be implemented. Of course the chance of the units being convinced is limited. With regard to these kind of problems, there is often not a single truth, and the truth propagated by IT specialists is especially likely to evoke distrust among professionals.

When the board uses command and control or management by expertise, there is a big chance that this will evoke resistance and will fail to convince the professionals. Moreover, a characteristic of using these two management styles is that they draw all attention to one issue: the new IT system. Multi-issue decision making, on the other hand, implies that other issues are put on the agenda as well – for instance issues regarding buildings, facilities, and perhaps also more substantive issues that touch upon the profession. These issues do not necessarily have anything to do with the IT system. It is more important that they are interesting to the professionals or professional units in question. Another way to compose a multi-issue agenda is to divide the implementation of the system into a number of different components: the choice of hardware, the choice of software, the pace of the implementation or options for local, tailor-made subsystems. Some aspects may, for instance, be negotiable, or opportunities are created for the adaptation of the system to local circumstances. What are the advantages of multi-issue change?

First, the change process is stripped of its massive either/or character. As long as decisions on single issues have to be made, units can either be in favour of or against the change. There are always advocates as well as adversaries, and by definition this creates a basis for conflict. Multi-issue change, on the other hand, results in a diffuse playing field, which generates fewer conflicts.

Second, when the issues on the agenda are interesting to one unit – perhaps these are issues which have been on their wish list for a long time – they will at least be stimulated to participate in the change process and to join the discussion. Moreover, when they feel there is something in it for them, they will be more prepared to pro-actively participate in the process. People who join a discussion in a one-issue meeting which is not interesting to them will often adopt a reactive attitude.

Third, a multi-issue change process will create varying coalitions. Suppose that there is a draft agreement on each of the issues. Each issue will have some advocates and some adversaries. If only issue I was being discussed, such a situation would create conflict – it is either/or. In this case, however, there is an issue II with a coalition of advocates and adversaries that differs from the coalitions on issue I. The same goes for issue III, and so on. We call these 'changing coalitions'; these coalitions do not create conflict. After all, if issue I is discussed, professionals A and B are in favour and professionals C, D and E are opposed. For issue II, B and C are in favour and A, D and E are opposed. For issue III, professionals A, C and D are in favour, and B and E are opposed, and so on. Actor A may see actor C as an opponent when it comes to issue I, but he knows that he needs actor C's support in relation to issue III. He will therefore treat actor C benevolently, even during the discussion of issue I. In jargon: changing coalitions create incentives for cooperative behaviour.

Fourth, all kinds of unforeseen opportunities will present themselves during the multi-issue process. After all, many issues can be connected, which may result in interesting combinations. Perhaps this will lead to new issues that no one could have identified as potential agenda items. Multi-issue processes therefore typically result in unforeseen but desired outcomes.

A multi-issue process will usually end in a package deal: a set of agreements about a number of issues. For each of the professionals involved, the package deal will have elements that are appealing and elements that are less appealing.

The idea is that professionals will accept the package deal if the net result is sufficiently appealing to them. This is what we call a win-win situation: every actor is faced with costs and benefits, and the net outcome is sufficiently appealing for them to accept the package.

3. LET THE PROCESS DO ITS WORK

So the basic idea is quite simple: invite different parties to share in the thinking and decision-making processes, and present them with an appealing agenda. Processes are much more powerful than they might appear to be. I will give two important examples.

First, can one of the professional units ignore the process? Or leave it at the very last moment? This is a lot less easy than it might seem to be. After all, the process with its multi-issue agenda will keep running. The units will be aware of this. Suppose that five out of an organization's six units join in the process and one does not. Non-participation is quite risky for this sixth unit: the other five may reach an agreement with the board and arrive at a package deal, which will be difficult for the sixth unit to ignore. After all, in that case the sixth unit would be set up against the other five *plus* the board – a very unattractive perspective for the sixth unit.

A party that leaves the process halfway through will also take a risk: the others may proceed with taking decisions that have implications for this party. Moreover, a party will also have a problem if it leaves the process and thereby jeopardizes the 'gains' of others. Take the example of the IT system. Perhaps there is a draft agreement that unit III and unit IV will get their local, tailor-made sub-system. If unit VI leaves the process and consensus is no longer possible, the board might no longer support units III and IV. After all, the sub-systems were part of a package and the package ceases to exist as soon as unit VI leaves.

Unit VI will need the others in the future, and these others will not appreciate it leaving the process. This will compromise future cooperation and limit the possibilities of leaving the process. And finally, there is the issue of reliability. A unit that leaves the process will be regarded as unreliable. Why would other units cooperate with this unit in the future if they know that it may always leave at the very last moment? If units decide to work together at all, the level of distrust will be high and this is not to the advantage of the sixth unit.

As a second example, suppose the IT system is rolled out by the board, without the professional units having been consulted in a process. What if serious problems emerge a few months after the roll-out? A board that did not involve professionals will be the single owner of the problem, and will therefore have to solve the problem by itself. Others may find this amusing. Problems in a one-issue situation are owned by the individual problem owner, and others do not always have an interest in solving them. However, if the decision to roll out the IT system was the result of a process, all units share the ownership of the problem, and all of them take an interest in solving it. That is a significant difference: shared problems involve everyone and everyone's expertise, and therefore they are easier to solve.

So the process has to do the work. The logical next step is that processes can be designed. Someone who has just embarked on a process of change, no matter how small, should think about the architecture of the process. Which parties should be involved? What agenda is sufficiently appealing to these parties? What rounds or steps will the process have? Should the relevant parties perhaps even be involved in the question, which process should be chosen? Who will lead the process?

4. SMART COMMAND AND CONTROL

A process approach is an alternative to command and control, but this does not mean that there is no room for command and control in processes. Sometimes a manager needs some command and control, for example to speed up a process. Normally, this will not work because of the many interdependencies in a professional organization – it will merely evoke resistance. But there is also something that might be called 'smart command and control': command and control embedded in a process. Take the example of the board that wants to implement an IT system using the process approach. When can a manager use command and control in the process?

- When the gains affect a large number of people. If the critical mass of the professional organization is faced with a package deal that is appealing to them, they will be more inclined to accept orders. After all, it is in their best interest that the process is finished and the decisions are implemented, including the ones about the IT system. The process, in other words, has created support for the orders.
- If a process has failed. When parties have discussed the subjects that are important to them and this has not resulted in anything, they have learned one thing: they cannot solve the problem among themselves. This may increase the legitimacy of top-down orders. If the units are unable to reach a conclusion on the IT system and the other issues, the next logical step is that decisions are made for them by the board. A variation on this theme: when there is a sense of crisis among the professionals, the legitimacy of

command and control will also increase. Crises, after all, occur when there is a need for action.

- If space is created at the same time. Sometimes units will tolerate an order because it is compensated for by space with regard to another issue. In the IT system example, the final deal may be that the units accept an order relating to the IT system in exchange for compensation and degrees of freedom in other areas.
- In order to influence the perceived gain. Someone who points a gun at another person and demands 'Your money or your life!' creates a win-win situation. The first person gains 50 Euros, the second his life. This may also happen in managerial situations: using commands, or threatening to use them, in order for the other person to perceive their avoidance as a gain.

Each of these commands typically hides some kind of intelligence.[2] They are all embedded in a process, and derive their effectiveness from this process. Commands work thanks to a process (the first and second points above) or because they are part of a process (third point) of because they are followed by a process (fourth point). It may also be clear that the person who gives the commands has to be highly sensitive, and therefore needs to have a large number of process-managerial skills. The command can be given just a little too early (the critical mass of professionals does not yet recognize the gain, or the process has not quite failed yet), or it can be perceived as a type of blackmail ('Your money or your life!'). In both cases there will be no effect.

5. CHANGE IS SUCCESSFUL IF THE STAKEHOLDERS PERCEIVE IT TO BE

The above has quite a few implications for the evaluation of change processes. The crucial difference between a project approach and a process approach is that evaluation in a project approach is a goal-rational activity. The main question is whether the previously formulated goals have been met, and at what cost. In other words, the keywords are effectiveness and efficiency.

In a process approach, it is not that simple. After all, during a multi-issue process goals may shift. Actors make a package deal, they will put their own views in perspective, and they may learn during the process. A party may even abandon its original goal and formulate another one during the process because other opportunities presented themselves. Someone who evaluates from a project point of view – have the previously formulated goals been met? – will conclude that the process wasn't a success. But it will be clear that this is not a good criterion for a process. Process evaluation calls for other criteria:

- A first question is whether the parties are *content* with the final result. It is very possible that they formulated several broad goals in advance, which changed during the process, but they are still content with the result. There is also the so-called criterion of tolerance: parties may not be content, but they tolerate the outcomes of a process because they still experience a net gain, or because they will need the other parties in the future and therefore do not intend to block the package deal.

- A second question is whether problems have been solved during the process. Of course these problems do not just include those of the person who initiated the decision-making process, but also those of other professionals. A process may have been initiated in order to tackle actor A's problem X, but if it proves to have contributed to the solution to actor B's problem Y, the process of course will have been valuable. The process may also have contributed to actor A's problem Y, and his problem X remained unsolved. In that case, too, the process has contributed to the solution to a problem. In other words, other problems are important besides those of the initiator.

- A third question is whether the parties have learned during the process. They have been faced with new issues and new information, and this may have stimulated them to take different viewpoints. A product development director, for instance, may have felt that there was a good market for a new product A, but during his interactions with other professionals within a company he may have reached the conclusion that this was not the case, and that the new product B was much more promising. Suppose this director's superior performs an evaluation on the basis of SMART criteria: the director is supposed to deliver on *s*pecific, *m*easurable, *a*cceptable, *r*ealistic and *t*ime-bound goals, which are evaluated after a year. If the director formulates the introduction of product A as a goal, there are two risks. Either the director focuses exclusively on the realization of A and is thus unable to learn, or he is willing to learn and thus runs the risk of being punished by receiving a bad evaluation.

- A fourth important question is whether sustainable relationships have been formed. Are the parties prepared to negotiate with each other in a future round, discussing other issues? Or have the negotiations been surrounded by so many problems – and has this resulted in so much distrust – that any future cooperation is out of the question? This too is an aspect that is of major importance with regard to decision making in networks, but it can easily be overlooked in classic situations. Suppose goals have been formulated in advance, and they have been met, but in such a way that future cooperation is impossible. Compare this with a situation in which goals may not have been fully met, but there is no objection to future cooperation.

The latter situation is preferable from a network point of view, but the first will score better in an evaluation that is strictly project-based.

- A fifth question, to conclude with, is whether the process has been fair. Have all the parties in the process had sufficient opportunity to fulfil their interests? Have their core values been respected? Have their views been taken into account? The parties may not be entirely content with the result of the process, but they may accept it anyway if the process has been fair and if they realize that there is more loss than gain in blocking the decision-making process.

WHY PDCA IS UNSUCCESSFUL, YET APPEALING

What does a formal decision mean in a process? Not very much. Parties in a process will first have to reach agreements that result in a package. These agreements then need to be approved by the bodies that are formally in charge. However, by the time this has happened, of course the decision has already been made. Decisions *originate* during processes, and are not *made* during formal meetings. Formal meetings are only needed to formally approve them. In fact, some decisions are simply implemented, and are never even addressed in the formal platforms. Many people will be familiar with the fact that lists of decisions issued by management teams in professional organizations hardly have any information value. They include some decisions that are already common practice, or that everyone already knew to be just a matter of time. This is a logical phenomenon in an organization in which the process logic dominates over the project logic.

With this in mind, let us return to project management logic – and in particular the well-known Plan Do Check Act (PDCA) cycle. This cycle was formulated by W. Edwards Deming, and represents a relatively simple way to initiate change. The cycle starts with a problem analysis and the formulation of solutions, which are laid down in a plan. The plan is implemented (Do). After a while, the plan's implementation is evaluated: are the formulated goals being met (Check)? If not, this may lead to the adjustment or cancellation of the plan. If the implementation is on track, the new method of action becomes part of the daily routine within an organization (Act). The cycle may be repeated, but this time at a higher level of complexity: more complicated problems are being addressed. The use of this cycle as a frame of reference for looking at change processes in network-like organizations, however, entails a number of risks:

- The PDCA cycle obscures the perception of the reality behind the formal policy, plan or decision. These documents cannot be understood without any insight into the underlying process. Someone who simply relies on plans ignores the reality of the process-like change, and is thus unable to fully participate in the game.

- The PDCA cycle obscures the reality that exists in parallel with the formal decision-making process. Some of the results of the interaction process will not make it into the formal documents. Some things simply happen: parties reach an agreement and conform to this agreement without having defined it in any formal document.
- The PDCA cycle obstructs change processes. Change is most likely to occur in a multi-issue process, and PDCA is in conflict with every principle of such a process. It requires clear goals – which often obstruct change. And it requires a clear plan – which is not conducive to a good process either.
- The PDCA cycle leads to increased bureaucracy. In processes, plans only have limited meaning. Someone who is obliged to formulate plans anyway, sometimes according to very detailed formats, will mainly perceive this as bureaucracy.
- The PDCA cycle frustrates. Looking at change processes from a PDCA point of view will only result in disappointment. The prevailing impression will be that processes are unpredictable and almost chaotic, that goals are not met, that there are hidden agendas, that political games are played, that ambitions shift continually, and so on. From a process point of view, however, a certain order will be visible behind this apparent chaos, as well as results that will not be visible from a project point of view.

Does this mean that any kind of PDCA-oriented thinking should be avoided? Of course not. PDCA is in fact applicable in contexts in which there is a certain kind of hierarchy, which is the case in some professional environments. Plans have meaning if they are the outcome of a change process, rather than the input for a change process. After all, if parties have reached agreement on a plan, there is an increased chance of a PDCA-like implementation. Sometimes plans serve the purpose of initiating a process. They may stimulate a change process, rather than a change project.

Why is the PDCA approach so popular, despite all these threats? There are at least two reasons.

The first is that the framework of the PDCA approach offers certainty. Someone who is confronted with the inconsistency of decision making in a network and who does not recognize the underlying mechanisms – professionals, interests, strategies – may be overwhelmed by the apparent chaos in which he finds himself. PDCA-like frameworks offer clarity, and more importantly, they carry a certain amount of promise: they suggest that the decision-making process can also be orderly and structured. The risks elaborated above, however, make clear that this promise is not fulfilled, at least not in a professional, network-like organization.

A second reason is the communicative power of the PDCA approach. When decision making and implementation are presented and communicated as the result of a PDCA cycle, this suggests that the decision-making and implementation processes have been prepared thoroughly and carried out systematically. When decision making and implementation are presented and communicated as the result of discussion and negotiation, on the other hand, this may create the impression that they result from opportunism and coincidence. The notion that this communicative power implies that PDCA can also be used for 'real world' decision making in a network, however, is deceptive. There is a difference between appearance and reality. Research shows that in 80 per cent of change processes, a choice is made for a planned change; 24 per cent of these cases are successful.[3]

PROCESSES ARE ENIGMATIC

The communicative power of PDCA and other project-oriented models has an important implication. Many people who have been involved in change in a professional organization will recognize the processes described above. However, they are not always visible. This is the result of an important mechanism: the *actions* in a network of interdependent relationships are often process-oriented, while the *communication* about the results of the process is often project-oriented. This is what is called the difference between front stage and backstage.[4] The process takes place backstage. Parties design a multi-issue game, broaden the agenda, try to make a package deal, and so on. Front stage, however, is where the public performance takes place and where the outcomes of this process are presented and communicated. The dominant language in this area is that of project management. Why? Because in addition to effectiveness (is it working?), expressiveness is an important value. Is a change communicable?[5] Project language – problems, goals, analysis, solutions – is often more expressive and better communicable than process language – discussion, negotiation, package deals.

Suppose a number of parties in an organization are negotiating in a multi-issue game about three issues: a potential investment in new equipment, a change in the planning and control cycle, and a revised marketing strategy. Eventually they reach an agreement and make a package-like decision. This decision will include a simplification of the PDCA cycle: the professional units need to produce fewer statistics, and the audits carried out by the centralized staff departments will be less strict. This is something that the professionals have been wanting for a long time.

This decision needs to be communicated. It can be legitimized through process logic: the planning and control cycle is simplified, and in return the units will comply with more centralized management in the area of marketing. The expressive power is limited, however: professionals may perceive this as ordinary bargaining. The decision may, on the other hand, also be communicated in project-oriented language:

- there was a problem: in the course of the years, the planning and control cycle had been expanded to such an extent that the bureaucratic load had become too heavy;
- there was a goal: reducing bureaucracy and revitalizing the planning and control cycle;
- there has been an analysis: which aspects of the planning and control cycle have become bureaucratic and thus dysfunctional, and which ones *are* functional?
- a decision has been made;
- this decision will be implemented and evaluated.

Such a strategy – acting in a process-oriented way backstage, communicating in a project-oriented way front stage – unites the best of two worlds: effectiveness that stems from the process, and expressiveness that stems from the project. On top of this, there is another advantage. When parties know *during* a process that they will have to communicate in project-oriented language *after* the process, opportunism and bargaining can be avoided. They will have to explain the result in the project-managerial vocabulary when the process is finished. It is problematic if there is no reasonable way to legitimize the decision other than as a bargain. Other parties can make use of this during the process. They can point out to other parties in the network that they cannot explain certain results of the process because they seem to result from bargaining.

The earlier question was: why is the project approach so appealing? Since actions are often – even though few people realize it – process-oriented, and communication is often project-oriented, the impression is sustained that project-managerial change is successful. This may be a reason why many people believe in a project-oriented approach. On paper, it is very promising: it is supposed to offer structure and control, for instance. Front stage this impression is reconfirmed, which makes it very appealing to rely on project management. In network-like organizations, however, the vast majority of change projects will naturally turn into processes.

NOTES

1 The storyline in this chapter is in large part based upon Hans de Bruijn and Ernst ten Heuvelhof (2008), *Management in Networks*, London: Routledge.

2 Other command- and control-like strategies are described in de Bruijn and ten Heuvelhof, op. cit.

3 See also the essay by Jaap Boonstra (2005, in Dutch), Veranderen en adviseren. Tussen beklemming en passie. In: Gabriël van den Brink *et al.* (eds) (2005), *Beroepszeer. Waarom Nederland niet goed werkt.* Meppel: Boom, pp. 155–67.

4 David Buchanan and David Boddy (1992), *The Expertise of the Change Agent*, Hemel Hempstead: Prentice Hall, pp. 27 and 133.

5 Expressiveness as a concept was introduced by Jock Young, who uses it in the context of criminal law. See Jock Young (2000), *The Exclusive Society*, London: Sage.

10

BEYOND THE ONE-HANDED ORGANIZATION

'GIVE ME A ONE-HANDED ECONOMIST' is said to be a heartfelt cry by the former American president Harry S. Truman. 'All my economists say, "On the one hand, on the other … "'. It wouldn't be entirely out of bounds to apply this statement to the discussion about managers and professionals that is held in many organizations. It is natural to long for a 'one-handed organization': the organization in which either the professional is right, or the manager.

I hope that this book has made clear that this one-handed organization is an illusion – and that there are many instances, particularly in professional organizations with their multifaceted environments, in which there is 'on the one hand' as well as 'on the other hand'. Protocols, plans, knowledge codification and performance measurement can lead one-handed professionals to a fast judgement, but they can also be quite meaningful to the profession. When an organization is patchwork-like, and decision making is merely muddling through, the one-handed manager will be quick to judge. These characteristics, however, can also be the strong side of an organization: patchwork-like organizations are innovative, and the process of muddling through protects it from making serious mistakes. Management is often a problem in professional organizations on the one hand, but on the other hand it can be a solution. Professional autonomy may be a breeding ground for superb professional performance on the one hand, but on the other hand it may nurse the preservation of defensive routines and professional failure.

THE MANAGING PROFESSIONAL

What does this mean for a manager in a professional organization?

First, of course managers should be knowledgeable about what they do: managing. In addition, however, they will need some degree of substantive knowledge about their profession. Without this knowledge it is very difficult for them to evaluate whether protocols, for instance, have any added value for the profession or whether they only result in hassle. The line between added value and hassle may after all be thin, and making sensible decisions calls for a large degree of sensitivity. Without this knowledge it is difficult to predict whether professional autonomy will result in superb performances, or in the continuous defence of existing routines.

Second, the question is where these managers should come from. If the above is true, the answer is self-evident: managers should mainly come from within the profession itself. If management is left to outsiders, it may result in management becoming a problem for professional organizations.

Third, in the early days, universities and hospitals – the classical professional organizations – had a category of employees called managing professionals: professionals who were charged with management tasks. This was often a temporary role for professionals who were past their prime, or who were close to retiring. It was a half-hearted affair, and people perceived it as a chore. Perhaps it is worth considering reviving the function of the managing professional – not as a half-hearted affair, but as a full-fledged aspect of the organization. Revival of the managing professional is first and foremost a cultural challenge: we need to learn to value professionals who do this work.

Fourth, there may be major differences between the managerial and professional ways of looking at an organization. A managing professional speaks the languages of both worlds, and this makes him valuable in a professional organization. This means he will have an important role: the role of *boundary spanner*. The managing professional is aware of the many managerial interventions that his professionals are faced with. Some of these interventions are useful, others are not, and some are simply disastrous. Since he knows the language of the profession, he can assess the value of these interventions. Sometimes he can phrase a managerial intervention in professional language, and sometimes he can ward off the intervention. Sometimes he can add a new aspect to a general intervention and thus make it applicable to the specific working environment of his professionals. And sometimes he may act intelligently from a bureaucratic point of view: he may pretend that the intervention is implemented, while in fact this is only true on paper. This is the function of a heat shield: the professionals are shielded from the managerial heat, and vice versa: since the managing professional speaks the language of the managerial world as well, he can bring developments in the profession to the attention of managers in the right language and hopefully at the right moment. This way he may really be the boundary spanner who can make the connection between the worlds of management and professionals.

Managing professionals come from within the profession itself, and can spare professionals much managerial hassle. What's more, they can even bring some good things to the professional organization – after all, management is a solution as well. Professional communities that regard management as a chore and managing professionals as the unlucky ones who drew the short straw will provoke another kind of management: the management that soon becomes a problem. Professionals who leave management to others, however, will create that problem themselves.

LITERATURE

Bachmann, Lucas M., Esther Kolb, Michael T. Koller, Johann Steurer and Gerben ter Riet (2003), Accuracy of Ottawa ankle rules to exclude fractures of the ankle and mid-foot: Systematic review. *British Medical Journal*, 326 (7386), pp. 417–19.

Ball, Philip (2005), *Critical Mass: How One Thing Leads to Another*, London: Arrow Books, pp. 152–53.

Barbuto, John E. Jr. (2001), How is strategy formed in organizations? A multi-disciplinary taxonomy of strategy-making approaches. *Journal of Behavioral and Applied Management*, 3, 1 (Summer/Fall), pp. 64–73.

BBC (2007), *Planet Earth*, DVD.

Bendor, J.B. (1985), *Parallel Systems: Redundancy in Government*, Berkeley: University of California Press.

Boonstra, Jaap (2005), Veranderen en adviseren. Tussen beklemming en passie. In: Gabriël van den Brink, Thijs Jansen and Dorien Pessers (eds) (2005), *Beroepszeer. Waarom Nederland niet goed werkt*, Meppel: Boom, pp. 145–67.

Borges, Jorge L. (1952), El idioma analítico de John Wilkins. In: Jorge Luis Borges (1952), *Otras Inquisiciones*, Buenos Aires: Emecé

Börzel, Tanja A. (1998), Organizing Babylon – On the different conceptions of policy networks. *Public Administration*, 76, 2, pp. 253–73.

Bower, Joseph L. and Clark Gilbert (2007), How managers' everyday decisions create – or destroy – your company's strategy. *Harvard Business Review*, 85, 2.

Brink, Gabriël van den, Thijs Jansen and Dorien Pessers (eds) (2005), *Beroepszeer. Waarom Nederland niet goed werkt*, Meppel: Boom.

Bruijn, Hans de (2007), *Managing Performance in the Public Sector*, London: Routledge.

Bruijn, Hans de and Ernst ten Heuvelhof (2008), *Management in Networks*, London: Routledge.

Bruijn, Hans de, Ernst ten Heuvelhof and Roel in 't Veld (2002), *Process Management*, Dordrecht: Kluwer Academic Publishers.

Buchanan, David and David Boddy (1992), *The Expertise of the Change Agent*, Hemel Hempstead: Prentice Hall.

Causer, Gordon and Mark Exworthy (2002), Professionals as managers across the public sector. In: Mark Exworthy and Susan Halford (eds) (2002), *Professionals and the New Managerialism in the Public Sector*, Buckingham: Open University Press, pp. 82–101.

Chan, Paul S., Harlan M. Krumholz, Graham Nichol, Brahmajee K. Nallamothu and the American Heart Association National Registry of Cardiopulmonary Resuscitation Investigators (2008), Delayed time to defibrillation after in-hospital cardiac arrest. *New England Journal of Medicine*, 358, 3, pp. 9–17.

Chisholm, Donald (1992), *Coordination without Hierarchy: Informal Structures in Multiorganizational Systems*, Berkeley: University of California Press.

Collins, J.C. and J.I. Porras (1997), *Built to Last: Successful Habits of Visionary Companies*, New York: Harper Business.

Crommentuyn, R. (2008), Fouten zijn geen natuurverschijnsel. *Medisch Contact*, 63, 21, pp. 908–11.

Currie, Graeme (2006), Reluctant but resourceful middle managers: The case of nurses in the NHS. *Journal of Nursing Management*, 14, 1, pp. 5–12.

Davenport, Thomas H. and Laurence Prusak (2000), *How Organizations Manage What They Know*, Harvard Business School Press.

Delft University of Technology (2000), *Evaluatie toepassing allocatiemodel 1996–1999*, Delft: Delft University of Technology.

Denis, Jean-Louis, Lise Lamothe and Ann Langley (2001), The dynamics of collective leadership and strategic change in pluralistic organizations. *Academy of Management Journal*, 44, 4, pp. 809–37.

Department of Health (2008), *Final Report of the National CAMHS Review*, London: UK Department of Health.

Draaisma, Douwe (2004), *Why Life Speeds Up as You Get Older*, Cambridge: Cambridge University Press.

Eden, Lynn (2004), *Whole World on Fire: Organizations, Knowledge, and Nuclear Weapons Devastation*, Ithac, NY: Cornell University Press.

Elbanna, Said (2006), Strategic decision-making: Process perspectives. *International Journal of Management Reviews*, 8, 1, pp. 1–20.

Elsevier Thema Studeren [yearly student questionnaire among Dutch university students], October 2007.

'Er is geen andere maat dan de mens', interview with Guy Verhofstadt, *De Morgen*, 4 June 2007.

Eshuis, Roland (2007), *Justice in Better Times. On the Effectiveness of Measures to Accelerate Civil Proceedings*, Rotterdam: Erasmus University.

Externe onderzoekscommissie (2006), *Een tekortschietend zorgproces. Een onderzoek naar de kwaliteit en veiligheid van de cardiochirurgische zorgketen voor in het UMC St Radboud te Nijmegen*, Zwolle: Inspectie voor de Gezondheidszorg.

Franklin, Aimee (1999), Managing for results in Arizona: a fifth-year report card. *Public Productivity and Management Review*, pp. 194–209.

Gawande, Atul (2007), The checklist: Intensive care can harm as well as heal, but there is a simple way of improving the odds. *New Yorker*, 10 December, pp. 86–95.

'Gekoesterd als een breekbare vaas. Actrice Carice van Houten is ontdekt door Hollywood, ze speelt met Tom Cruise en Leonard di Caprio', *NRC Handelsblad*, 22 October 2007.

Glisson, Charles and Anthony Hemmelgarn, The effects of organizational climate and interorganizational coordination on the quality and outcomes of children's service systems. *Child Abuse and Neglect*, 22, 5, pp. 401–21.

Goddard, M. (2000), Enhancing performance in health care. *Health Economics*, 9, pp. 95–107.

Groopman, Jerome (2007), Medical dispatches: What's the trouble? *New Yorker*, 29 January, pp. 36–41.

Harvard Business School Press (ed.), *Harvard Business Review on Knowledge Management*, Cambridge, MA: Harvard Business School Press, 1998.

Haselbekke, A.G.J., H.L. Klaassen, A.P. Ros and R.J. in 't Veld (1990), *Prestatie tellen. Kengetallen als instrument voor een bedrijfsmatig(er) bestuur en beheer van decentrale eenheden*, The Hague: VNG, pp. 131–32.

Houwing, R.H., E.S.M. Koopman and J.R.E. Haalboom (2007), Vochtigheidsletsel is 'gewone' decubitus. *Medisch Contact*, 62, 3, pp. 103–5.

Inspectie voor de Gezondheidszorg (2007), *Zorgverlening door Jeugdgezondheidszorg, GGZ en huisartsen aan Gessica vanuit het perspectief van een veilige ontwikkeling van het kind*, The Hague: Inspectie voor de Gezondheidszorg.

Inspectie voor de Gezondheidszorg (2007), *Het resultaat telt 2006. Prestatie-indicatoren als onafhankelijke graadmeter voor de kwaliteit van in ziekenhuizen verleende zorg*, The Hague: Inspectie voor de Gezondheidszorg.

Jacobson, Bobbie (2003), Hospital mortality league tables. *British Journal of Medicine*, 326, pp. 777–78.

Janis, I.L. (1982), *Groupthink: Psychological Studies of Policy Decisions and Fiascos*, Boston: Houghton Mifflin.

Kennedy, J. and R. Eberhart (2001), *Swarm Intelligence*, San Francisco: Morgan Kaufmann Publishers.

Keuning, D. and D.J. Eppink (2000), *Management en Organisatie. Theorie en Toepassing*, Groningen: Stenfert Kroese.

Klein, Gary (1998), *Sources of Power: How People Make Decisions*, Cambridge, MA: MIT Press.

Koffijberg, Jos (2006), *Getijden van beleid*, Delft: Delft University of Technology.

Koppenjan, Joop and Klijn Erik-Hans (2004), *Managing Uncertainties in Networks*, London: Routledge.

Krogstad, Unni, Dag Hofoss and Per Hjortdahl (2004), Doctor and nurse perception of interprofessional co-operation in hospitals. *International Journal for Quality in Health Care*, 16, 6, pp. 491–97.

Lansbury, Russell D. (1978), *Professionals and Management: A Study of Behaviour in Organizations*. Englewood Cliffs, NJ: Prentice Hall.

Lindblom, Charles E. (1968), *The Intelligence of Democracy: Decision-making through Mutual Adjustment*, Englewood Cliffs, NJ: Prentice Hall.

Lindblom, Charles E. (1968), *The Policy Making Process*, Englewood Cliffs, NJ: Prentice Hall.

Maarse, H. and M. van Velden (2004), Nutteloze informatie. *Medisch Contact*, 59, 44, pp. 1722–24.

Maister, David (1993), *Managing the Professional Service Firm*, New York: Simon & Schuster.

Mak, Geert (2005), Over eenzaamheid, moed en vertrouwen. In: Gabriël van den Brink, Thijs Jansen and Dorien Pessers (eds) (2005), *Beroepszeer. Waarom Nederland niet goed werkt*, Meppel: Boom.

Mak, Geert (2007), *In Europe: Travels through the Twentieth Century*, London: Harvill Secker.

Mintzberg, Henri (1979), *The Structuring of Organizations*, Englewood Cliffs, NJ: Prentice Hall.

Mintzberg, Henri (1994), *The Rise and Fall of Strategic Planning*, New York: Free Press.

Mintzberg, Henri and J.B. Quinn (2003), *The Strategy Process: Concepts, Contexts, Cases*, Upper Saddle River, NJ: Prentice Hall.

Moore M.H. and A.A. Braga (2003), Measuring and improving police performance: The lessons of compstat and its progeny. *Policing: An International Journal of Police Strategies and Management*, 26, 3, pp. 439–53.

Murray, John F. (2000), *Intensive Care: A Doctor's Journal*, Berkeley: University of California Press.

National commission on terrorist attacks upon the United States (2004), *9/11 Commission Report*, New York: W.W. Norton.

Newell, S., H. Scarbrough, J. Swan, M. Robertson, R.D. Galliers and R. Holloway (2002), The importance of process knowledge for cross project learning: Evidence from a UK hospital. In: HICSS (2002), *Proceedings of the 35th Annual Hawaii International Conference on System Sciences*, Los Alimitos, CA: IEEE Computer Society Press, pp. 1019–28.

Nonaka, I. and H. Takeuchi (1995), *The Knowledge-creating Company*, Oxford: Oxford University Press.

'Nooit meer die dieptepass', *NRC Handelsblad*, 3 July 2004.

Noordegraaf, Mirko (2008), *Professioneel bestuur. De tegenstelling tussen publieke managers en professionals als 'strijd om professionaliteit'*, Utrecht: Lemma, pp. 28–32.

Nussbaum, Bruce (2007), Inside innovation: At 3M, a struggle between efficiency and creativity. *Business Week*, June, pp. 3–26.

O'Leary, John (2005), Determined challengers keep heat on the elite. *The Times Higher Education Supplement*, 28 October.

O'Reilly III, Charles and Michael Tushman (2004), The ambidextrous organization. *Harvard Business Review*, April, pp. 74–81.

Orr, Julian (1996), *Talking about Machines*, New York: Cornell University Press.

Osborne, David and Ted Gaebler (1992), *Reinventing Government*, Reading, MA: Addison-Wesley.

Payne, Malcolm (2007), *What is Professional Social Work?*, Chicago: Lyceum Books.

Penn, Mark (2007), *Microtrends: The Small Forces behind Tomorrow's Big Changes*, New York: Hachette Book Group.

Peters, B. Guy (1998), Managing horizontal government: The politics of co-ordination. *Public Administration*, 76, 2, pp. 295–311.

Polanyi, Michael (1966), *The Tacit Dimension*, Garden City, NY: Doubleday.

Poortvliet, M.C. van, D.L. Gerritsen, A.P.A. van Beek, P.P.M. Spreeuwenberg, J.R.J. de Leeuw and C. Wagner (2007), *Kwaliteit van leven in de V&V sector: De samenhang tussen kwaliteit van leven van cliënten en kenmerken van de instelling*, Utrecht: NIVEL.

Posthumus, F. (2005), *Evaluatieonderzoek in de Schiedammer parkmoord, Rapportage uitgebracht in opdracht van het College van Procureurs Generaal*, The Hague: Openbaar Ministerie.

Pronovost, Peter, Dale Needham, Sean Berenholtz, David Sinopoli, Haitao Chu, Sara Cosgrove, Bryan Sexton, Robert Hyzy, Robert Welsh, Gary Roth, Joseph Bander, John Kepros and Christine Goeschel (2006), An intervention to decrease catheter-related bloodstream infections in the ICU. *New England Journal of Medicine*, 355, 26, pp. 2725–32.

Propper, Carol and Deborah Wilson (2003), The use and usefulness of performance measures in the public sector. *CMPO Working Paper Series*, No. 03/073, Bristol: Centre for Market and Public Organisation.

Quinn, R.E. and J. Rohrbaugh (1983), A spatial model of effectiveness criteria: Towards a competing values approach to organizational analysis. *Management Science*, 32, 5, pp. 539–53.

Regnér, Patrick (2003), Strategy creation in the periphery: Inductive versus deductive strategy making. *Journal of Management Studies*, 40, 1, pp. 57–82.

Resnick, Mitchel (1994), *Turtles, Termites, and Traffic Jams*, Cambridge, MA: MIT Press.

Ridderstrale, J. and K. Nordström, *Karaoke Capitalism*, Harlow: Pearson Education.

Roberts, J. (2000), From know-how to show-how? Questioning the role of information and communication technologies in knowledge transfer. *Technology Analysis and Strategic Management*, 12, pp. 429–43.

Sabel, C.A. Fung, and B. Karkkainen (1999), Beyond backyard environmentalism: How communities are quietly refashioning environmental regulation. *Boston Review*, 24, 5, pp. 1–20.

Sacks, Oliver (2007), A bolt from the blue: Where do sudden intense passions come from? *New Yorker*, 23 July, pp. 38–42.

Salm, Harriët (2006), Bevlogen, maar niet professioneel. *Trouw*, 14 June, De Verdieping, pp. 1–2.

Surowiecki, James (2004), *The Wisdom of Crowds: Why the Many Are Smarter Than the Few and How Collective Wisdom Shapes Business, Economies, Societies, and Nations*, New York: Doubleday.

Taleb, Nassim Nicholas (2007), *Fooled by Randomness: The Hidden Role of Chance in Life and in the Markets*, London: Penguin Books.

Termeer, Catrien J.A.M. and Brechtje Kessener (2007), Revitalizing stagnated policy processes:

Using the configuration approach for research and interventions. *Journal of Applied Behavioral Science*, 43, pp. 256–72.

Thalmann, Markus, Ernst Trampitsch, Norbert Haberfellner, Elisabeth Eeisendle, Raimund Kraschl and Georg Kobinia (2001), Resuscitation in near drowning with extracorporeal membrane oxygenation. *Annals of Thoracic Surgery*, 72, pp. 607–8.

Vaughan, Dianne (1996), The Challenger Launch Decision: Risky Technology, Culture and Deviance at NASA, Chicago: University of Chicago Press.

Veld, R.J. in 't (2001), *Relations between the State and Higher Education*, The Hague: Kluwer Law.

Vermaat, Adri (2007), Zedra het over Gessica gaat: Diepe stilte. *Trouw*, 26 November, De Verdieping, pp.2–3.

Visitatiecommissie Rechtspraak (2006), *Rapport visitatie gerechten*, The Hague: Raad voor de rechtspraak.

Wanrooy, Marcel J. (2003), *Leidinggeven tussen professionals*, Schiedam: Scriptum.

Warin, Jo (2007), Joined-up services for young children and their families: Papering over the cracks or re-constructing the foundations? *Children and Society*, 21, 2, pp. 87–97.

Weick, Karl E. (2001), The vulnerable system: An analysis of the Tenerife Disaster. In: Karl E. Weick (2001), *Making Sense of the Organization*, Oxford: Blackwell Publishing, pp. 124–47.

Wendel de Joode, Ruben van (2005), *Understanding Open Source Communities: An Organizational Perspective*, Delft: Delft University of Technology.

Wenger, Etienne and William M. Snyder (2000), *Communities of Practice: The Organizational Frontier*, Cambridge, MA: Harvard Business School Press.

Wetenschappelijke Raad voor het Regeringsbeleid (2004), *Bewijzen van goede dienstverlening*, Amsterdam: Amsterdam University Press.

Wilde, Rein de (2001), *De voorspellers. Een kritiek op de toekomstindustrie*, Amsterdam: De Balie.

Young, Jock (2000), *The Exclusive Society*, London: Sage.

INDEX